# Green Computing

## Tools and Techniques for Saving Energy, Money, and Resources

# Green Computing

## Tools and Techniques for Saving Energy, Money, and Resources

## Bud E. Smith

**CRC Press**
Taylor & Francis Group
Boca Raton   London   New York

CRC Press is an imprint of the
Taylor & Francis Group, an **informa** business
AN AUERBACH BOOK

CRC Press
Taylor & Francis Group
6000 Broken Sound Parkway NW, Suite 300
Boca Raton, FL 33487-2742

© 2014 by Taylor & Francis Group, LLC
CRC Press is an imprint of Taylor & Francis Group, an Informa business

No claim to original U.S. Government works

Printed on acid-free paper
Version Date: 20130531

International Standard Book Number-13: 978-1-4665-0340-3 (Hardback)

Visit the Taylor & Francis Web site at
http://www.taylorandfrancis.com

and the CRC Press Web site at
http://www.crcpress.com

# Dedication

This book is dedicated to everyone who looks beyond the demands of providing cutting-edge computing services to the larger social impacts that computing can have for society and for future generations.

# Contents

# Preface

The rationale for green computing starts with the "green" part. The world is beginning to experience the serious environmental and sustainability problems that entered the public consciousness in 1961 with the publication of Rachel Carson's breakthrough environmental book, *Silent Spring.*[1]

The chickens that Carson discussed are now, if you'll excuse the pun, coming home to roost. In addition, climate change is a new problem that has arisen since Carson wrote her book. It is accompanied by extreme weather, droughts, forest fires, and crop failures—all slated to worsen in the future. Also driving the green agenda are overpopulation, pollution, and resource scarcity—especially scarcity of energy resources, a major theme of this book.

The aforementioned problems are almost certain to steadily intensify throughout the years and decades to come, especially climate change and related problems with extreme weather and crop harvests. Increasing public awareness and regulatory pressure will accompany these changes. Therefore, those who choose green computing today will be seen as forward-looking leaders; those who wait until tomorrow, as reluctant followers and laggards. You and your organization can benefit greatly by getting out in front of these trends.

The other reasons for green computing are much more positive and enjoyable to explore. The green computing vision steadily delivers good ideas and solid benefits for all aspects of IT. Green is all about getting more from fewer resources. And ever-growing IT demands have to be met with fewer resources for companies and other organizations to survive and thrive. In particular, green computing can help you save a lot of money.

Green computing continually suggests ways for you to serve your users better while generating less heat from computing devices, using less electricity, and taking up less floor and desk space for equipment. This increasingly efficient computing infrastructure can be supported by fewer people, who will have more enjoyable jobs, and at the same time empowers users to do more real work and less fiddling around with technology.

A simple example of this occurred when I came home from a trip with several ideas for revising this Preface. I waited more than a minute and a half for my state-of-the-art Windows PC to boot up and open Microsoft Word. If I had instead reached for my Apple iPad, I would have been typing my ideas into the Notes app within ten seconds. (I use "iPad" here as a proxy for all tablet computers.)

An Apple iPad uses just 3 watts of power each hour that it's on. The screen—the most power-hungry component—turns off very quickly when it's not being used. A Windows laptop uses 30 watts per hour, and the screen can easily be left on, unused, for hours.

An iPad weighs about one pound and uses a correspondingly smaller number of resources. A Windows laptop weighs about four pounds, using resources corresponding to that. The iPad is also easier to refurbish, recycle, or dispose of.

There are usability implications to the iPad's lower profile as well. The iPad is easier for me to carry and to use while carrying on a conversation or gazing around the room while gathering my thoughts. It requires less onsite support.

A laptop is less likely to be handy when I need it, more demanding of my full attention to operate, and, of course, slower to make itself available for use. And don't get me started on IT's obligations in purchasing, provisioning, and supporting what is, relatively speaking, a beast—if not, for many purposes, a dinosaur.

Now on this occasion, since my ideas developed straight into paragraphs and a couple of pages of text, I needed the power of Word and access to a large screen and a full keyboard. But the number of situations where I need this more powerful solution is gradually decreasing. The easier—and less resource-intensive—solution will be "good enough" more and more of the time.

And the solution when I don't use either my laptop or my iPad is even smaller and less resource intensive: I can speak my thoughts into a smartphone and have them translated to text by speech recognition almost as easily as typing them. The smartphone uses far less material resources and energy than an iPad or other tablet.

Again, there are times when I need the computer, and other times when I need the iPad. But as the smartphone becomes more and more capable, it can do the job at hand—no pun intended—more and more of the time.

I've focused on the iPad as an example, but there are many other tools and techniques you can use to save energy, money, and resources in IT. For instance, with green computing, you have the need and the opportunity to move the user interface to smaller, less resource-intensive devices. And, with the growth of cloud computing—including private clouds—you have the opportunity to either move computing resources offsite or into ever more efficient onsite data centers.

In making these and other changes, which I'll describe in this book, you will prepare yourself, your department, and your whole organization to meet the challenges that are present today and that will only grow in the future. You will not only save time, energy, and—most importantly—money throughout your organization, but you can also position yourself to make a contribution to solving problems that will need an ever greater share of public and organizational attention in the years to come.

CRC Press, the publisher of this book, has a long and honorable history of publishing books on green computing topics—as well as a wide range of books on broader "green" concerns and broader computing topics. I was particularly interested to find, in the CRC Press backlist, a book called *A Global Warming Forum*[2]—from 1992!

This book serves as an introduction to other CRC books on related topics, making it easy for you to dive into many of the topics that make green computing work. CRC has scores of relevant books; top recent highlights include the following:

* *Green Computing: Large-Scale Energy Efficiency* (Wu-chun Feng, CRC Press, 2012). A research-level book bringing together contributions from leading experts in hardware, systems software, applications, and more.

* *Engineering for Sustainability* (Dennis F.X. Mathaisel and others, CRC Press, 2012). Helps engineers design products with "minimal impact on resources and the ecosystem"; part of a series focused on military technologies.

* *Green IT Strategies and Applications: Using Environmental Intelligence* (Bhuvan Unhelkar, CRC Press, 2011). Describes how to implement environmentally responsible business strategies, deals with sociopolitical challenges, and more.

* *Green Project Management* (Richard Maltzman, CRC Press, 2010). Gives green techniques and methods for maximizing resources and minimizing costs; includes illustrative case studies and grants, tax incentives, and other resources for financing green initatives.

* *Handbook of Energy-Aware and Green Computing* (Ishfaq Ahmad and Sanjay Ranka, CRC Press, 2012). Totaling more than 1200 pages, this two-volume set explores the latest research and design standards for devices, software systems, and much more.

* *Roadmap to Greener Computing* (Raoul-Abelin Choumin Nguemaleu and others, CRC Press, 2012). This book covers methodologies, software

development tools, Computer-Aided Design (CAD), and related techniques for wringing maximum performance from systems.

* *The Green and Virtual Data Center* (Greg Schulz, CRC Press, 2009). How to build a data center with the maximum cost savings, best use of floorspace, and minimal use of energy, with nods to other resource usage and sustainability concerns.

* *Global Cooling: Strategies for Climate Protection* (Hans-Josef Fell, CRC Press, 2012). Planet getting too warm? Cool it down! Fell describes instruments for directly fighting climate change and global warming, starting by terminating further carbon emissions.

This book focuses on tools and techniques that you can use in each area of computing to carry out your green vision. Use it, and its companion books, to save energy, money, and resources. At the same time, adopting a green profile puts you in sync with long-term trends in environmental sustainability and energy use.

# About the Author

Floyd (Bud) E. Smith is one of the most accomplished authors of computing books around—and a green writer and activist as well.

Bud has written about technical topics, such as microprocessor programming and video cards; online subjects, including Internet marketing and Web usability; and social media, from Google Plus to Facebook for business.

His writing career parallels his work for some of the biggest names in technology. Bud has worked for search engine pioneer AltaVista, Web browser pioneer Netscape, and computing and electronics pioneer Apple, among other technology leaders.

Recently, Bud has focused on environmental concerns. He has become active in the international Transition Towns movement and is a member of the Initiating Committee for Transition San Francisco.

Bud wrote his first book about climate change, *Runaway* (published by Business and Technical Communication Services [BATCS], in 2008) and has written a book on green roofs. *Green Computing* gives Bud the opportunity to bring together his two strongest interests: technology and the environment.

Bud's next book will describe the impact of climate change on the San Francisco Bay Area.

# Acknowledgments

Bud would like to acknowledge Theron Shreve, Director of DerryField Publishing Services, who helped him imagine how this book could encourage the influential readers of CRC Press to do even more for sustainability.

He would also like to acknowledge Marje Pollack, copy editor and compositor extraordinaire. Bud's passion for the subject sometimes ran ahead of his precision, and Marje helped pull things into shape.

Finally, Bud would like to acknowledge Carole Jelen, a long-time publisher, now Bud's agent and a Vice President at Waterside Productions.

# Chapter 1

# Green Computing and Your Reputation

## Key Concepts

How green computing can help build up your company's reputation—and yours:

- Why reputation is important for green computing
- How to avoid greenwashing
- Using green computing as part of your career
- Using green computing for recruiting and retention
- Getting the word out

## 1.1 Reputation as Motivation

This chapter discusses reputation management and green computing. The two other chapters in this Part discuss saving money and protecting the environment as key drivers for green computing.

Reputation management includes promotion, PR, conversations, and other ways by which people learn about your efforts. It can serve as a framework for your entire green computing effort. It also complements the financial and environmental drivers described in other chapters, helping you get broad support for green computing initiatives.

The nice thing about using reputation management as a starting point is that it has a long-term focus. Using reputation management as a framework, you avoid obsessing over PR "hits" or advertising pageviews, and instead focus on the big picture.

Reputation management relates strongly—and in some surprising ways—to reasons that you "do" green computing. The main "buckets" encompassing these reasons, which mutually support each other, are:

- Because it's the right thing to do. (Activist explanation; external focus)
- Because it saves money. (CFO explanation; internal focus)
- Because it helps make money. (Marketing explanation; external focus)
- Because it helps with recruitment and retention. (HR explanation; internal focus)

Table 1.1 summarizes these explanations.

The reasons for doing green computing all support each other. The people whose support you need for green computing will be attracted to different rationales for doing it.

There are other reasons you need to be aware of, as well. For instance, you may get your IT staff interested in green computing as a technical challenge. That's a super-internal focus—it only applies to some of the people inside your company, not all of them. The motivation is a problem-solving one.

The egos of your CEO or board members may be part of the push toward green computing as well; this is a super-external focus (it only applies to the people outside the company whom the executives care about) and the motivation is egoistic.

However, in building support for green computing in your organization, you should mostly focus on the main "buckets" listed above.

### Table 1.1 – Four Types of Reasons for Supporting Green Computing

| | | Motivation | |
|---|---|---|---|
| | | Ethics | Money |
| Focus | External | Activist "right thing to do" | Marketing "make money" |
| | Internal | HR "right thing to do" | Finance "save money" |

How do reputation and promotion fit into this? Let's take a look at our main buckets and how reputation might apply:

- **Right thing to do (internal and external):** The goodness of doing the right thing increases if you publicize your work, so you're visibly setting a good example. This applies to both the activist (external) and HR (internal) motivations for doing the right thing, although, of course, the focus of your publicity and promotion is different depending on which direction you're following. Promotion and publicity: Important. Style of promotion: Low-key, targeted.
- **Make money:** You can't make money on the back of doing the right thing if no one knows you're doing the right thing. Luckily, marketers—the people who drive a "making money" motivation for doing green computing—are really good at promotion and publicity, so no worries there. Promotion and publicity: Vital. Style of promotion: High-energy, broad reach.
- **Save money:** This is the fascinating bit; if your motivation is only to be saving money, it makes no sense to spend time, money, and management attention promoting your efforts. Zero; zilch; nada. You might convince others that it's worth putting up a page or two about a money-saving effort on your company Web site; otherwise, those who are motivated by saving money will oppose, undermine, deride, and otherwise be manifestly unhelpful with your promotion and publicity efforts. Promotion and publicity: Problematic. Style of promotion: Spend no money.

The surprising thing in this breakdown is how different the attitudes toward promotion are, depending on the motivations of those supporting green computing efforts. No promotion; low-key promotion; high-energy promotion; there's a good argument for each, depending on what motivates you to do green computing.

It's actually even worse than that: two of the groups find their whole rationale for doing green computing wiped out by the other group's promotional approach. A big promotional campaign from the marketers can greatly reduce or eliminate the cost savings sought by the finance guys; doing no promotion, as the finance guys might favor, wipes out the ability to generate new revenues (as opposed to saving money) off the back of green computing efforts.

So when you have meetings to talk about the benefits of green computing efforts, you'll often find people talking past each other. They think they're after the same goals, but their motivations are really quite different. Help people see that these overlapping motivations need different approaches; for instance, the marketers can't simply go out and spend the money that the operations people just saved. The marketers have to show how their spending will pay for itself in new revenues. (Thus, leaving the initial savings untouched.)

Figure 1.1 shows the US Environmental Protection Agency's Green Power Leadership awards. These awards might please all sides, at least at first: They don't cost any money to enter or win, they're great for promoting green leadership to current and prospective employees, and they can be used in advertising and more active promotion to the outside world. (Notice, though, that this last motivation only works if money is spent after winning the award, which needs to be justified by new revenues that the spending will generate.)

So what's the answer to meeting the needs of all groups—and getting their continued support for your green computing efforts? I think there are two main ingredients.

The first is to sell all your reasons for doing green computing, all the time. Talk about marketing opportunities to the finance guys; talk about the importance of saving money to the marketers. That way, no one's surprised when different people in your organization have different goals around promoting green computing efforts.

The second is to handle the marketing efforts, in particular, with care. To the rest of the company, marketing spending often seems wild and out of control. Help other groups understand what marketing may do with your results.

**Figure 1.1**   The US EPA gives out Green Power Leadership Awards. (*Source*: http://www.epa.gov/greenpower/awards/winners.htm)

Marketing will tend to wait until an effort has succeeded; then, they'll weigh that successful effort against other positives and decide what to put marketing money behind. There's never a guarantee that marketing will promote your green computing efforts, and there's never a guarantee that it won't.

Help people understand that marketing money is intended to help the company make more, new money. So marketing your green computing accomplishments is not wasting the money that they saved. Instead, the cycle goes like this:

- Your company invests in a green computing effort.
- The effort becomes a success, saving money as part of the benefits.
- Marketing looks for good things happening in your company that they can market—in order to make new money. Marketing "spending" should really be called marketing "investment," at least when it's done right.
- If a green computing effort gets marketed, then hopefully that marketing effort helps the company make more money, as any marketing effort should.

Keeping the focus on reputation also helps. With this big-picture focus, a really frenetic marketing effort will seem inappropriate. The slow work of building your brand is easier for others to get behind than a concerted push to get a newspaper headline or to start "trending" on Twitter—although that can be valuable, too.

## 1.2 Avoiding Greenwash

One of the most evocative terms to come out of the move to sustainability initiatives is "greenwashing." Greenwashing is putting a layer of green PR over efforts that are really driven directly by the good, old-fashioned pursuit of profit.

Now, distinguishing greenwashing from truly solid green initiatives is difficult. As I hope this book will show, real green initiatives are driven by the pursuit of profit, too. In most cases, however, there's a larger dimension as well. The difference is simply this: Greenwashing is when you're pursuing raw financial interest, or even self-interest or career advancement. It often involves overinflating the benefits of the initiative that's being promoted. A solid green initiative is when you're pursuing enlightened self-interest: profit, yes, but also other benefits for a wide range of stakeholders and the community at large.

One of the key markers of greenwashing is publicizing something you're going to do, as distinct from something you've actually done. You may be familiar with the old saying, "There's many a slip twixt the cup and the lip." Another way of saying the same thing comes from the Scottish poet Robert

Burns: "The best laid schemes o' Mice an' Men, Gang aft agley"; that is, they often go awry. When you aggressively promote something you're going to do, you ignore the very real possibility that you won't follow through all the way to getting results.

People who follow green issues know that the easiest green effort to undertake is to issue a press release with green-sounding words in it. Yielding to this temptation has two ill effects:

- By announcing your plans in advance, you leave yourself very little to say if the effort actually succeeds. You sacrifice the chance for a meaty announcement of your successes by firing off the celebratory cannonade before the battle to get something worthwhile done even begins.
- You also set yourself a high bar that may be impossible to clear. Let's say you plan for a greenhouse gas emissions reduction of 10% in the first year. But in reality, it takes you six months to get going, and eighteen months to achieve the planned reductions. Now, this may be a big accomplishment, well worth celebrating—but outsiders started counting when you issued the press release, and "one" (year) and "ten" (percent) are pretty

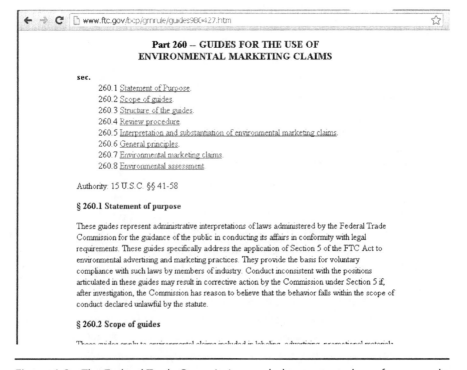

**Figure 1.2** The Federal Trade Commission can help you steer clear of greenwashing. (*Source:* http://www.ftc.gov/bcp/grnrule/guides980427.htm)

easy numbers to remember. So you will have done something really hard and really important—and left people remembering only that you underachieved your announced plans by a factor of two.

While avoiding the urge to preannounce, be sure to be scrupulously honest in everything that you do publicize. (This is so much easier when you're promoting accomplishments instead of plans.) If you set out to achieve a 10% reduction and only got 9%, say so. Describe the many accomplishments you did complete, but also share the obstacles that led to your shortfall. Such a press release might actually get more attention than the usual, purely celebratory blather.

Honesty is particularly important because environmentally related marketing claims can get you into legal trouble. Figure 1.2 shows the Federal Trade Commission's guidelines for environmental marketing claims. These guidelines can help you stay out of trouble—and help you fend off colleagues and top management who want you to make broader claims than you think are justified by the facts.

In addition to promoting accomplishments rather than plans, make sure you can identify the non-profit-motivated parts of your efforts. Who benefitted from extra efforts you made beyond the quarterly profit outlook? You can take credit for long-term investments, even if they do yield a profit over time; often, operating on a longer timescale is the main difference between enlightened self-interest and the rapacious pursuit of short-term profit.

## 1.3 Social License to Operate

A big component of reputation management is also something that's hard to define, hard to measure, and hard to discuss: an organization's social license to operate.

The social license to operate means that society as a whole, and local communities where you operate, broadly accept that your activities are constructive. This touches on the issue of community standards, which are inherently vague. As US Supreme Court Justice Potter Steward once said about pornography, it's hard to define, but "I know it when I see it."

If your organization's reputation in some important area becomes too negative, you can lose your social license to operate. There are entire industries that are in danger of losing this. For instance, the tobacco industry has lost a good part of its social license to operate. Many people avoid investing in tobacco companies, and many people who work for tobacco companies find their career choices embarrassing and hard to explain to people close to them.

This can vary in different local communities, of course. A tobacco-growing area that hosts a large office for a tobacco company will likely grant more social acceptance to the industry, and its employees, than a big city where tobacco use is comparatively rare and heavily restricted.

The nuclear industry is also challenged with regard to its social license to operate. Many people would fight hard to keep any kind of nuclear facility from locating in their area, and a good number of them would consider moving if that were to happen. A Web page about stewardship—an important component of sustainability—is shown in Figure 1.3.

Underlying your reputation-management work is maintenance of your social license to operate. If your organization is seen as a "bad guy," people won't want your facilities in their neighborhoods, and formerly routine permissions and licenses can become quite difficult to obtain.

Rankings and awards on green issues can quickly undermine your social license to operate. If you're the "dirtiest" or worse in some measurable way, the pressure to improve can grow quite intense. Apple got negative press for having the most-polluting data centers, inefficient and powered by coal-fired electrical generating plants. It quickly moved to create a very green data center powered largely by renewables, and publicized the effort energetically.

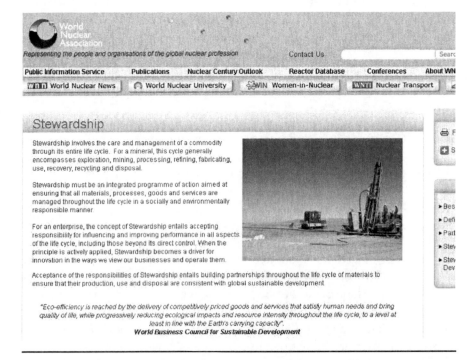

**Figure 1.3**   The nuclear industry shows concern for its social license to operate. (*Source*: http://www.world-nuclear.org/uranium_stewardship/stewardship.html)

When describing reputation management and its importance in green computing to others, make the effort to bring up the social license to operate and its importance. Doing so will help reinforce the value of green computing efforts; those who are working hard to be at the top of well-regarded efforts such as green computing are far less likely to risk the difficulties and opprobrium that accompany finding themselves at the bottom.

## 1.4 Green Computing and Your Career

Your personal reputation is very important to you—and also quite hard to measure. One way of looking at your personal reputation is by looking at the effect of green computing efforts that you involve yourself in on your career.

How can green computing impact your career? It can be a huge positive—or a negative. It all depends on how good you are at making change that your organization is at least somewhat ready for.

Your ace in the hole, whatever the political environment in your company, is that most green computing initiatives save money and reduce business risk. Saving money has always been popular, and reducing business risk is becoming more and more highly valued inside organizations—especially larger ones. You can go a long way as a green computing maven by building your plans on saving money and reducing risk as two of the three legs of your stool for justifying green computing efforts.

The remaining—and tricky—piece is the third leg of the stool, which is the sustainability piece. I believe you should always include this piece in your green computing plans and related marketing, whether for internal or external audiences. You aren't doing your efforts, nor your company, any favors if you leave this important piece out of the picture.

The tricky part is how to position sustainability alongside cost savings and risk reduction. I believe you should be guided by the position of sustainability within your company as a whole:

- **Sustainability-led:** If your green computing initiatives are part of a company-wide sustainability effort, you can lead the justification, and the marketing spin, for your green computing efforts with sustainability. However, I would try to ensure that initial efforts are fully justifiable on narrow cost- and risk-reduction grounds, so the sustainability benefits are icing on the cake. As you develop momentum and credibility, you can consider putting more financial (as well as marketing) weight on sustainability as the third leg of the stool.
- **Sustainability-supported:** If your green computing initiatives are departmental—in the computing area only—rather than company-wide, make a

solid case for a project's sustainability benefits. Don't oversell them, however, in comparison to the cost-saving and risk-reduction benefits. Give your company's senior management room to become innovators by taking your green computing initiative company-wide.

- **Sustainability as a plus:** If your green computing initiatives have little support, or even active opposition, among key stakeholders, position the sustainability benefits as important additional benefits, rather than as a driving rationale behind the project. This minimizes politically motivated opposition while you "get stuff done," and helps you build a track record for getting things done. Starting with a solid string of successes—rather than making a lot of noise—is usually the best way to raise the profile and importance of green initiatives across your company.

Many companies have a "green team" that pursues sustainability initiatives. These efforts often start in the employee lunchroom—reducing waste, and providing new "kits," such as metal water bottles to replace ever-growing piles of discarded paper and plastic cups. A green team can grow into a major player in your organization's sustainability efforts. Consider starting a green team in your IT department.

## 1.5  Green Computing and Your Department

Green computing is really, really going to help your department. That's because it will inoculate you against the most damaging trends and events that could otherwise hurt you, relating to your reputation and, ultimately, your social permission to operate.

A good way to think about the worst thing that could happen to your department is to imagine a management consultant coming in who really, really doesn't like you. Let's say it's the CEO's new son-in-law, and he wants to finish his consulting gig by being awarded your job. Still, the tyro has to stay in spitting distance of the facts. What's the worst thing he could do to you?

A consultant will note the overall trend toward steady increases in IT spending, as shown for the US Federal government in Figure 1.4. He may note that the resulting benefits are hard to quantify.

In most cases, the harshest recommendation a consultant could make for an IT department, while staying credible, is "outsource everything." That is, use cloud computing instead of in-house software wherever possible; use the smallest sensible devices, perhaps terminals powered by Citrix running virtual Windows instances, plus tablets; and outsource most service and support.

There may be real problems with these recommendations, but there will be real benefits as well, and the recommendations will sound great. It won't be that

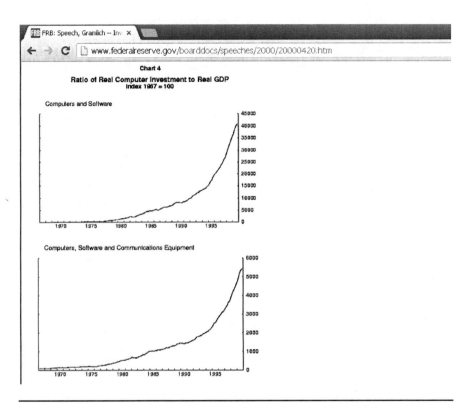

**Figure 1.4**    Not only federal IT spending is growing rapidly. (*Source*: http://www. federalreserve.gov/boarddocs/speeches/2000/20000420.htm)

hard to make assumptions that seem to yield big, immediate cost savings, and ongoing savings as well. All with fewer employees and less hassle.

Now you may know that several cloud software companies could raise prices quickly over the next few years, that having core service and support saves money, and that not everyone in your organization can do their job with a tablet. But these arguments could fall on deaf ears; or, they could simply lead to some modifications, not real changes, in this theoretical consultant's proposals.

The consultant could point out all the risks your company will avoid by moving hardware and software costs off your books and onto someone else's.

A consultant can also take a "green" computing path. If he's savvy, he'll recommend everything the cloud-computing maven would, and also project big savings from buying less, and cheaper, equipment; a stock price or sales boost from good press for the new effort; better hiring and retention; and much more.

The way to save yourself from such a theoretical consultant—or from your CEO or peers coming to you, in a hurry to have you implement the same ideas—is to get out in front of this and do it yourself. You can implement cloud computing in a balanced way, move to smaller devices with pilot projects and clear criteria, and keep some affordable internal people while using external resources for well-defined projects. In other words, you can achieve all the actual savings a consultant might have achieved, with far less drama and disruption.

On the green computing side, you can use your deep knowledge of your company to push sustainability efforts that will actually work in your company and your industry. You will know who in your company can be challenged with new opportunities today, and who will want to go second—or third, or fourth—no matter what. And you can "put the pedal to the metal," where the opportunity arises, in a way that doesn't produce problems and push-back.

This is why green computing is so important to your career. Even as you make the "old you" obsolete, you position yourself to help yourself as well as your company in the new, cost-saving, risk-reducing, sustainability-enhancing world. You'll help yourself even as you help your company.

## 1.6  Green Recruiting and Retention

When people are deciding whether to take a job with an organization, and whether to stay there, reputation matters hugely.

Although it's only the tip of the iceberg, the reactions of new graduates from top colleges and professional schools, such as MBA programs, are a leading indicator of people's reaction to your green reputation as it relates to employment. There are a few reasons for this:

- Young people are, of course, the future. They're a leading indicator of where overall public opinion will go in the future.
- Graduates of the top schools have just received a cutting-edge education, anticipating longer-term educational trends. If this group is getting a "green" education, then that will likely become the norm at all schools in the future.
- CEOs and other top execs are very competitive about "bagging" the hottest graduates from "name" schools. It's not just business—it's personal; the execs themselves, and their own children, and their friends and their friends' children, often are or were highly desired graduates themselves. If this much-desired group named free hot dogs as their most-desired benefit in work, your CEO might be manning a free hot dog stand in the employee cafeteria at lunchtime each day. By which I mean, even non-green executives will have substantial willingness to "go green" if that attracts the hottest graduates.

- Getting the hottest graduates has a knock-on effect with all graduates. If young people hear their highly accomplished friends are going to company X, they'll want to "get in," too.
- Getting highly accomplished, energetic new people in has a strong effect on the atmosphere within a company. I've been involved in breathless conversations about how sharp this or that intern or new hire is. If it takes going green to get this kind of liveliness and energy into the company, top management may well be willing to do it.
- The people who are attracted in as employees today are the ones who have to be retained tomorrow. If people are brought in under a "green" banner, and get the chance to help maintain and grow that reputation once they join your organization, they'll be highly motivated to stay.

Today's young people want their work to make a difference, as well as give them a paycheck and career growth. Green initiatives are perhaps the most obvious, widely appealing way to do that.

Young people also have doubts about the morality of the business world, and more so for specific companies within it. Green programs can help allay these doubts. I know of at least one major tobacco company that tries to overcome its understandably bad reputation as an employer by maintaining several green initiatives! Employees participate quite energetically.

Figure 1.5 shows a guide for young women looking to get into green jobs. These kinds of programs are very popular with school administrators as well as students.

**Figure 1.5**   Green jobs programs are very popular with students and administrators. (*Source:* http://www.dol.gov/wb/Green_Jobs_Guide/GreenJobs%20Ch%204.pdf)

Part of the opportunity for you is that, so far, the green economy has been a bit of a disappointment. Because of tough economic times, and with the dearth, so far, of strong national legislation around carbon emissions, the fully green sector hasn't taken off as much as some people have expected and hoped.

This is sad—and will probably change in the future—but for now, it's also somewhat of an opportunity for you. If you are fully in the green economy, many people will want to work for you. Even if you're not all the way there yet, a green computing initiative can be very attractive to people who are hoping for a green job. You can, as green consultant Andrew Shapiro said, help to "make every job a green job."

You might want to make the case that, in tough economic times or troubled industries, young people will be happy to take any job they can get. (Or, other people might put this argument to you.) But remember, you don't want just anyone to take a job with you—you want the very best candidates. These people always have choices, and you want your organization to keep coming out on top of the decisions they make.

What about green retention? Everyone wants to work at companies where exciting things are happening. Green computing initiatives are certainly different from the run of the mill, purely profit-oriented decision making that goes on at most companies. They offer people new ways to look at their work and the opportunity to make a name for themselves in a new area. Even working at a company that has green initiatives going is exciting, whether every employee gets to work on them or not.

On the other hand, it's worth considering that employees who are not concerned about climate change, or who think it's a hoax or overplayed, might be less interested in working for you if you have green initiatives going. (This could also be an argument that gets thrown at you in a meeting or in email.) There are at least three good reasons not to worry much about this, though:

1. Concern about climate change is steadily growing, especially as extreme weather, melting ice, drought, and other climate-change impacts make the news. A majority of Americans see evidence for climate change as "solid." Figure 1.6 shows one of many headlines on this topic.
2. Younger employees who were maturing as climate change was becoming news, such as millennials—people born between 1980 and 2000—are very likely to be concerned about climate change. Their share of your company's workforce grows every year.
3. "Lead, follow, or get out of the way." Experienced employees have seen all sorts of initiatives come and go in our companies. The positive effect on those who are excited about green initiatives—the majority of employees, and the younger group as well—is likely to far outweigh grumbling from the minority who are less excited about them.

**Figure 1.6** Acceptance of global warming as a concern is growing, among Americans and worldwide. (*Source:* http://www.whitehouse.gov/blog/2012/03/06/poll-shows-more-americans-accept-global-warming-say-seeing-believing)

While your green reputation will help you with recruiting and retention, your success in recruiting and retention will almost certainly help your green reputation. What do people talk about more with friends and families—the minutiae of their daily jobs, or the overall impression their organization makes on the world at large? People who come to, and stay with, your company for its green reputation are likely to add to it by the way they talk about your company with others.

Recruiting and retention are among the very best drivers for green computing initiatives, and for green initiatives beyond the computing area. Make sure to include this area in the justifications for initiatives you're proposing.

## 1.7 Getting the Word Out Inside the Company

Reputation management only works if you get the word out about what you're doing. It's often amazing to see how little a company can know about great things happening in-house.

You need to think of multiple ways to let people know about your green computing initiative. You should plan around:

1. What you need people to do. (This is question #1.)
2. What you want people to know. (Especially where information is needed to support action.)
3. Who has to know the information to do their jobs.
4. Who are key influencers who you want to know about the initiative.
5. Who are the people immediately around the influencers.
6. Who is "everyone else."

Then think about how you'll reach these audiences. Techniques include:

- Including people in the planning process
- Personal meetings
- Direct emails (to people by name, rather than internal mailing lists)
- Emails to internal mailing lists
- Internal company newsletters, magazines, intranets, etc.
- Presentations to specific people
- "Lunch and learn"-type presentations
- Departmental or company-wide presentations

Let's put this into a table so you can do some thinking and planning. The resulting table is shown in Table 1.2.

Use this table, or one like it, to plan your communications around major milestones in your green computing efforts. Here are a few guidelines to remember:

- **Get—and use—executive sponsorship.** Get a top-level company sponsor and have him or her be involved regularly. People need to know that you have buy-in, both for the project itself and for any rewards for good work on it. (And for any opprobrium for poor work on, or noncompletion of, assigned tasks.)
- **Focus first on people who need to act.** Lots of things happen in organizations, and most people are good at prioritizing their use of their time. If it's critical to you that someone do something—but not critical to them that they get it done—expect to spend some time and effort setting out goals, getting agreement, and following up on completion.
- **Get clear agreement from people who need to act.** If someone needs to do something, get clear agreement from them, hopefully in email, so you can track it. You're not out to get people in trouble, just to establish a feedback loop to make your project a priority.

**Table 1.2 – Plan How You'll Get Key Stakeholders Informed**

| | Include in planning | Meet in person | Direct email | Mail lists | Newsletters, etc. | Presentation meetings | "Lunch and learn" | Broad presentations |
|---|---|---|---|---|---|---|---|---|
| People who have to do something | | | | | | | | |
| People who have to know something | | | | | | | | |
| Key influencers for the above | | | | | | | | |
| People around the influencers | | | | | | | | |
| Everyone else | | | | | | | | |

- **Follow up.** This is the hardest part, but you have to keep your eyes on the (your) prize. Remember, your green computing project is likely to be more important to you than to others, so you have to stay on top of things until stuff actually gets done.
- **When you can, do it yourself.** If something is a "must have" for you, and a "nice to have" for the person you're assigning it to, consider doing it yourself—especially if it's only a few minutes, or up to a couple hours, of work.
- **Remember that not everyone attends every meeting.** Many people miss key meetings and don't take the time to read key emails. (Especially when the meetings and emails are key to you, but not to them.)
- **Limit core communications.** Figure out who really needs to know something, what it is, and why, before communicating. Then find three ways to get the information to them. Given this level of effort, you want to keep core communications as narrow (a target group) and as brief (key points only) as possible.
- **Use "broadcast" messaging.** Use scattershot techniques, such as emails to big lists and internal company newsletters, for general awareness-raising. These means are very visible, but not really very useful for getting things done.

Every company communicates differently. When I worked at a large computing company many years ago, we had quarterly all-hands meetings, presentations at conferences, restricted email lists, and many other ways to get the word out. One favorite of some people, though, was to leak information to industry-specific magazines. Once something appeared in a magazine as a company initiative, people within the company were pretty much guilted into following through.

Your company will have its own unique ways of communicating.

## 1.8 Getting the Word Out Outside the Company

One of the biggest sources of frustration and disagreement about any internal effort can be whether and how to let the outside world know about it. Typically, an internal project leader wants to shout their plans out to the whole world; a savvy PR pro is looking for earth-shaking news with major external impact and "thought leader" involvement. Between these two extremes, much news is never released to the public, or gets only the briefest mention.

The best way to make a case for external PR for a green computing initiative is to look at what competitors, and similar companies that aren't competitors, have done. Try to use your contacts to find out what your IT colleagues in the other companies went through in order to get PR support.

Also, consider looking for external speaking opportunities. These may or may not get PR support, but they're great ways to get the word out regardless. (And these are also good for internal PR.)

Work with your PR people to find out what their desires are before you do PR. You may be surprised by the "little" things that make the difference between a PR-worthy initiative and one that isn't. (They'll seem little to you, perhaps; but, of course, they are vital to the PR person.)

There's lots of good information online about writing press releases—or, as they're sometimes called, news releases. You may well be asked to submit a draft; even if the writing work gets done for you, it's great to understand something of what goes into it.

I don't actually suggest that you use most existing press releases as a model, because so many of them are so poorly written and formatted. Find a quality press release that you like from a company that is known for communicating well with the public, and use it as a guide to help you do the right (write) thing.

You can also look into a VNR, or a video news release. Figure 1.7 shows a video version of a news release. Often a 3- to 5-minute video showing and telling what you've done is a great way to get the word out, internally and externally.

**Figure 1.7**   Good press release writing is both an art and a craft. (*Source*: http://www.nsf.gov/news/news_videos.jsp?org=OLPA&cntn_id=102829&media_id=54275)

## 1.9  Summary

This chapter described how green computing can help build up your company's reputation—and your own. Topics include the importance of green computing, avoiding greenwash, using green computing as part of your career, using green computing for recruiting and retention, and getting the word out. The next chapter discusses green computing and saving money.

# Chapter 2

# Green Computing and Saving Money

## Key Concepts

This chapter shows how money-saving and green-computing efforts complement each other:

- The green Zen of saving money
- The advantages of energy efficiency
- Getting the most out of the cloud
- Greening your energy-saving moves

## 2.1 Why Saving Money Is Green

Saving money seems like such an obvious win in business. Profit is revenues minus costs. So cutting costs is just as important to a company as making sales, but it doesn't seem to have the same glamour or get the same attention and focus.

People who think up new ways to make money—marketers, engineers, product managers—are heroes. People who keep the budget under some semblance of control are thought of as boring green eyeshade people (a green eyeshade is the stereotypical accoutrement of the accountant).

But saving money may be even more powerful than making money. Many cost savings, once put in place, continue to repeat year after year, making the company's revenue successes more powerful and valuable. And a cost-cutting mentality can help in all sorts of unexpected ways.

Now, there's another reason to focus on cost-cutting: Cost-cutting is usually green. Most expenditures a company makes also involve resource use, generate waste products, and/or have a carbon footprint. Cutting the expenditure cuts the environmental impact as well.

Figure 2.1 shows a chart from a talk by Amory Lovins of the Rocky Mountain Institute about energy efficiency as a way to address the climate crisis (www.ccnr.org/amory.html). She uses the concept of negawatts—that is, negative megawatts. Generating a megawatt of electricity always has an environmental impact; even if it's solar power, the solar panels have to be built, sited, installed, connected to the grid, and, eventually, disposed of.

Saving energy, however, means that none of those things have to happen. (What actually may happen instead is that the solar power still gets installed,

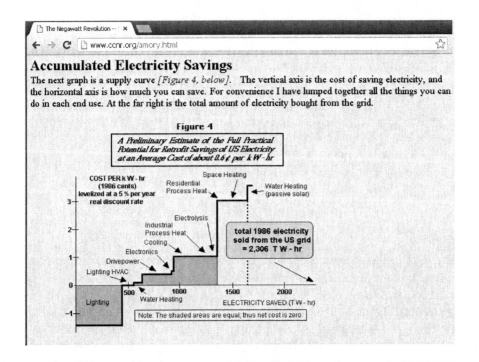

**Figure 2.1**   Negawatts can ease the need for electrical-generating capability. (*Source*: http://www.ccnr.org/amory.html)

but an old, highly polluting coal-fired plant is moved to backup status, where it does far less damage—or is mothballed entirely.) Whether energy efficiency saves on new generating capability or helps in retiring the worst of the old generating capability, it has a strong and positive environmental impact.

Energy savings, measured in megawatts, are called negawatts. Negawatts are the easiest way to increase our effective generating capacity and point the way to economic growth without increasing environmental impacts.

So money-saving efforts, especially energy-efficiency efforts, are usually green as well. It works the other way, too: Green efforts usually save money. Whenever you cut resource use, cut waste, or cut greenhouse gas emissions, you're usually eliminating some unnecessary activity that costs money. Profit-driven and green-inspired cost-cutting efforts can work together, each making the other more effective.

Saving money, usually through energy efficiency, is often the strongest single justification for green-computing efforts. Using green-computing principles, you can extend money-saving IT projects in three related ways:

1. Finding additional ways to save money
2. Adding additional efforts to make the effort more truly "green"
3. Publicizing both the efficiency and "green" parts of the effort together

In this chapter I'll talk about how to use green computing to save money—and how to make your money-saving efforts as green as possible. In addition to being good for the world, the greener your effort, the more positive the impact on your company and your community—and, potentially, the greater the impact on revenues, as customers, partners, potential employees, and others have a greater desire to work with you.

## 2.2 Getting Focused on Money-Saving Efforts

When you set out to save money, and the planet, through efficiency, there are two problems to overcome that seem strictly psychological, but that have real effects. The first is companies' bias toward making money—that is, generating revenue. Saving money and cutting costs don't get nearly the same focus.

To overcome this, the main tool is logic. Saving money has a measurable return on investment, just like making money. In fact, cutting costs often has several advantages, when considered as an investment:

1. The cost of cost-cutting efforts is often more predictable than the cost of revenue-generating efforts. (Manage your cost-cutting efforts carefully and conservatively to keep it that way.)

2. The savings of cost-cutting efforts are almost always more predictable than the revenues from revenue-generating efforts. (Projected revenues are often inflated; you may have to find ways to gently point this out.)
3. A cost-cutting effort usually pays off year after year after year, whereas revenue-generating efforts often have a more finite lifespan. Inventing the iPad may only get you into a profitable business for a decade or two; moving everyone in your company to iPads may, in some form, pay off for much longer. (The iPad's predecessor, the iPod, was a huge success ten years ago; today, iPods are trinkets.)

If your company has a strong project management culture, "selling" cost-cutting efforts is MUCH easier. (Sorry for "shouting" there, but this is important.) In organizations with a strong project management culture, everything is analyzed for its return on investment (ROI).

Projects are stack-ranked, meaning the strongest ROIs, in percentage and absolute dollars returned, get done first. Weaker projects, however sexy, are often shunted aside. (And yes, I know this isn't always good for an organization

**Figure 2.2**    The Project Management Institute is a good resource for your cost-cutting efforts. (*Source:* http://www.pmi.org)

in the long term; it's up to executive management to make sure that a few seemingly weaker, but higher-potential projects, make it through the annual project-assessment process.)

In a company with a strong project management culture, it's not just the objective parts of the process that help give money-saving efforts a fair shake. There's also a cultural difference. People experienced in project reviews will be accustomed to regarding revenue projections with a jaded eye. And they'll have an inherent respect for the impact of saving money on the bottom line.

If your organization doesn't have a strong project management culture, you can still use project management-type thinking to sell your cost-cutting projects. Use resources such as those made available by the Project Management Institute (PMI) to help organize the case for your project. (The PMI home page is shown in Figure 2.2; www.pmi.org.) Project managers are good people to share ideas with; consider going to PMI meetings to swap stories and learn.

## 2.3  Implementing Energy Efficiency

This book discusses green-computing efforts—and it also mentions how much easier it is to do green computing when an entire organization is going green. This dynamic is particularly true for energy efficiency.

If your entire organization has an energy-efficiency focus, you'll easily get management and peer support for your efforts in IT. You can share ideas and best practices.

It's particularly fun to implement energy efficiency in IT as part of a company-wide effort because IT is set up to be a hero in this kind of process. IT usually has as great or greater a scope for saving energy than other parts of a company. The exceptions include companies in manufacturing and transport—"making stuff" and "moving stuff." Even there, IT can be a big part of implementing, measuring, and tracking efficiencies.

For the purposes of this chapter, however, I'll assume you're going it alone. If your money-saving and green-computing efforts are part of larger efforts at the organizational level, things will be easier, and there may be even greater opportunities than described here.

Much of what you do in implementing energy efficiency is not IT-specific. There may be some question over your jurisdiction on such issues as office lighting or building insulation. I recommend that you start with the IT-specific issues, develop a track record, and then use that to help get support for initiatives that go beyond your own department.

If you have one or more data centers, those are fully your responsibility. You can use a data center to try out ideas, including in areas such as lighting, which have broader applicability.

For end-user devices, you can save energy in a few different ways:

1. Changing how current devices are used. There's no capital cost involved here.
2. Buying new devices that are similar to current devices, but more energy-efficient. The new devices might be slightly more expensive, or slightly cheaper, than what you would otherwise buy; the focus is on operational efficiency.
3. Buying new devices that are a different class of devices. If you replace desktop computers with laptops, you may spend more or less money. If you downsize to tablets, you'll almost certainly save money. Operational efficiencies from the change should be greater.

Let's take a closer look at each of these money-saving steps.

## 2.4 Changing How Current Devices Are Used

You can save a lot of energy by changing how current devices are used—mainly by running them less. For end-user computers, simple steps can make a big difference:

1. Turning off monitors when they're not in use.
2. Turning off computers when they're not in use.
3. Turning off printers—and other office machines, if you have input into that decision—when they're not in use.

For end-user computing devices, you can configure existing or additional software to put devices on standby, or even turn them off completely, after a certain period of non-use. This can be a big money saver. If you take a step like this, educate users about it—partly so they don't subvert the process, such as by tapping their keyboard every few minutes to keep the screen lit up, and partly to encourage a cultural shift where employees take ownership of both money-saving as well as green efforts.

You can also use policy to achieve the same goal, asking users to turn off extra monitors and their computers when they go off to a meeting (and don't bring their laptop), for instance. You can tie these efforts to healthy workplace practices, such as taking a break from computer work every so often, helping to prevent repetitive stress injury and eyestrain.

EyeProtector Pro, shown in Figure 2.3, is a software product that helps keep people ergonomically safe. You can include this kind of consideration in your money-saving and green efforts.

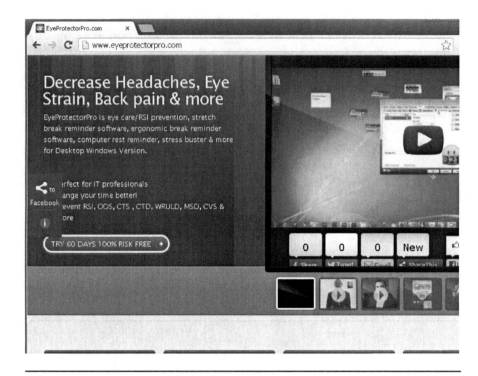

**Figure 2.3**  Ergonomic efforts can help save money through efficiency and avoided workplace problems. (*Source*: http://www.eyeprotectorpro.com)

For servers and data centers, much more is possible. In a data center, a large percentage of capacity is superfluous most of the time; it's kept running to avoid the possibility of a system crash if a sudden usage spike exceeds the currently available, online capacity. The designers of servers are way behind the times in implementing graceful spin-up and spin-down of large numbers of devices without causing system crashes—which, sadly, are far more career-limiting than wasting very large amounts of money to make sure to avoid them.

There's a lot of specialized software and hardware out there for running existing machines more efficiently. It does cost money up front, and there's always the chance that adding more components (whether software or hardware) can increase the chance of failures. In some cases, when a failure does occur, it can be very hard to find out what the cause was, which unfortunately is a strong incentive to keep things simple.

Investigate alternatives carefully and look for savings. Double-digit reductions in costs and concomitant environmental impact may be possible. Even a 10% savings in energy usage by a data center can be huge, and save a lot of money on cooling costs for a facility, as well.

## 2.5 Moving to Cloud Services

Moving from services hosted on-site to services hosted through the cloud can be a huge energy saver. This saves you energy in two ways:

1. Services are delivered more efficiently. One study found that cloud companies delivered computing services many times more efficiently than in-house data centers, mainly because this was the only business for the cloud companies. They were far more motivated, as well as structurally more able, to be efficient.
2. The cost and environmental impact of providing the services goes off your, and your company's, books, and onto the provider's.

You may feel badly, or get criticized, for the savings and greening that come from moving services out of your facilities and into those of some other company. Don't feel bad; first, the provider, as mentioned, is likely to be much

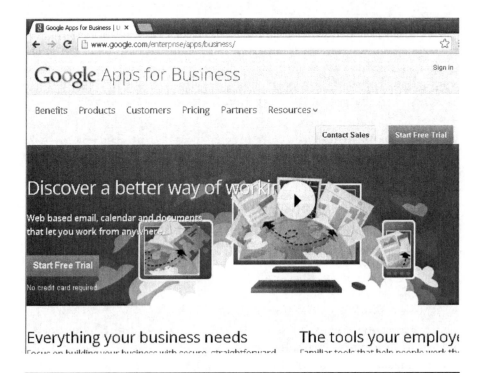

**Figure 2.4** Google Apps is a cloud-based solution for office software. (*Source:* http://www.google.com/enterprise/apps/business; Google and the Google logo are registered trademarks of Google Inc., used with permission.)

more efficient than you would be in providing the same level of service. Also, it makes economic sense to move functionality to specialists where possible, just as it makes sense for companies to use a power company and connect to the grid rather than generate all their own power.

Moving to cloud services can be a very big money-saving effort. You have to be a bit careful, however. Many on-premise software packages are at a high point of maturity, complexity, and price. Just for one minor example, Adobe Photoshop used to be given away for free with the purchase of a scanner; it now costs hundreds of dollars a copy.

At the same time, we're early in the life of cloud-computing solutions. Many of them are at the same stage as Photoshop was when it was being given away: they're simple, immature, and the companies involved will come close to giving them away in order to rapidly gain market share.

In years to come, the complexity and price of some of these products may go up. It may also drop, depending on the competitive situation, but you have to allow for the possibility of bad news—a rise in price.

Even factoring in this pricing risk, cloud computing is often a great savings, and one that's likely to at least mostly endure for the long term. It's certainly a green step.

At the current growth rate of cloud-computing solutions, it may well be worth it for your company to do a holistic review of all its software usage and what should be on-premise vs. outsourced. For instance, centralized Windows servers can cut your cost per seat a lot. So can using more or less dumb terminals and cloud-based office applications from Google instead of buying into the Microsoft operating system and office software complex. The home page for Google Apps for Business is shown in Figure 2.4.

Microsoft has also introduced its own solution, called Office Live 365. Expect lively competition in the years to come. A holistic review can help you chart a sensible path forward for your organization, so you're not just reacting to every new press release claiming greater efficiency, collaboration opportunities, and savings.

## 2.6 Digitizing Non-IT Functions

As your computing functionality becomes greener and less expensive, you gain increasing capability to virtualize previously non-IT functions. Let's look at a few examples:

*Mail.* People used to eagerly await each day's mail delivery. (Or, two deliveries.) Now most important messages are delivered by email.

*Checks and official documents.* For a long time, checks and official documents had to be physical, and fast, secure delivery services, such as FedEx, grew and grew. Then, faxing took over big parts of the traffic. Now, more and more payments and "signings" take place online.

*Telephone.* Telephony used to be reliable, but staid, with long waits for new phone lines. Now, "real" telephone numbers are digital, and cell phones and Skype carry more and more of the traffic.

These changes save huge amounts of money and increase speed and flexibility. What they aren't is very green, except in aggregate. That's because the movement of small pieces of paper (snail mail, express mail) and analog data (plain old telephone service) is being replaced with digital data.

Google Voice is a kind of uber-digitalization of phone service. You tie multiple phone numbers—cell phones and/or land lines—to a Google Voice number. Your voicemails are automatically transcribed; the results are usually accurate

**Figure 2.5**   Google Voice virtualizes phone calls—"One Number to Ring Them All." (*Source:* http://www.google.com/googlevoice/about.html; Google and the Google logo are registered trademarks of Google Inc., used with permission.)

enough, but occasionally hilarious. And calls are extremely cheap. The Features page for Google Voice is shown in Figure 2.5.

Now, however, new functions are being replaced with IT-supported equivalents—and the results can be much greener:

*Meetings and conferences.* Webinars and online learning are replacing many in-person seminars; teleconferences are replacing many in-person meetings. Flying decreases as more interaction happens from the desktop, or from a specially equipped video conference room.

*Going to the office.* Fast data connections and secure log-ins to corporate systems make working from home an occasional benefit for huge numbers of office workers and the norm for many others.

I have a couple of anecdotes about working from home. A huge part of the success of Silicon Valley is the agglomeration of many different kinds of high-tech talent, all in one place—allowing "working at work" to bring together the best and the brightest. However, even in Silicon Valley, some people and some professions are challenging the "work at work" norm.

Technical writers are among those famous for working virtually. When one hires a technical writer, the question often isn't how many days he or she might work at home—it's how few days the writer will be physically present in the office. Many writers come to the Valley one day a week from their homes in Santa Cruz or Sacramento. This saves a lot of commuting and is, therefore, quite green. It also saves money on relocating people, or paying more to hire from the limited pool of employees who live in Silicon Valley proper.

I've also had experience with fly-in commuters. A vice president of one Silicon Valley startup I am acquainted with was based in Chicago; one of his key lieutenants had her home in Virginia. They each spent about one week out of three in the office.

However, this didn't really work; the VP didn't use technology well to keep up. When he wasn't there, emails and phone calls were few; videoconferences didn't replace in-person meetings. Often, he might as well have been on Mars. And his habit of often scheduling his visits at the same time as his employee's didn't promote collegiality or relationship building for either of them with the people who routinely worked in the office.

So this points to the need to use technology aggressively to fill in gaps in physical presence. It also shows a green downside to virtual technology. Instead of moving from Chicago, which would mean a few flights back and forth to make the move, our VP took about 20 trips a year, with technology filling in the gaps in between. The carbon footprint of this strategy is much greater than the previous strategy—moving to where the job is—which it replaces.

The bottom line is that moving physical functions to the virtual world can save a lot of money, and be very green indeed—but that the two aren't synonymous. You have to manage both cost savings and environmental impact in order to optimize both.

## 2.7 Greening Your Energy-Saving Moves

As pointed out in this book, green computing saves money and helps save the environment; you can do well while doing good. However, when an initiative begins with saving money as the primary, or even the sole goal, knowing how to handle the "green" part of the project's benefits can be tricky.

There are three ways that money-saving initiatives can intersect with a green agenda:

1. *Saves money and traditionally green.* Replacing outdated Web servers with new, greener ones will save a lot in operating costs and also reduce environmental impact. Publicity around this effort can tout the cost-saving and environmental benefits equally.

2. *Saves money and not all that green.* Entering into a volume purchase agreement for laptops may save money, and the new supplier may be greener than the previous one. That fact is probably worth mentioning—maybe a paragraph or two in a press release about the new arrangement. It's not worth headlining, however.

3. *Saves money and not green at all.* Using videoconferencing to avoid going to meetings is green. Using videoconferencing and related technologies to enable the hiring of remotely located executives, who then fly into the office once a month or more, may actually be counterproductive from an environmental point of view. Don't mention the green benefits of using technology for a nontraditional hiring approach, for example, if they're not there.

The creative way to go, with the most benefits, is to start some conversations with green benefit, and others with cost savings—and then find new and interesting ways to make the same initiative serve both purposes.

For instance, you may realize that you can save money by entering into a master purchase agreement for much of your IT hardware. If you use a green-weighted selection process, however, you're likely to get environmental benefits as well as strong cost savings. You can then publicize the whole effort as both a green and a cost-saving initiative.

Your data center may be out of date. Replacing outmoded equipment with newer hardware is likely to save you money, whether it's a green effort or not.

However, if you use the opportunity to really green your data center, you may create a story worth retelling for many years to come.

One discipline that will help you stay on the right side of the greenwashing tendency is to calculate the carbon footprint for different strategies. This works even better if you've calculated the carbon footprint for your IT efforts—and, optimally, for your organization's operations as a whole. The more hard numbers you have for reference, the more credible new announcements will be.

## 2.8  Some Big Thinking About Money-Saving Efforts

Money-saving efforts often seem "nickel and dime" oriented, "small potatoes" efforts that lack the drama of exciting new products and services.

There are two responses to this. First, in modern business, a "nickel" (5% savings) or "dime" (10% savings) effort is a big deal. These kinds of savings can make a huge difference to the bottom line, especially if successive "nickel and dime" efforts cascade off one another to steadily cut costs over time.

Second, there's plenty of room for cost-saving efforts to be big and dramatic. Here are key ways to go large on saving money:

- *Stop doing stuff.* When you're in a hole, stop digging. If your travel budget has grown by double-digit percentages for a few years in a row, why? Stand back and take a big-picture look at why your people travel. Replace a big percentage of travel with videoconferencing (which will thereby pay for itself quickly), make an additional big cut in the travel budget, and enjoy the resulting savings.
- *Do similar stuff differently.* How much would you save if a quarter of your employees used iPads instead of computers? If you used the first-year savings to write or commission new apps, you could move a whole lot of functionality onto iPads—and maybe exceed your original goal.
- *Do new stuff.* As mentioned above, you can do things in IT that are currently done in "meat space," such as travel. Don't stop there, however. How do you make products? How do you sell and support them? Radically re-examine these functions to see how you can cut costs while greening them.

Ironically, big new ideas in cost-cutting tend to generate new product ideas as well—and to make the product development process better and cheaper. So don't fall for the idea that these efforts have to fight each other; ultimately, they're mutually supportive, not competitive.

## 2.9  Summary

This chapter described how money-saving and green-computing efforts complement each other: the green Zen of saving money, the advantages of energy efficiency, getting the most out of the cloud, and greening your energy-saving moves.
The next chapter describes how green computing contributes to the environment.

# Chapter 3

# Green Computing and the Environment

## Key Concepts

This chapter shows how environmental concerns contribute to the green agenda:

- Traditional environmentalism and IT
- The new green agenda and climate change
- Climate change and IT
- The future of climate change

## 3.1 Environmental Drivers for Green Computing

The drivers behind green computing come in two main flavors: allegiance to a green agenda, which has both costs and benefits, and allegiance to the direct business benefits that come from going green.

IT groups often go green primarily for the immediate benefits—saving money, reducing the use of various resources, reducing business risk, and providing better services to users. These benefits—what they are and how to get them for your IT department—are the main subject of this book.

But the benefits are a result—somewhat of a side effect—of other driving forces for going green. You need to understand these driving forces for motivation, and in order to communicate with others around what you're doing and why.

This is especially true because IT departments often go green within organizations that, for the most part, are not yet doing so. So, in pursuing green computing, the IT department is out front on issues that have major financial and even political implications. This can be uncomfortable. So, it's good to know what you're getting into as you're getting started.

In the next chapter, I'll describe a green-compatible vision for computing that makes life better for everyone involved, and is sustainable—in the business sense—as well. In this chapter I'll address three key points:

- What's driving the green agenda.
- The new imperative of climate change.
- What it means to "go green." (People, profit, and planet—even if it costs more!)

Understanding how all these threads work together will help you get both short-term benefits (mainly around cost) and long-term benefits from green computing. Each effort you make can build on the others. So, the combined effect is more than the sum of its parts.

## 3.2 What Drives the Green Agenda?

"Greens" can seem very strange indeed to a typical businessperson, whether in IT or outside it. Greens are stereotyped as having long hair, wearing Birkenstock sandals, shaving partially (or not at all), showering irregularly, and otherwise dressing and behaving unconventionally. More seriously, they are also seen as caring about nature more than people, and certainly more about nature than about economic growth or the needs of business.

Much of this is true. A tie-dyed shirt, jeans, and sandals can be just as much of a uniform for one group of people as a business suit is for another. And part of being "green" is making a priority of many things other than profit.

There are more and more greens, however, who are comfortable with business. Some are former or current businesspeople or entrepreneurs. Others just take the time to "get" business concerns in order to be more effective in pursuing their green agenda—whether that's working with business one day, or working to oppose it the next.

And still others bounce back and forth between business and environmental activism—not always an entirely positive arrangement.

It's valuable to understand some of the high points of environmentalism so you can see where the broader green agenda in society at large connects to a green agenda in IT– and understand why green computing has so many beneficial effects within IT. Green computing's effects include strong contributions, ironically, to making a profit.

## 3.3 Key Roots of Environmentalism

The United States has been a leader in environmentalism for more than a century. President Andrew Jackson set aside a hot springs in Alabama as a preserve in the 1830s; a few decades later, President Abraham Lincoln signed the land cession that became Yosemite National Park. Yellowstone National Park, the first national park in the world, was established in 1872, with a then-young Theodore Roosevelt helping convince fellow Republicans to back the bill.

So, preserving natural resources has a long history in the United States. This movement was long called "conservationism," and generally had bipartisan support. Republican President Richard Nixon may appear in the history books as one of the greatest environmentalists of all time, having signed into law major parts of the Clean Air Act and what became the Clean Water Act.

Saving endangered species, a specific concern within the conservationist movement, got a big boost with the publication of Rachel Carson's *Silent Spring*[1] in 1962. *Silent Spring* brought the problem of endangered species to wide public attention, tying it to the growing use of dangerous pesticides, such as DDT, and the harm DDT caused to birds.

Conservationist, preservationist, and antipollution concerns have spawned a wide array of nonprofit groups and a smaller array of for-profit companies. Well-known green groups include the Sierra Club; the Natural Resources Defense Council; Greenpeace; the World Wildlife Fund (whose website is shown in Figure 3.1); and many, many more.

It's worth taking a few minutes to peruse the websites of these and other organizations, or search Google News to find recent press stories about their activities. Even a small amount of research will give you a feel for what the modern green movement is all about.

There is even a Green Party in many democratic countries, with the Green Party in Germany being the largest and most powerful of its kind. Germany's Green Party website is largely available in English, as shown in Figure 3.2. This political activism ties into a reality about green groups and their individual members that's hard for business to deal with: Many of them question, and some even oppose, capitalism. This hasn't stopped green activists and business, however, from greater and greater collaboration in recent years.

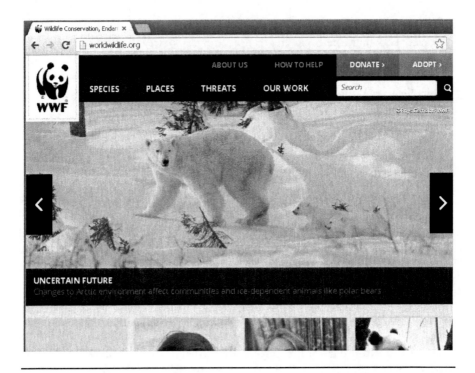

**Figure 3.1** The World Wildlife Fund is an old, large, and well-respected green organization. (*Source*: www.wwf.org)

Many green groups are quite well connected to industry and government. When I was working for a large company some years ago, it gave tens of millions of dollars to a small set of green groups. Some executives in green organizations have moved back and forth between the green organizations and trade groups for polluting industries, or government bodies, often with handsome pay packages. This job-hopping has the potential to confuse the agendas of both sides of the issue in a way that isn't necessarily healthy for anyone.

On the other hand, some groups are quite radical, and green causes have inspired energetic protests, the destruction of property, and a few acts that have been described as terrorism. Even mainstream green groups sometimes compete to show who is most "down" with the most committed activists. Greenpeace is one of the more uncompromising among the mainstream groups; Deep Green Resistance, which calls for the destruction of industrial society in order to save both people and the planet, doesn't even try to be acceptable to mainstream politicians and businesspeople.

So what drives the green agenda? A key concern of all green groups is sustainability. The underlying concern behind sustainability is that humanity is using available resources—for example, timber and phosphorus—faster than the natural environment can replace them. That makes the usage unsustainable, by definition. It's been calculated that the current population of the Earth is using several Earths worth of crucial resources—a way of measuring how short the time is until some of those resources start to disappear.

Human rights concerns are sometimes part of the green and sustainability agendas, and sometimes not. Practices such as the use of child labor and human trafficking are often targeted by green groups, and conferences such as GreenFest, which takes place in several cities in the United States each year, often include human rights groups alongside traditional greens.

The traditional green agenda also has a complicated and often surprisingly uncomfortable relationship with efforts to stop climate change, which only gained widespread public attention quite recently. If the environment is going to warm by several degrees Fahrenheit, for instance, efforts to save some of the more obscure species—which, in the pre–global-warming context, can be quite important—are now, at the same time, both a bit trivial and doomed.

**Figure 3.2**   The German Green Party has an English-language area on its website. (*Source*: https://www.gruene-bundestag.de/service-navigation/english_ID_2000025.html)

The broader green agenda now includes climate change concerns, which I'll describe in the next section, but sometimes awkwardly. You can meet greens who are markedly unconcerned about climate change, and greens who are concerned about little else.

## 3.4 Environmentalism and IT

The traditional green agenda targets resource-intensive industries, such as logging; the production of goods, such as paper; and highly polluting industries, such as the automobile industry. This traditional green agenda has not had as great an effect on IT. In fact, IT-driven innovations, such as the "paperless office" of the 1980s, teleconferencing, and telecommuting, have often been presented as a solution to key conservationist concerns.

Greens are often quite advanced in their personal use of consumer electronics and are quite savvy about using the Web, Facebook, Twitter, and other products of IT—especially the low-cost ones—to advance their agenda and to just generally have a good time, while inflicting little obvious environmental impact. Some Silicon Valley and other high-tech executives have taken strong stances in favor of green concerns.

More recently, though, it's become clear that IT has its own concerns within the traditional green agenda:

- Pollution from mining for needed materials, such as rare earth minerals (needed for computers, monitors, and, ironically, clean-energy equipment, such as solar panels and wind turbines)
- Use of electricity to power all this stuff, which contributes to traditional pollution (from coal-fired and other polluting power plants) as well as global warming
- Pollution from the disposal of smartphones, computers, monitors, servers, and so forth, after their (often short) useful lifetimes
- The mistreatment of workers who build electronic devices, particularly in China and the developing world, including the use of child labor, long working hours, prison-like housing conditions, and intense and repeated exposure to toxics. Again, some green groups see this kind of issue as a core concern, some as a related concern to their main drivers, and some as a totally separate issue.

Even with these concerns, IT people are much better received among traditional greens, at green conferences and so on, than people from traditional "bad guys," such as paper mills or auto companies—let alone tobacco companies.

You can also attend such events as an individual, which is especially easy if you become active in a green group yourself. Going to green events is a great, quick, and immersive way of getting both information about, and a feel for, the green agenda.

## 3.5  The New Imperative of Climate Change

Climate change is a new driving force behind green and sustainability concerns, and at the same time is a crisis all its own. Some people, including me, see it emerging to become as big a crisis as humanity has ever faced, right up there with the threat of nuclear war.

Climate change has also been very controversial, especially in the United States, while at the same time serving as a key driving force—perhaps the key driving force—behind green computing. So it's worth taking some time to understand climate change concerns, the controversies behind them, and what we can expect to happen going forward.

The question of whether you "believe" in climate change is complicated. There are at least four levels to the effects of climate change on you and your organization:

1. Laws and regulations relating to climate change that your company has to comply with
2. Your company's public and internal statements and actions relating to climate change
3. What you personally believe about climate change
4. Where you and others think your company should position itself with regard to climate change and your customers' and stakeholders' concerns about it

Note that the first two sets of concerns are "musts." You simply have to act in compliance with laws and regulations around climate change, such as the existence of carbon-trading requirements in areas where you do business (such as Europe; California; and, separately, the San Francisco Bay Area). And you are also strongly affected by your company's past statements, public and internal, about climate change. It's a career-limiting move to stray very far from your company's public position in your own public statements. It may also be unhelpful to stray very far from your company's internal positioning in your own statements, even within the walls of your organization.

You can, to a certain extent, hold your own personal beliefs about climate change in a bubble, separate from your actions as an employee. This becomes difficult, though, if your beliefs are strongly held.

If you strongly believe that climate change is baloney, it may be very difficult for you to act, in your professional role, to support strong action about it by your company—such as a strong green computing initiative. However, you have to do what's required to help, unless and until you can gain sufficient influence to stop it. Or, try to find an employer whose actions don't clash with your beliefs.

If, on the other hand, you're strongly concerned about climate change, there's not likely to be much that your company can do that will entirely satisfy you. Companies—especially public ones—operate under very strong short-term business drivers. They can't simply stop operations and devote all their resources to preventing climatological disaster, however valuable such action might be.

If you're in a publicly held company, the company is legally obligated to maximize financial return to shareholders. If you're in a government organization, you're responsible to voters. If you're in a privately held company or non-profit, exactly who you're responsible to depends on the documents the organization is constituted under.

But unless you own your own company or other organization, the policy you create and follow has to meet the needs of other people. Concern about climate change can inspire you—and you can use it to fashion a strategy that's winning for your IT organization, and your company or other organization, on many fronts.

But you can't do big stuff unilaterally solely because you, personally, are concerned about climate change. You need to tie your concern—or lack of concern—back to doing the right thing for your organization.

Luckily for those of us who are concerned, there are a lot of other people who are also concerned about climate change as well. There's also growing legal and regulatory pressure in different jurisdictions around the world. Cost- and risk-management concerns, as I'll show in this book, point in the same direction as well. If you're concerned about climate change, tie your desire to do the right thing back to these external drivers.

## 3.6 A Brief History of the Climate

If you do anything at all around green computing, you're likely to end up discussing—or debating—climate science with others. It's valuable to understand the basics so you can participate effectively in these discussions.

Much of the current confusion around climate change relates to prehistoric changes in the climate. The Earth's climate has cycled through a wide range of climatic changes, over periods of millions and hundreds of millions of years.

At one extreme, the Earth seems to have had one or more periods when it was "Snowball Earth"—almost totally covered by ice and snow, from the poles to the equator. This seems to have occurred about 650 million years ago—an eighth of the planet's 5-billion-year lifespan. It may have occurred before that as well. Because the white surface reflected sunlight effectively, "Snowball Earth" was a fairly durable state of affairs, but it eventually ended (possibly because burrowing worms evolved and helped take $CO_2$ out of the environment, burying it in the Earth).

The Earth has also been much warmer than today, with average temperatures 10°C warmer, and sea levels 600 feet (about 200 meters) higher than today. This was partly because there was almost no permanent ice and snow at that time, which accounts for about half the sea level rise from our current levels, and partly because much of the water was in shallow inland seas that warmed extensively. Warmer water takes up more space, thus raising the sea level.

Over the last 800,000 years—the period in which humanity has evolved to our current form—the climate has oscillated between Ice Ages (in which glaciers advanced from the North Pole down over Canada and much of Europe) and interglacial periods. We're in an interglacial period right now. The Wikipedia article on "temperature record" (http://en.wikipedia.org/wiki/Temperature_record) is a useful introduction to, and summary of, this information. Among the resources it points to is a map of the world's forest cover shortly after the last Ice Age ended. Vast areas of this forest cover have been cleared for various purposes in the years since.

The current era, called the Holocene, started about 12,000 years ago, when glaciers retreated from Europe and North America. The retreating glaciers left much of the planet covered by forests, as shown in Figure 3.3.

The temperature during the Holocene period has been remarkably stable, despite a slight downward trend, until recently.

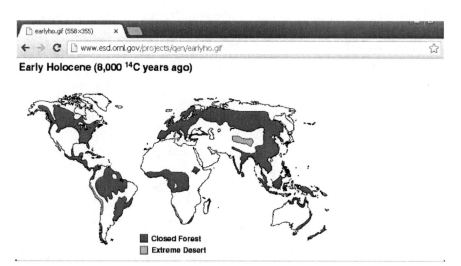

**Figure 3.3**   The beginning of the Holocene era saw much of the Earth covered by forests. (*Source:* http://www.esd.ornl.gov/projects/qen/earlyho.gif)

Some scientists theorize that a stronger cooling trend, which would have otherwise trended us toward another advance of the glaciers, has been offset by human-caused warming over most of the Holocene. Early agriculture in Mesopotamia turned a fertile river valley into a desert. The clearing of Europe's forests, largely by monks, liberated a great deal of carbon dioxide as wood rotted and was burned. Scientists believe that these and other human-caused changes had a relatively strong effect—enough to forestall the emergence of another Ice Age until industrialization began, causing the current warming.

It's really important to understand the relative stability of the Holocene to frame our current concerns about climate change, and to understand how short a time period 12,000 years—the length of the Holocene—is in relation to larger climate cycles of hundreds of thousands and millions of years. It is definitely true that the Earth's climate has cycled in the past, without human intervention. But it's also true that we are looking at likely temperature rises of 6°–10°C (about 9°–15°F) in a century—much faster than nature, let alone humanity, can adapt to.

There are also many subtle issues about how nature works that make the rapid disruptions of climate change hugely problematic. For instance, in the oceans, the littoral zones—the shallow edges of the ocean, nearest where it touches land—are tremendously productive, biologically. The rich ecosystem found in littoral zones takes hundreds of years of stability to develop.

Any rapid change in the sea level, as we are looking at in this century—perhaps two meters of sea level rise by the end of the century—destroys the productivity of most littoral zones. That productivity needs centuries of stability to re-establish itself. Under current projections, it will be many centuries before the necessary stability of sea level returns—which is a long time for people who depend on the oceans for part of their protein intake, meaning just about all of us, to go hungry.

There are also subtle issues about how people behave that make the rapid disruptions of climate change hugely problematic as well. For instance, economic drivers—and pure pleasure—drive people to build as close to the coastline as possible, and to value oceanfront property very highly indeed. A sea level rise of a meter or two this century will only submerge a small part of the planet's land area—but a huge proportion of its populated areas, causing huge disruption to humanity all over the world.

Some scientists and activists, such as ecologist Eugene Stoermer, assert that we are now leaving the Holocene—the stable weather patterns of the Holocene, the 12,000 years since the glaciers retreated from Europe—and entering the Anthropocene, a new period in which human activities dominate the planet, including the climate (see http://en.wikipedia.org/wiki/Eugene_Stoermer). In general, people have not yet grasped how dependent we are on the specific climate patterns of the Holocene, nor how likely we are—in my own view—to act to restore those patterns if they're threatened, whether it was due to human activity or not. I expect to see a great deal of activity on the geoengineering front as the reality of climate change kicks in, but the effectiveness of such efforts is very far from being proven.

## 3.7  Al Gore and Climate Change

Al Gore, whether you love him or loathe him, has done perhaps the most amazing job of scientific communication of all time. He has received a lot of praise, and a lot of criticism, for his efforts to educate people worldwide about climate change and global warming. After losing the Presidential election in 2000—with the US Supreme Court casting the tie-breaking vote—Gore dug out a slide show he had developed about climate change. The slide show, and the resulting book and movie: *An Inconvenient Truth*,[2] represent perhaps the greatest single-person effort ever in science education for the public. Figure 3.4 shows the slide show being shown in the New York State Senate.

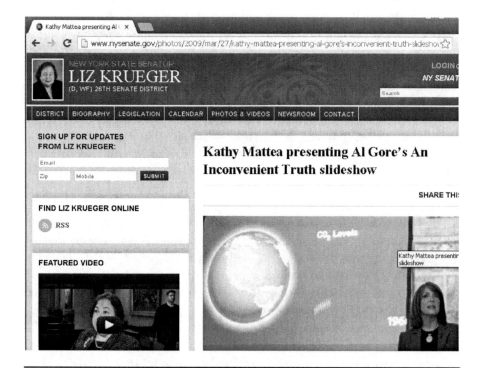

**Figure 3.4**  *An Inconvenient Truth*, in various forms, reached millions. (*Source:* http://www.nysenate.gov/photos/2009/mar/27/kathy-mattea-presenting-al-gore %E2%80%99s-inconvenient-truth-slideshow)

Al Gore and the Intergovernmental Panel on Climate Change, also known as the IPCC, shared the Nobel Peace Prize in 2007 for their efforts. *An Inconvenient Truth*[2] was largely a vehicle for publicizing the IPCC's Fourth Assessment Report, which came out in 2007 as well.

Whatever you believe about climate change, I strongly recommend that you read the book, *An Inconvenient Truth.*[2] It's an excellent summary of the state of climate science as of that time. In addition, the book has a lot of helpful pictures. It only takes about an hour to read through the book's contents, and there's a lot packed into it. Even if you disagree with Gore's conclusions, you'll at least understand the mainstream scientific argument that climate change is occurring, is caused by human activity, and requires drastic action.

Ever since *An Inconvenient Truth*[2] appeared, climate change has regularly appeared on lists of issues people worldwide are worried about. However, at this writing it's fallen quite a bit in the rankings, given that economic problems hit the world hard in 2008 and have continued to cause problems since then. At the same time, opinion polls from around the world seem to show support for stronger action than has been taken, so far. Support for climate action in the United States has risen in the wake of Hurricane Sandy, which caused so much damage—especially in New Jersey and New York—in November 2012.

*An Inconvenient Truth*[2] recommended action to address climate change by individuals as well as governments. However, governments have not taken any global action to address climate change, as they did some years earlier with chlorofluorocarbons and the then-famous "hole in the ozone" (a problem, and solution, described in some detail in Gore's book).

Especially notable is the failure of the Copenhagen summit on climate change in 2009 to produce any binding agreement. It seems that the world's governments, notably including the United States and China, are not ready to commit to solid actions to reduce greenhouse gas emissions and avert big impacts from climate change.

This puts countries, and companies, in a bind. Greenhouse gases are clearly pollutants, in that they contribute to global warming. As pollutants, they're already regulated in many countries, including the United States. However, unlike smog-causing auto emissions and most other pollutants, the effects of greenhouse gas emissions are global, not local. So, action in any one city, state, or country—or by a given company or other organization—will hardly make a difference globally. Only a global agreement can provide "air cover," if you'll pardon the pun, for governments and other entities to take effective action.

This is why local and specific actions to forestall climate change are so controversial, even among those who agree about the need for action globally. Many people who question the science, or who have economic reasons not to want action, try to use both arguments, of course—climate change isn't happening, but even if it were, no one government or company can do much to solve it.

Others see the climate issue as so serious that action is required, now, by anyone who's ready, willing, and able, to move. That sounds good, but in the absence of an international agreement, it's very hard to know just how fast and how far to cut. Europe and California, for instance, have specific targets, but they seem more likely to be missed than hit. Organizations are left to fend for themselves.

## 3.8 The 2°C Warming "Limit"

The Earth's climate system is very complicated, and any effort to predict its course over time is filled with uncertainty. The key assertion of mainstream climate scientists about warming, though, is that the temperature in the surface region of the Earth will increase as people emit increasing amounts of carbon dioxide, or $CO_2$.

The level of $CO_2$ in the atmosphere before the Industrial Revolution—that is, in the middle of the 1700s—was about 280 ppm, or parts per million. Since then, it's risen faster and faster and is now at about 390 ppm—and increasing about 3 ppm per year. Scientists have long estimated that a doubling of the Earth's $CO_2$ level, to 560 ppm, would cause the Earth's average surface temperature to rise by about 2°C, or 3.2°F.

$CO_2$ emissions are generated by power plant emissions, emissions from transportation and shipping, agriculture—cows have their own "tailpipe emissions," activities such as making cement, and clearing land for farming and other purposes. Burning coal for power emissions is the single biggest cause of $CO_2$ emissions worldwide, and China, in particular, is adding one major coal-fired power plant a week.

China, India, and other countries are raising their emissions as their people move into the global middle class. The United States has average $CO_2$ emissions of about 20 tons per person per year; China used to be at about 2 tons per person per year, but is now up around 6 tons per person per year. This is an average; some Chinese now live like Americans, but many still live low-emission lifestyles.

In his book,[2] Al Gore, and the scientists he quoted, urged that people worldwide start limiting their use of fossil fuels. Estimates were made that cutting global $CO_2$ emissions by 80% by 2050 would limit warming to a total of about 2°C.

If warming caused directly by humans is allowed to rise beyond 2°C, it's believed that the $CO_2$ cycle of the Earth will become increasingly unbalanced. As ice melts, forests weaken and die, and the ocean reaches its limit of $CO_2$ absorption, warming will take on a momentum of its own.

The 2°C limit is also important to controlling ocean acidification. As they absorb $CO_2$, the world's oceans are steadily becoming more acidic, which severely affects tiny creatures that normally form shells. Acidification threatens to prevent this, putting entire food chains, not just individual species, at great risk. Scientists calculated that emissions up to the 2°C limit were tolerable for ocean acidification; anything beyond that, very threatening.

There are two main problems with this diagnosis, as well as the proposed solution. The first is that Gore's numbers were too optimistic. It looks like the current level of $CO_2$ in the atmosphere, 390 ppm, might already be too high to prevent runaway climate change. (It's certainly too high to prevent extreme weather, which is already increasing dramatically.) That's why 350.org, the famous climate change organization led by Bill McKibben, was formed—to urge people to rapidly cut $CO_2$ emissions and get atmospheric $CO_2$ levels down to 350 ppm in a hurry, and then cut them further still over time.

The other problem is the sheer scale of the change that would be needed to reduce $CO_2$ emissions. It's hard enough for economically developed countries like the United States to start cutting their emissions by about 2% a year. But in order to reduce their $CO_2$ emissions starting now, countries like China and India would have to more or less stop conventional economic growth.

Gore and others tried to finesse this problem by letting the developing world continue to grow its emissions for a while, offset by faster cuts—and rapid development of green technologies—in the West. But Gore had outdated numbers. One of the few major errors in *An Inconvenient Truth*[2] is that it shows China, just after the year 2000, with about half the total emissions of the United States. The really inconvenient truth is that China was already catching up with the United States at that time, and has since surpassed America in total emissions—though still being well behind in emissions per person.

So, the only solution to climate change is to somehow start cutting emissions, now, without cutting the economic growth that feeds the world. Gore sketches out a too-weak solution in *An Inconvenient Truth*,[2] and websites such as Climate Progress (www.climateprogress.org) show more updated solutions. However, it would take an unprecedented worldwide effort—"the moral equivalent of war," in President Jimmy Carter's famous phrase—to even begin to cut emissions enough to stay below the 2°C warming limit.

## 3.9 Climate Change and IT

How does IT fit into the picture of climate change that Gore popularized worldwide?

On the somewhat negative side, Gore pointed out that IT generates about 3% of emissions worldwide. This is far less than construction or transport, but it is still a substantial—and growing—contributor.

The use of IT is rapidly increasing; so, in a "business-as-usual" scenario, emissions would increase rapidly, too. However, the Gore effort caught IT at a good time, as concern about costs and resource use were already growing in the IT community. So, initiatives such as those described and promoted in this book have become more popular, driven by traditional environmental concerns, carbon footprint reduction, and cost concerns.

Still, the emission of greenhouse gases in the use of IT has cast doubt on the formerly green reputation of the discipline. This combines with the widely publicized use of exploited and, in some cases, underage labor in the production of consumer electronics for major companies, to make IT less of a "good guy" than it had previously been.

Green computing is a necessary antidote to these concerns. By reducing emissions, other resource use, and getting out in front of social issues, IT departments—and computing and consumer electronics companies—can get positive attention and support for the increasing use of IT for all kinds of purposes.

IT can even help with much bigger efforts to reduce greenhouse gas emissions. For instance, air travel is the single biggest way for an individual to increase or decrease his or her carbon emissions. A flight from the United States to Europe and back, for instance, has the same carbon footprint as an entire year of a typical American's activities, about 20 tons of $CO_2$. But IT can help replace flights—for business meetings, conferences, and so forth—with videoconferences.

If the IT area can steadily reduce its emissions, while steadily taking on functions such as reducing air travel, it can be a part of the solution to climate change, rather than a small, but growing, part of the problem.

## 3.10  What's Next with Climate Change?

Al Gore made climate change a major issue in and around 2007. However, it's likely to become larger and larger in the years ahead.

Here are ten drivers that will make climate change an even bigger issue:

1. **Blowing through the 2°C limit.** According to recent reports from institutions such as MIT, $CO_2$ emissions worldwide are increasing, not decreasing as needed. There's now virtually no chance of emissions being reduced to keep warming below the 2°C limit (just over 3°F), and it could well be breached by 2050.
2. **Rapid warming this century.** Leading climate change research institutions, such as MIT and the UK's Hadley Center, are now projecting global average surface temperature increases of roughly 4 to 6°C (7 to

10°F) this century. This is still so new, and so immense, that it's not yet widely publicized or understood.

3. **Faster sea-level rise this century.** The Fourth IPCC Report projected sea-level increase of about one to two feet this century, due to warmer water taking up more space, but excluded the effects of ice melting in, well, nearly everywhere. This made the IPCC's projection a gross underestimate, and recent work is projecting a sea-level increase of one to two meters this century. Sea-level rise directly threatens infrastructure and greatly worsens the effects of hurricanes, "normal" storms, "freak" high tides, and other natural events.

4. **A great die-off in the natural world.** Even a 2°C temperature increase is likely to cause a great loss of biodiversity. Any increase beyond the 2°C limit will threaten entire food chains, and a great, "Noah's ark"–type effort to move and shelter current ecosystems may be needed to preserve some fraction of the natural world of today. The situation in the oceans may be even worse, with acidification eliminating the basis for much current marine life.

5. **Food and water shortages.** In addition to the indirect effects of ecosystem collapse, agriculture and the availability of fresh water are both under threat from extreme weather and desertification. Farmers are already experiencing problems getting the harvest in, and these could worsen severely. Figure 3.5 shows expected desertification in 2060–2069, but this timing could move up by one or more decades. (To see the article

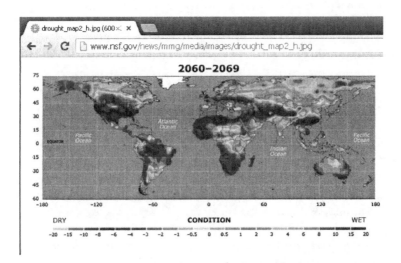

**Figure 3.5**  Even conservative projections see strong desertification this century. (*Source*: http://www.nsf.gov/news/mmg/media/images/drought_map2_h.jpg)

this image came from, visit http://www.nsf.gov/news/news_summ. jsp?org=NSF&cntn_id=117866.) Water is increasingly privatized worldwide, So, scarcity for many means a business opportunity for a few.

6. **Increased use of coal.** The use of coal for generating electricity is rapidly increasing in the developing world, swamping slight decreases in the United States and elsewhere. Coal causes $CO_2$ emissions at double the rate of oil and triple the rate of natural gas, making emissions reductions impossible.

7. **Increases in extreme weather.** Extreme weather is increasingly being blamed on climate change. Hurricane Sandy in November 2012 was the tipping point here—the first time a major weather event was directly tied to climate change across the mainstream media. Future extreme weather events will now be understood as part of the climate change picture.

8. **Use of unconventional fossil fuel resources.** Alongside fracking for natural gas, fossil fuel resources, such as deep-sea deposits and the hugely damaging Alberta tar sands, are being exploited. Greens were able to stop the Keystone XL pipeline for a while in 2012, but this is a holding action; these unconventional resources, some even more polluting than coal, are likely to be exploited.

9. **Hopelessness on limiting emissions.** Humanity, fully alerted by Al Gore and the Fourth IPCC Report, has steadily increased—even accelerated—its greenhouse gas emissions in the years since. The odds of limiting emissions while achieving conventional economic growth are increasingly understood as next to nil.

10. **The 2014 IPCC Report.** At this writing, the Fifth Assessment Report of the IPCC is expected in 2014. The previous report was a political football; the next one could fully include, partially include, or mostly exclude, the concerns cited above. Whichever way the process goes, the report will be hugely controversial, and is likely to spark a whole new level of concern about climate change worldwide.

It's hard to predict how these drivers will affect public opinion, international agreements, the legal picture, and regulation around climate change and related environmental issues. The temperature of the debate will go up—no pun intended—but, in the short term, resistance and backlash might almost match increased concern and desire for action.

In considering this, I'm reminded of the historical example of America's involvement in World War II. As Hitler launched war across Europe, including the invasion of Poland and the Blitz on London and the United Kingdom, isolationism in the United States increased. Franklin D. Roosevelt, as President, had to use a combination of bluster and subterfuge to help arm Churchill and the Brits through 1941. It was only the bombing at Pearl Harbor in December 1941 that finally—and instantly—changed public opinion, bringing the United States fully into the war.

In the long term, public opinion almost has to converge with the emerging, fast-changing objective situation—but, as the economist John Maynard Keynes famously observed, "In the long term, we're all dead." How these realities play out in the next several years is hard to predict and hugely important to any effective response to climate change.

The way these issues play out is also important to green computing. There could be a sudden demand on entire sectors of the economy to "go green"; intense political debate about what's really happening; or both at once.

Given the big picture, though, the prudent approach is to start now—to get the benefits of green computing today, and to lay the groundwork for a bigger shift in the future.

## 3.11  What It Means to "Go Green"

The emergence of climate change as an issue—and the prospect that it will only become more important in the years ahead—changes what it means to "go green."

Business has traditionally looked almost exclusively at the "bottom line"— profit. Green movements have promulgated a "triple bottom line": people, planet, and profit.

The business-friendly way of stating this is that business still exists primarily to pursue profit, but looks hard at reducing negative impacts—and creating positive impacts—for people and the planet along the way.

The more truly green way of saying the same thing is that organizations of all types should evenly balance positive impacts—no negative impacts anywhere—on humanity, on the environment, and on the bottom line, in creating strategy, pursuing business objectives, and reporting results.

All of this dovetails in an interesting way with traditional PR around the provision of a social license to operate, as described in Chapter 1. This means that a company needs to have a generally positive public perception in order to win customers, establish partnerships, get needed permissions for new facilities, and much more.

Royal Dutch Shell—an oil company, of all things—has a good summary of what a company's "license to operate" means. Figure 3.6 shows a Web page on which Shell refers to the "license to operate" idea and how Shell positions itself in relation to it.

As an example, to bring the concept to life, tobacco companies have lost part of their "license to operate." You would not want a tobacco company to

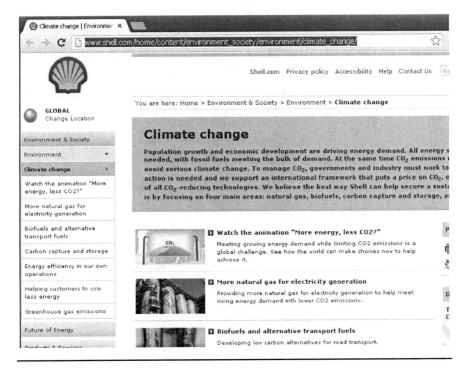

**Figure 3.6**  The impact of climate change strongly effects a company's license to operate. (*Source*: http://www.shell.com/home/content/environment_society/ environment/climate_change)

sponsor your kids' soccer team, even if the actual intentions were completely benign. Taking a job at a tobacco company is the furthest thing from cool, and a great many people will simply refuse to do so. No one wants their company or industry to be in this kind of position.

A general perception of "goodness" around environmental issues is increasingly part of this still vague, but important, concept. Within the traditional environmental framework, it wasn't that hard for a company to maintain a positive image, even if many companies still didn't bother to do so.

The triple bottom line and the license to operate have strong effects on the people parts of a company's operations. Attracting top-notch employees, retaining them, and establishing partnerships are all made easier by a generally positive impression around a company. So is getting needed permissions from government.

Bringing all of these concepts together: people, planet, and profit; the license to operate; traditional PR; and the need for people to respect an organization, one can make a case that not putting profits first actually leads to more profit over time, and that it's actually easier to advance a basket of related agendas, each of which meet different needs, than to focus exclusively on profit, to the exclusion of all other concerns.

There are a few organizations with visionary leadership that can truly put sustainability concerns at the forefront of what they do, and how they do it, every day. For most organizations—including IT departments within "main-stream" organizations—the impact of adopting a sustainability agenda is likely to be more subtle.

The idea is that you use the sustainability agenda to generate ideas, then implement them. This is a five-step process.

1. Ask yourself: "If we were putting sustainability first, what would we do?" Record the answers.
2. For each answer, ask yourself: "In traditional business terms, what are the costs and benefits of this idea?"
3. Separate the ideas into three buckets: "yes" ideas with a clear business benefit; "maybe" ideas with an unclear business benefit; and "no" ideas with no (or negative) business impact.
4. Implement the "yes" ideas immediately; research the "maybe" ideas further; and shelve the "no" ideas, or seek to implement pieces of them as volunteer efforts, partnerships with outside organizations, and other approaches away from the main path of your business.
5. Review results, report them, and repeat.

## 3.12  Why IT Is a Climate Change Solution

We've talked about how IT is one of the drivers behind climate change—responsible for 3% of emissions now, a share that's likely to grow as IT's role in business and society grows. Green computing is part of the answer to that concern.

IT is also a climate change solution, however. There are two main reasons for this: the "greenability" of IT, and "substitutability"—the ability to use IT in place of other, more environmentally damaging activities.

The "greenability" of IT has a great deal to do with the way that IT uses energy. Increasingly, the main power demands of IT are due to the needs of data centers—vast arrays of servers that answer Internet or in-house requests.

The nice thing is that data centers are fungible; one can easily be substituted for another. So one can easily replace a data center that gets its electricity from a coal-fired power plant, for instance, with one that gets its electricity from renewable energy, such as wind. The geographical location is not all that important.

This flexibility dovetails nicely with something that is normally a big negative for renewable energy: the fact that sources such as wind and solar power are intermittent. The sun doesn't shine all the time, and neither does the wind always blow when it's needed.

However, data centers can be sited in various locations, with various forms of power. Most of the time, most of the renewable energy will be available to power them; when it's not, fossil fuel–fired plants can be used instead. One hundred percent uptime might be achieved by using fossil fuels 10% of the time, which means a 90% savings on fossil fuel usage.

Other aspects of IT are greenable as well. IT devices can be made with fewer rare minerals, by better-paid workers, and with a strict prohibition on the use of child labor in any part of the supply chain. And disposal can be handled better and more safely than it is today.

In the short term, companies can prioritize using suppliers and partners who have greened their operations. In the medium and long term, the prospect exists for entire companies, and even the entire IT industry, to be a model of green behavior and green supply chains.

The other win for IT is substitutability. Videoconferencing is an obvious example.

Instead of having people travel for a meeting, they can videoconference. Or, people in a given facility can meet in person, and a speaker can appear via videoconference.

Cisco Systems is pioneering the development of conference rooms that are built out as if they were one half of a whole—a semi-oval of chairs around half a conference table. Videoconferencing equipment then brings two such halves together, creating a complete, virtual conference room. The people alongside you are physically present with you; the people across from you might be 1,000 or 10,000 miles away.

This is vastly greener than having physical meetings—and roughly as effective. The slight remaining time lags and cognitive overhead induced by virtuality is roughly competitive with the effects of jet lag and distraction if people physically traveled instead. As the technology improves, the downsides of virtuality can be further reduced, possibly making a virtual solution preferable in every way to a physical meeting.

I experienced such a conference room in 2010. Using the room—for a discussion about the advantages of, you guessed it, virtual conference rooms—was as big a "wow" as I've had in thirty-plus years in IT.

Just as IT can help people meet without traveling, it can help them read a "book" that is never transported nor printed; visit a city without going there; order products online, for efficient multicustomer delivery, rather than driving to the mega-mall.

IT can also help with the smart use and management of energy, from keeping just the needed parts of an office building lit and heated (or cooled), to power management in an individual home. The much-discussed "smart grid" might, if implemented, be the largest IT project ever. The often-criticized models that climate scientists use to predict the finer points of climate change are products of the world's most powerful supercomputers.

Overall, IT has a powerful opportunity to be a "good guy" in the struggle for sustainability and the battle against climate change, and even more so as concern about climate change, in particular, grows in the years to come.

## 3.13 Career Development and "Going Green"

Before you dive into one or more green computing projects, it might be worth a moment to consider the career impacts of "going green."

There are two driving forces you may want to consider: The first is the growing importance of environmental issues; the second is the growing importance, in business and in society, of IT itself.

I am, of course, a fan of going green, and find myself in the forefront of those concerned about climate change. The only thing I assume from the fact that you're reading this book is that you're interested in the topic. Or you may be a skeptic, ordered to look into green computing by your boss. I do believe, however, that you—like most people in IT—are willing to be influenced by evidence, and that the evidence for addressing sustainability concerns, in general, and climate change concerns, in particular, will only grow in the years ahead. So, I'm happy to have you engaging in this topic now, confident that it will only grow more important for you, and that you and others will only become more "down" with this cause, in the years ahead.

Getting strongly involved in green projects will make you more attractive to many employers, and less attractive to a few. I believe that the "more" group is much larger today, and growing, even in the United States, where climate science denial is more common, and that the "less" group is smaller, and shrinking.

Taking on and completing green projects also shows you to be flexible and able to deal with a wide range of stakeholders and a wide range of concerns, while still, hopefully, "getting stuff done." I was able to build such a reputation for myself by delivering a long-delayed video portal project for one company's worldwide operations in a single year of consultancy. The project was green—but more than green as well. Completing it did a great deal for my credibility, not only as a green computing advocate, but also just as someone who "gets stuff done."

As the importance of IT grows—within companies and societies—the demands on all of us are only going to increase. Showing yourself as flexible and capable—on green issues, and other issues as well—can only be beneficial.

Whether or not you're a convinced green, as I am, use the green agenda for inspiration and effectiveness. Make sure that your projects deliver traditional business benefits as well.

Keeping the business, as well as environmental, benefits in mind will actually make your efforts—and your career—more sustainable.

## 3.14 Summary

Traditional environmental concerns, including those specific to IT, are part of the green agenda. The green agenda was slow to accommodate climate change. It's widely understood that IT is a growing contributor to climate change—which will become a bigger and bigger worldwide concern in the years ahead. The next chapter describes a new, less expensive, and greener vision for computing.

# Chapter 4

# A New Vision of Computing

*"If you fail to plan, you can plan to fail"*

– attributed to Benjamin Franklin

## Key Concepts

This chapter describes a new, greener vision for computing:

- Simplicity: Beyond the PC
- The new green agenda and climate change
- Cloud computing
- The Zen of green computing

## 4.1 Cloud Computing Emerges

The average person's view of computing's future is largely shaped by Star Trek and similar science fiction TV shows and movies. On the bridge of the Enterprise, people talk out loud to the computer; it answers back by voice, and via screens dispersed around the bridge, the walkways, recreation areas, and personal spaces. Meeting rooms are served by large displays, but the displays serve a supportive role; they're often dark to allow the focus to be on discussion between people. Videoconferencing, though often interstellar, is not all that different from what we see today.

In Star Trek, we see an early version of cloud computing, at the Enterprise level (if you'll excuse the pun). People say, "Computer," and expect to access all the resources on the ship. There may be local processing, but it's hidden; people are talking to a unitary system. Unlike today, there aren't separate logons for separate systems, and there's no separation between different clouds; everything is united.

Technology trends and user demands are driving computing toward a future not very different from what we saw on Star Trek, as far back as the 1960s—a surprisingly durable vision from half a century ago. The great thing about this new agenda is that it's more powerful, yet less expensive and less resource-intensive, than the microcomputer-based model that it's largely replacing.

The biggest difference between the emerging computing model and the Star Trek vision is the strong dependence of today's users on smartphones. Very personal, and very easy to use, they bring computing even closer to the user and their needs than the distributed computing resources of the Star Trek model.

The most difficult thing about this agenda for IT departments is how badly people want it. Users are bringing their own devices to work, expecting—OK, demanding—that people support them, and asking that almost all the software functionality they need be delivered as an app or app-type software application. Tools for taking on bigger tasks should, according to users, be delivered in familiar forms—via Microsoft Outlook, through familiar workbench tools such as Adobe Photoshop and Microsoft Excel, or as an easy-to-use application running in a browser window. But people want the benefits of cloud computing even when working with familiar tools.

In this chapter, I'll set out a new vision for computing that includes all of the hardware and software trends going on today and casts them in a sustainable model, allowing you to implement ever-greener computing in a way that surfs the breaking wave of longer-term hardware and software trends, rather than trying to ignore or overcome them. The new approach is a less expensive and more powerful approach to getting computer services to all the people in your organization, and beyond.

## 4.2 The End of the PC Era

For years, the driving force behind changes in computing was the ever-increasing performance of microprocessors. Moore's Law famously says that the number of transistors that could be etched onto a microchip doubles every 18 months. Figure 4.1 shows the first 30 years of Moore's Law as reflected in Intel microprocessors. (The 8086 microprocessor was used in early IBM PCs.)

Moore's Law is now somewhat hamstrung by the difficulty of cooling ever-denser transistors. But whether it continues to be fully achieved or not, it's no longer the most important dynamic in computing.

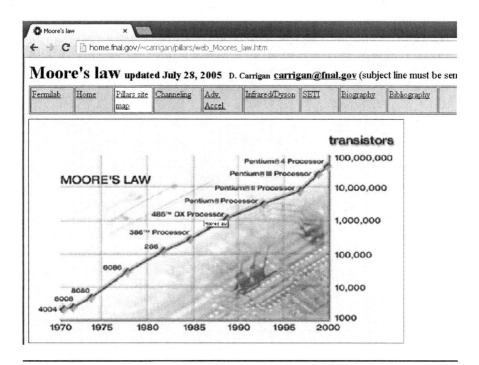

**Figure 4.1** The number of transistors in new microprocessors has rocketed upward. (*Source*: http://home.fnal.gov/~carrigan/pillars/web_Moores_law.htm)

There are now two trends that are driving computing: ever-faster networking and ever-larger hard drives. Both of these fundamental trends in computing are following Moore's Law–type trajectories.

Mainframe computing was the reigning paradigm for computing for more than 30 years—from the emergence of computers for business use after World War II until well after the arrival of personal computers in the 1970s. Computer processing power and storage were expensive and precious; telecommunications (of kilobytes of text, not megabytes of graphics) were relatively inexpensive. So users worked at terminals connected to a mainframe computer.

The slowness of computer operations and data transmission led to big problems for users. I remember, early in my career, watching skilled data entry people wait, and wait, and wait for their screens, which were green on black, text-only, to refresh. It was endlessly frustrating, and a waste of time and money for everyone involved.

Microcomputers, such as the Apple II and the IBM PC, put computer power, hard disk storage, and the communications between them right in front of the user. Response time was almost miraculously faster. As microcomputer capability increased—following the Moore's Law curve—personal computers could run graphical user interfaces (GUIs) rather than text-only, command-line

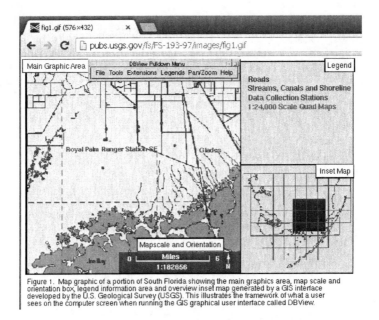

Figure 1. Map graphic of a portion of South Florida showing the main graphics area, map scale and orientation box, legend information area and overview inset map generated by a GIS interface developed by the U.S. Geological Survey (USGS). This illustrates the framework of what a user sees on the computer screen when running the GIS graphical user interface called DBView.

**Figure 4.2** Graphical user interfaces are now the standard for computing. (*Source*: http://pubs.usgs.gov/fs/FS-193-97/images/fig1.gif)

interfaces. A primitive GUI for geographic information systems is shown in Figure 4.2. Many cloud computing systems cleverly limit the use of graphics onscreen to help the screen refresh faster across the network.

Networking capability gradually increased to allow people to send documents to each other, then to send email across different systems, leading to the global connections of today.

Now we're in a new era. Because of ever-faster networking, including global communications over the Internet, the elements that made up the personal computer are being broken apart again. For many functions, including cloud-based software, the main processing capability and disk storage are once more remote from the user; only the user interface runs on the user's personal computer, tablet, or smartphone.

This is a wonderfully simple and powerful model for the user. The need for users to manage their computers steadily declines as more and more of the computer power they access is hosted elsewhere. The personal computer becomes a thinner and thinner client connected to ever-more-powerful computing resources.

The use of tablet computers and smartphones—and apps that run on both—is speeding and deepening this trend. Software designers have to make functionality available to users in small, easily digested chunks. Users mix and match scores or hundreds of small programs that handle discrete tasks, plus a few "workbench" programs that often host app-like tools of their own—think of Photoshop and its wide marketplace of filters, or Excel add-ins.

I will argue here that users are pulling the current computing ecosystem, inside and outside the workplace, into an even more radically different model. But first, let's look at how the current computing model impacts IT.

## 4.3 Some New-Model IT Challenges

My overall take is that the direction in which users are leading IT—toward smaller, more convenient, more personal devices—is ultimately the right one. It's not easy, though, to get there.

Let's take a look at some of the problems IT is experiencing, and make a few suggestions as to how to solve them in light of the emerging big picture.

The new model of computing is putting a great deal of strain on IT departments. The root problem can be called "the consumerization of IT." Challenges include the following:

- Ever-greater requirements for ubiquitous and secure access to work-related email, information, and applications
- The need to support employees' personal devices—smartphones, tablets, and computers—in the workplace and off-premises
- The need to support employees' personal email accounts and favorite software
- Complicated interactions among the employees' own software and devices and work-issued software and devices
- Viruses and malware on employees' personal and work-issued devices

Not only do users demand support for all of these scenarios and their problems; more and more, they win. IT policies on supporting a wider variety of devices are no longer just a matter of the organization's convenience. These policies are an issue in attracting hot prospective employees, making people productive, and retaining them. For instance, there are some potential employees, inside and outside IT, who just will not take a job at a company that uses the "wrong" kind of emailing software—that is, the kind they're not used to.

Trying to control users closely is less and less of an option. Some large enterprise organizations held the line for a long time, insisting that work only be done on work-issued smartphones (usually BlackBerry devices) and work-issued computers (usually laptops).

What broke this down was, as much as any one factor, the late Steve Jobs. The iPhone and the iPad have been just too popular, and too useful, for those of us in IT to turn our collective noses up at them. When the CEO starts bringing an officially proscribed iPad to board meetings, you know you've lost.

Yes, some companies still try to insist on the use of company-issued devices, but most are adapting to a mixed world of user-contributed and company-issued hardware and software. This is a massive pain for IT in the short and medium term, but a useful goad toward where computing is really going in the long term.

## 4.4 A Few Examples from a Multinational

I can give a couple of examples of the emerging blended approach to computing from my experience working at a multinational during the recent financial crunch.

During my time there, one of the biggest projects was an effort to extend a new information service to the company's 100 top executives worldwide. This was a daily update, to be kept highly confidential: Not only were outsiders not allowed to see it, but other executives had to be kept out of it as well.

During a trial run of the new service, it turned out that executives had to use their Windows system password to set up access for their mobile phones to the service (not the screen password, but a deeper-level and, usually, different one). Many of the executives concerned didn't even know they had a Windows system password, let alone what it was. The secretary, IT person, or predecessor who had set this up for them was, as often as not, long gone.

IT first refused, then acquiesced, to the evident need to hand hold each and every one of the chosen executives in getting their initial login completed (and to repeat the exercise every time a mobile phone disappeared down an airport toilet or other unplanned destination).

The mobile phones in use in the company at that time were relatively up to date, but video on a mobile phone was then fairly new, and only the very latest and greatest models had really reliable video playback. The company's chief executive wanted all of his top 100 people to see and hear him share about key issues on an almost daily basis, so this was another issue to work around. (And a total mobile phone replacement cost of somewhere around $1,000, once IT and executive time was included, was nothing to sneeze at when multiplied by 100.)

It took many months to get this high-profile project to work.

Other IT challenges were part of daily life at this company, as well. Its wired and wireless networks did not, at that time, support access to the Internet. To use a public-facing wireless network and check one's personal email, you had to go to a specific floor and log onto one of a small number of PCs that had access to the regular Internet. This caused endless problems for employees trying to juggle a (usually) small amount of personal business with the big workloads that the company's best people tended to sign up for.

The final project that may be worth mentioning is one that I led. Some large companies are (in)famous for using very thin pipes—that is, very low-bandwidth data connections—to support individual branch offices, especially when the company has worldwide operations in countries or regions with less-developed IT infrastructures. It was common for branch offices to have connections that were highly secure, highly reliable, but very low bandwidth; think 128 KBps for all the employees in a branch. Downloading a PowerPoint presentation from a PC in a branch office could cause delays for other users.

My project was to implement a video portal so users could download videos, often of their own executives explaining quarterly results, which were rather good for the company at the time, despite the financial crash. The only way to make this work over the thin wires that many branch offices were on was through an impressively distributed cached system specifically designed for serving videos in bandwidth-constrained environments. A few hundred highly desired videos could be made locally available for fast access; other, less-often-used videos might not be available until the next business day.

Using existing infrastructure, we were able to get the system agreed, designed, tested, and deployed in less than a year. Not all of the company's worldwide employees (more than a quarter of a million, at the time) got access by launch day, but an awful lot of them did. The remaining areas and branch offices received clear instructions as to what they had to do if they wanted to get access as well.

## 4.5  How a Company Adopted the iPhone

The process by which this company began to adopt the iPhone for internal use can be summed up in a single word: unwillingly.

Mobile phones are often worn in holsters on men's belts, much like six-shooters in the Old West. However, cowboys typically had two six-shooters; most mobile phone users only have one mobile phone.

At this company, however, two mobile phones were almost the standard during the global credit crunch in 2008. That's because corporate standards mandated the use of a different kind of phone for business, but the company's office workers—wanting access to the latest and greatest—insisted on iPhones. So hundreds of workers at the company's headquarters carried both—a company-issued phone for business use and an iPhone for personal use, music, and fun.

While one phone can potentially be slipped into a pocket, two phones is too much. So both phones tended to end up on opposite sides of the male employees' waists, in leather holsters, just like Old West six-shooters.

The ironies that resulted were rich and humorous. At the very time that we were struggling to get reliable video playback on the mobile phones the bank supported, users could pull up a YouTube video on their iPhones at any time of the day or night, with attractive and reliable playback on the large iPhone screen.

So the company has adopted the iPhone as an informal alternative for personal use. Now, it's under increasing pressure to adopt the iPhone formally.

## 4.6  A Mental Model for IT Simplicity

Where are knowledge workers, such as a company's employees and millions of other corporate workers worldwide, leading IT departments? IT already functions as an extension of people's minds. I've heard the following words said when people leave behind or lose their smartphone or other device: "I feel like I've lost part of my brain."

A useful way to think of the IT of the future is as a literal extension of the user's mind. Direct connections between the brain and the cloud may or may not be the future of computing, but it's a useful way to think of computer access in the future.

Imagine if you literally had direct mental access to computing resources. Your thoughts could be "heard" by the cloud (when you wanted them to be), and the cloud could speak to you, as a voice in your head, and show you results in, let's say, 1280 x 800 resolution (the resolution and aspect ratio of a widescreen laptop, which is similar in its proportions to the more useful part of the human visual field).

Now we're beyond Star Trek and heading toward the world of The Matrix— where the computing interface is a plug in the back of your head, and you can enter immersive environments and interact with others in a world that's half like reality, and half like a dream.

If you're anything like me, this sounds great—and only a little scary. But imagine, in using a direct mental connection, how you would feel about, and react to:

- Bugs in software
- Slow response times
- Unclear interfaces
- The need to install and update software
- System crashes

- The idea that dying in cyberspace tended to cause the actual physical body in "meat space" to die as well

Not much fun to think about, is it?

Still, this is a useful mental model, for two reasons. The first is that it might literally be true someday; scientists are already experimenting with direct mental control of computing interfaces. ("Yes/no" works well, while running a mouse cursor across a computer screen is pretty imprecise.)

Android's voice interaction, and Apple's Siri, are speech-driven interfaces that feel very personal indeed. It wouldn't take many Moore's Law–powered doublings in these system's capability for each to become a primary access point for a lot of today's computing tasks, though, as well as new ones we haven't imagined yet.

The second reason for considering a direct mental interface is that people are already reacting to their devices and software as if the computing experience were almost this personal to them. I know that I spend a lot of time using my smartphone (a "green" Samsung Replenish running Android) and my iPad (a fast iPad 4) because I experience few PC-type problems with them.

Smartphones and the iPad are good models for another reason. Their software is delivered via apps, which compete for users' interest and cash in app markets overstuffed with hundreds of thousands of offerings, many with overlapping functionality. Apps compete on the basis of power, ease of use, and a hard-to-define "cool factor."

Many IT departments are managed via service-level agreements. Service-level agreements are great, but they're basically promises not to mess up. As you acquire and develop new systems and services for your users, challenge yourself: Apply the direct mental access model when thinking through how users will interact with them. Seek to make them as easy to use, reliable, and interesting as if they were going to be directly accessible to the user from their thoughts. This will help you meet the true standards of users, who have been conditioned by thousands of app developers eager to make users' lives easier and more fun.

## 4.7 Why Green Computing Fits the New Model

The key enabling technology powering the new computing model I'm describing is ubiquitous, fast networking, both wired and wireless. The key contribution of this kind of networking is the ability to physically split the jobs of doing calculations, holding data in storage, and running the user interface.

The archetypal model for this use of fast networking is a cloud computing service such as Salesforce.com's Customer Resource Management (CRM) software. Users access the software, which is delivered as a service, through their browser. The acronym SaaS, for Software as a Service, sums this up. The other name for this approach, which is somewhat broader, is cloud computing—the delivery of computing services to the user, whereby the user accesses networked resources in a truly seamless manner.

What's green about cloud computing? Cloud computing allows the different elements of computing to be split up, with specialization taking place at each point in the chain. This allows efficiency, which allows for much lower use of resources.

Let's look at the various elements of computing services and how they work in cloud computing. Table 4.1 sums up the comparison between PC-based, networked services; in-house services; and cloud computing.

There are three key reasons why cloud computing is superior to either in-house hosted software or PC-based software, from a green computing point of view:

- **Efficiency.** In the PC-based software model, every user is their own system administrator (IT has to try to take over remotely, which is not easy). This is simply not the user's job, and inherently inefficient. For software hosted by IT, the IT team has to administer a very wide range of software tools, many of which might have only a few users in-house. This allows for greater, but still suboptimal, efficiency. With cloud computing, the vendors administer the software they sell and maintain. This gives the greatest scope for focus and the efficiency that results.
- **Greenability.** For PC-based software, the user's computer has to be quite robust, and inherently un-green. For in-house hosted software, the in-house servers have to be quite robust. In both cases, processing power and data access, and the electricity to support them, have to be provided at a specific place and time. This is inherently un-green. Cloud computing also allows a large number of small devices—thin clients, including smartphones—to access a smaller number of data centers. Each can be optimized to do what it does best, with lower resource use at both ends.
- **Responsibility.** There are two levels to responsibility and green computing. The first is who handles computer support for each piece of software—the individual user, for PC-based software; the organization as user, through IT, for software hosted in-house; and the vendor, for cloud computing. The second is who owns the carbon footprint and other resources associated with the software's use. Cloud computing moves the direct responsibility outside the firewall, and outside the organization's literal and metaphorical walls as well. The organization still "owns" the carbon footprint, and so forth, in the sense that it "owns" its supply chain,

**Table 4.1 – Comparing PC Software, Data Center Hosting, and Cloud Computing**

| | PC-based software | Software hosted in-house | Cloud computing |
|---|---|---|---|
| **Where software resides** | User's PC | Servers inside the firewall | Vendor's servers offsite |
| **Where processing occurs** | User's PC | Servers inside the firewall | Vendor's servers offsite |
| **Where data resides** | User's PC | Servers inside the firewall | Vendor's servers offsite |
| **User interface runs** | User's PC | User's PC or other device | User's PC or other device |
| **Optimization of resources** | Very little | Some | A great deal |
| **Data backup** | Only as extra-cost item | Yes | Yes |
| **Software upgrades** | User or IT | IT | Vendor |

but this is much less direct, and more easily managed, than having direct ownership and responsibility.

Separate discussions about the advantages for cloud computing in the areas of efficiency, greenability, and responsibility follow. However, before we consider those, let's look at whether cloud computing is the whole answer, and at some of the disadvantages of cloud computing.

## 4.8 Is Cloud Computing the Whole Answer?

When PCs first became available, they were not the whole answer to organizations' computing problems. However, over a period of about 30 years—from 1980 to 2010—PCs became ubiquitous. There were still many other problems and opportunities, besides the mammoth task of moving computing functionality to PCs and getting the most out of them. But that task was the main story for that entire period.

It's likely that the next few decades of computer use will similarly be defined by the increasing move of software functionality off of users' PCs and other devices, and off of IT's in-house servers, and into the cloud. Some functionality, including organization-specific functionality, will continue to be designed, developed, and delivered by IT, but this will be built on open-source frameworks, industry-standard tools and techniques, and other resources not owned by IT. The "secret sauce" for each organization will be how it selects, combines, and adds value to these largely externally sourced resources.

Even internally developed solutions will be delivered as if they were cloud based, from the user's point of view. In fact, IT will be managing, and the user will be—I hate this phrase—"consuming," a mix of public, private, externally based, and internally based clouds. IT will make this all a relatively seamless whole by providing necessary infrastructure, shared services such as single sign-on, and support.

So the short answer to most questions about IT trends will be some variant on the phrase, "cloud computing." Longer answers, though, will be quite rich and varied. A key ingredient in those answers will be the speed with which organizations move the majority of computing functionality to some version of cloud computing.

Over time, most of the computing functionality "consumed"—that word again—by an organization's users will be delivered via cloud computing. There are various potential ways to measure this, but a simple one is the user's face time with various software tools. As cloud computing takes over, becoming the dominant method of delivering computer software, a greater and greater proportion of users' computing time will take place in the cloud.

## 4.9  Disadvantages of Cloud Computing

Like the move to PCs before it, broad and deep adoption of cloud computing will have its problems. Here are a few of the more prominent ones:

- **Slow response time.** A famous study by IBM, "The Economic Value of Rapid Response Time," is shown in Figure 4.3. You can access it at http://www.vm.ibm.com/devpages/jelliott/evrrt.html. The productivity of users, based on system response time, was analyzed in this study. The most famous finding was that response times of greater than one second had a huge effect on users' productivity. Cloud computing systems often fail to meet this and other sensible response-time benchmarks.
- **Lack of customizability.** Cloud computing achieves much of its power and efficiency through delivering a "one size fits all" experience. Since one size doesn't truly fit all, organizations need to customize the experience, and doing so is often impossible, or unachievably difficult.
- **Lack of pricing leverage.** Cloud computing companies can easily get clients to adopt their software widely, then steadily raise the price, charge

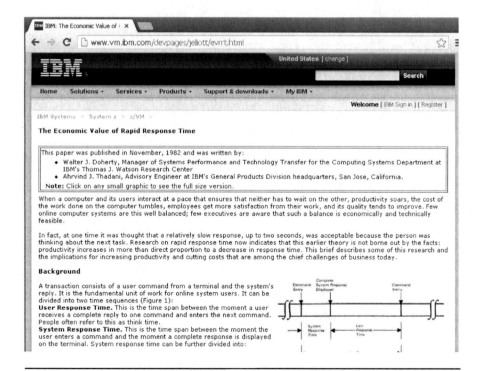

**Figure 4.3**    IBM has a famous paper on the importance of rapid system response time. (*Source*: http://www.vm.ibm.com/devpages/jelliott/evrrt.html)

the same high rates for power users and occasional users, and otherwise make it very expensive to continue using the software. It can be very difficult for organizations, as customers, to fight back. Multiply this issue by numerous cloud computing relationships, and an organization could get into real difficulties in keeping its computing costs reasonable.

- **Variability in user experience.** Cloud software interfaces are meant to be simple, but "simple" can mean a lot of different things. Users can have a vastly different experience with one cloud computing solution versus another.

Experienced IT people will recognize each of these problems as variants of issues that arose during previous generations of computing usage. A few examples include:

- **Response time: PCs as the answer.** PCs became popular largely because mainframe-based solutions were so darn slow. Moore's Law allowed the industry to throw ever-increasing amounts of processing power and storage at the problem, bringing response times down (with hiccups, such as slow response times on early Mac and Windows machines).
- **Customizability—the never-ending battle.** PC software is also notoriously difficult to customize, and the suffering caused by this is only ever managed, never solved. For one example, millions of low-end users struggle with the complexity of Microsoft Word, while power users struggle with its lack of, well, power. A rich ecosystem of solutions ameliorates this problem.
- **Variability in user experience—largely resolved by standards.** First Apple, with the Macintosh, then Microsoft, with Windows 3.x and Windows 95, created and implemented strict user interface standards. Although software variability remains a problem, it's much less than it was at one point, and users get a surprising amount done without getting training or resorting to a user manual.

The point here is that the market is likely to, more or less, work to provide tolerable solutions to the challenges thrown up by cloud computing. It may take a long time, though, for any one problem, such as the price of one key solution or the response time of another, to be resolved favorably. Sometimes, the resolution will be to move to a competing solution, as difficult as that can be.

## 4.10  Managing Disadvantages of Cloud Computing

Managing the disadvantages of cloud computing mainly depends on a very old, and very important, maxim: caveat emptor, or "buyer beware." You have to manage cloud computing vendors and their claims just like you do any other vendor.

There are a few specifics, though, that will help you get the benefits of cloud computing while insulating yourself from any downsides:

- **Don't just become an enthusiast.** Cloud computing is the wave of the future, but don't let yourself be associated with a simplistic approach that can be boiled down to "cloud is good." Most computing capability may be cloud based in a decade or two, but you don't always have to be the first one to get there.
- **Make one bet at a time.** When moving major systems from PC-based or internally hosted software to the cloud, make just one big bet at a time—and then make that bet a winner. If you can't make the transition successfully, walk away. Either way, figure out the lessons to be learned. Don't just keep throwing money into the cloud without follow-up.
- **Use the cloud metaphor internally.** Cloud computing is easy, even though moving to it can be difficult. If you make your internally hosted services available within the cloud metaphor—following through on a commitment to radical ease of use—then these services contribute to your users, no matter where they're actually hosted.
- **Watch costs and cost possibilities.** Cloud computing is becoming popular because it's so easy and, initially, inexpensive for users. By the time you notice that a new cloud service is gaining traction—even as its price keeps rising—it may be too late to change things. Get involved in these decisions early, and budget for whatever growth might be in the offing.
- **Become an expert on managing clouds.** Managing clouds is going to become just as important as managing internally hosted services has been in the past. In fact, externally and internally provided services will all become increasingly cloudy. So get good at managing cloud-based services.
- **Get green benefits spelled out.** Which cloud computing services consciously support green computing—lower power usage, lower resource use, positive impacts on the environment and society? Which Web host a cloud company chooses, for instance, is a big part of the overall impact; a green host makes for a green service, overall. Hold your cloud computing suppliers to high standards for green computing.
- **Become an expert in SLAs.** Service level agreements (SLAs) are the documents that describe just what you get for your cloud computing dollar. Feel free to negotiate SLA terms, and follow up energetically to make sure you're getting what you pay for.
- **Have a backup.** Any given cloud-based service can become unavailable, raise its prices too fast, fail to add needed features, or otherwise become a lesser option at any time. Have a planned alternative for any of your cloud services that you may need to move away from, and have a migration strategy ready in case that dreaded day ever comes. (One good discipline is to

be ready to move from any of your cloud computing services to the best alternative approach—cloud-based or not—quickly and efficiently.)

As with the move to computing based on PCs and networks, things have a way of working themselves out.

By being a careful and thoughtful adopter of cloud computing, and related trends, you can avoid mistakes and stay out of dead-end streets. A steady, managed, and assertive adoption will put you ahead of others.

## 4.11  What to Do Besides Cloud Computing

Cloud computing is a huge contributor to green computing by being inherently more efficient and easier to "green," and by moving responsibility for computer-related impacts away from you and your users (who have many other things to manage) to the cloud computing company (for whom efficiency in providing services is crucial to their image and their bottom line).

However, besides a carefully managed transition to cloud computing, what else can you focus on?

The most visible single element is devices. Users want inexpensive, portable, easy-to-use devices with a long battery life. And, increasingly, they're choosing such devices on their own, and then pressuring you to support them. The Apple iPhone (which is steadily replacing other mobile phones in many companies) and the Apple iPad (which pioneered a newly popular category) are perhaps the two most prominent examples.

Smaller, lighter devices are inherently greener than bigger, heavier ones. The impact of the physical components; power use; "embodied energy" needed to make a device; the expense and resources incurred by moving larger things around, in addition to breaking or losing them—these are all elements that make small + light = green. Chapter 6 covers these aspects of devices in detail.

The most subtle but powerful element in going green, however, is the human factor. An organization's most important—and, in most cases, most expensive—resources are its human resources. Look very hard at reducing support costs and increasing usability.

Actually, support costs are likely to drop, and usability is likely to increase, with or without your help. That's because users will take matters into their own hands, whenever needed. You can either lead the move to carefully planned, integrated, secure, and otherwise desirable green and easy solutions—or follow a move by your users that accomplishes their goals, without supporting any of yours that they don't happen to have front of mind at the moment they're making a choice.

So cloud computing is just part of the move to green computing. Use all the tools, techniques, and approaches described in this book, and in other resources, to make a planned, strategic move to green computing, and maximize the benefits as you go.

In addition, be ready to be flexible. If your users get out in front of you in the move to green computing—for instance, by bringing iPads or Android tablets into the office before you're ready—embrace the transition as quickly and enthusiastically as you can. Combine planned moves toward a green computing future with reactive and opportunistic efforts that accomplish the same goals.

## 4.12 Efficiency and Cloud Computing

It's not immediately obvious that cloud computing is inherently more efficient than PC-based networked computing or computing based on internal servers. But it is.

Cloud computing has efficiency benefits at both ends of the fast connections that make cloud computing possible. The more computing is delivered by the cloud, the thinner clients can be. And the more centralized the provision of each service is, the more effectively it can be delivered.

Google is a great example, as shown in Figure 4.4. The company has built its current immense profitability on a backbone of innovative data centers. It all starts with the unique server model pioneered by Google—basically, a bunch of circuit boards lashed together, without cases that trap heat inside. But the entire data center is designed for maximum efficiency.

Google is said to pay as much as one-third less for, say, a search, than many of its rivals, gaining a huge competitive advantage. Such a big cost advantage makes existing services profitable and new services feasible. Google gets more out of its hard work by marketing its advantages in this area as a plus, both as a demonstration of competency and an indicator of Google's commitment to the environment.

Oh, and those relatively inefficient rivals of Google that I alluded to? They may not be as efficient as Google, but they're far more efficient than most IT departments. Unless you basically gut your current infrastructure and replace it with a carefully planned and (initially) expensive new approach, you're not likely to approach the efficiency of the people whose entire business depends on low-cost, low-heat, low-energy operations.

Of course, you should green your own operations as much as you can. But in most cases, where it's possible, the most efficient—and therefore the greenest—approach is to let someone else do the heavy lifting.

The underlying idea is specialization. With a cloud computing–based infrastructure, users can run the minimum machine that gives them access to the cloud. Users concentrate on what they know best: their jobs.

**Figure 4.4**   Google touts its energy-efficient data centers. (*Source*: http://www. google.com/about/datacenters; Google and the Google logo are registered trademarks of Google Inc., used with permission.)

Vendors provide services through the cloud. This gets vendors focused on their own expertise: providing the services that they sell to customers. This happens at multiple levels: the economic customer who makes purchasing decisions, the end user who gets the advantage of the services provided, and various stakeholders who influence IT purchasing decisions.

IT has two roles: providing services in a cloud-like fashion, which can't be obtained (cost-efficiently, or at all) from outsiders, and managing the whole thing.

An organization's IT group really only has one sustainable competitive advantage in getting assignments from the organization: The IT group knows the organization inside and out. Everything the IT group does should be based on this fundamental advantage. Any service that doesn't require IT's specialized, insider knowledge should be treated as a candidate for outsourcing.

## 4.13 Greenability and Cloud Computing

There are two dimensions to the fit of a technology such as cloud computing into a green computing agenda. The first, more obvious, dimension is the extent to which a technology is green, in the here and now. But another, more subtle, dimension is the extent to which a technology is "greenable."

This is a tricky concept, and one that requires both deep thought and healthy skepticism. The deep thought is required to identify those products, technologies, and approaches that can most easily be made green. The healthy skepticism is required to assess the degree to which a greenable choice might actually become a green one.

Let's look at an example slightly out of the IT realm: an electric car. I say "slightly" outside because cars are full of computers—my new Prius plug-in has radar that slows and accelerates the car in traffic; car models are differentiated by consumer electronics, such as GPS and entertainment systems; and tech companies are actively involved in the future of cars, as with Google's experiments with self-driving cars.

An electric car is partly green, and partly greenable. The good news is that a fully electric car—or a gas/electric dual-mode car, like the Chevy Volt, when run in electric mode—isn't *directly* burning gasoline, diesel, or other fossil fuels, as nearly all other cars do.

The bad news is that a fully electric car, if charged in an area where coal, oil, or natural gas supplies the power behind the electrical grid, does burn fossil fuels *indirectly*. The grid, even with transmission losses, is roughly twice as efficient as a car engine, so electric operation generates about half the $CO_2$ as an internal combustion operation. Still, half of a lot is still a lot.

Looking at the electric car through a greenability lens gives us some more good news, however. Many individuals can opt for renewable power supplies— by choosing a billing option from their current provider, by putting solar panels on the roof of their house, or by switching to a renewables-focused electricity provider. This makes those individuals' electric car miles, and much else besides, far greener.

The electric car has even more green potential if a smart grid is put into operation. In a smart grid, green cars can serve as sources of power during a peak, such as an afternoon where all the air conditioners in an area are running at full capacity. Electric car owners can arrange to sell off up to, say, 20% of their electric storage capacity at peak times in return for a lower rate when they recharge, often overnight.

As more individuals make green and greenable choices, such as electric cars and renewable energy electricity supplies, the arc of profitable electricity generation and sales bends toward renewables. Demand goes up and supply rises to meet it. A single large organization—perhaps one like yours—can match the impact of thousands of individuals by doing the same thing.

Government mandates and subsidies for green power accomplish this from the supply side. As the electrical supply becomes greener, the advantage of electrically powered car miles over gasoline powered miles increases.

So how does greenability apply to IT? A good example is, again, cloud computing. The data centers run by vendors of cloud-powered software are far more efficient than yours—therefore, greener.

But their data centers, unlike yours, can be made greener still. It doesn't take a big push—a price on carbon, pressure from locals, or pressure from customers such as yourself—to push that cloud computing vendor to source renewable power for their data centers. They can even slightly overbuild their data centers, mixing power supplies from potentially intermittent wind and solar power with others powered by natural gas. The vendor can then mix and match availability and demand in such a way as to maximize renewable-powered computing services.

There will be a wide range of green computing, and greenable computing, claims made in the years ahead. Here are some ways to assess whether a given option is greenable, and the odds that it might actually become much more fully green:

- **Lifecycle length.** Long-term infrastructure often has more potential for green impact, positive or negative, than a specific consumable item. A green light bulb should last for several years, but a smart grid is likely to last for decades and have impact on future choices for a century or more.
- **One change.** An option that only requires one change to become fully green is often more greenable than an option that needs several. A greener device—smaller, using less power and fewer high-impact materials—might be made fully green if energized by renewable power, whereas a non-green device, such as a large, gas-guzzling car, basically needs to be replaced entirely in order to get all the troublesome elements out of the way.
- **Public and private pressure.** If there is already public pressure at work toward the elements that make a greenable item fully green, the odds are good that needed steps will be taken. The public pressure needed to make the entire electric grid fully green isn't present yet; but your ability to secure green power for some or all of your operations might be quite high, making every device you buy and use that much greener.
- **Current trends.** Understanding the greenability potential of various purchases you make requires a keen eye for underlying trends. A supplier that's a green leader today might become fully green tomorrow; a renewable energy supplier owned by an oil company might be less inclined to take energetic steps toward scaling up and toward lowering prices.
- **Inherent flexibility.** A user's personal computer has to get power where the user is; your organization's in-house data center has to get power where the data center is. In either case, geography may be destiny as far as access to renewable energy is concerned. But an outside supplier providing fungible computing services, and operating at a larger scale, is more able to

respond to market demand by locating data centers where green power is available and by bringing new green power to existing data centers.

A good example of greenability is a recent campaign conducted by Greenpeace. Greenpeace assessed the use of renewable versus nonrenewable power by companies that provide cloud computing–based services to consumers It looked at some of the biggest names in technology to see how much they paid for electrical power, and whether that power was generated by more- or less-polluting power sources. Greenpeace "named and shamed" some companies for the environmental impact of their decisions and encouraged consumers to look first to rivals for their cloud computing needs. Figure 4.5 shows a Google page that supports its environmental claims. To improve their standing in Greenpeace's eyes, companies will have to source renewable power for existing data centers, where possible, and locate new data centers where green—not coal-generated—power is available.

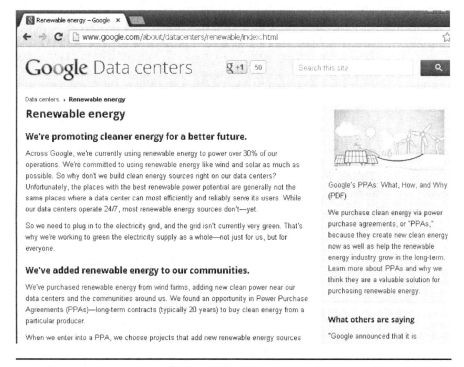

**Figure 4.5** The Google Renewable Energy Page highlights the company's efforts to reduce its carbon footprint. (*Source:* http://www.google.com/about/datacenters/energy.html; Google and the Google logo are registered trademarks of Google Inc., used with permission.)

This Greenpeace campaign illustrates many of the principles behind green computing. Not only does it illustrate "greenability," but it also shows the cost trade-offs companies make, and the risks they take, in making non-green decisions.

## 4.14 Responsibility, Usability, and Cloud Computing

A subtle impact of cloud computing, and the entire green computing agenda, is the issue of responsibility—who has what job.

A related issue is usability: making things as easy as possible for the user. It may seem odd, but the greenest thing a user can do is often the easiest thing a user can do.

Let's take a look at this from the standpoint of devices. The iPad, as I've previously mentioned, is inherently greener than a laptop. It's also inherently easier to use.

An iPad app has to be "fat-finger-friendly." The software can only present a small amount of information and a few choices to the user at one time. A laptop interface tends to have far more text, and a mouse or trackpad, in addition to a keyboard, makes it all too easy to inundate the poor user with information and options. So, to make a successful iPad app, software developers have to radically focus on a given task, or a smaller set of tasks, and radically simplify what they ask the user to do.

A company I recently worked with offers a useful example. They just rolled out their first iPad app. To use the app, a more expert user sets up an event on a personal computer, with a list of potential attendees for the event included. The event can then show up as an option on the iPad app that the company rolled out. Whereas one expert user set up the event, dozens of non-expert users can use an iPad and the app to check people in at the event. The user just picks an event (once per session), taps a name on a list, and presto! The customer or potential customer is checked in.

All of this is very green. The check-in staff are using iPads instead of laptop or desktop computers. Reams of paper are saved, with no printed lists to produce, to check people against—and then use for error-ridden data entry.

The app is also extremely usable. Relaxed, happy staff members wander among equally happy visitors, checking each of them into the event with a few taps. This replaces stressed, hurried visitors lining up to wait their turn while anxious, harried staff try to find their names on printed lists or awkward laptop or desktop computer interfaces. (And the iPad has fewer and less nasty crashes than any kind of PC.)

My company, the software vendor, has solved most of the check-in problem by providing this capability. A single user at our customer's organization then solves most of the rest of the problem by setting up the event online and attaching the right people to it. The task of the check-in staff, and the stress level of the attendees, is reduced to the bare minimum—"they only do what only they can do."

There is a strange and powerful synergy to the interaction between green computing and intense usability. Even the iPad app that I'm describing here is only a step in the right direction, compared to voice interaction. Apple's Siri could be used to make checking-in easier still.

Entering data onto a smartphone is painful, and so is reading the response on tiny smartphone screens. So both Android phones and Apple devices have highly capable voice interfaces. Apple, being very adept at marketing, has named its voice interface Siri. Apple has received tons of publicity for a capability that Google has actually been offering since well before Siri came along.

Siri is about as green as you can get and still be doing computing. The user interface is a tiny microphone (for input) and a tiny speaker and smartphone screen (for response). The smartphone does a bit of preprocessing, then sends the main task of voice recognition to Apple's highly efficient data centers.

But Siri is not lauded as a green computing solution, nor as an inexpensive one; it gets bouquets, instead, for being very easy and very cool. Learn to look for greenness and greenability in the easiest computing solutions, and for usability in the greenest ones. Expect to see very low prices accompanying both of them. You'll be surprised how often all these elements—low cost, low environmental impact, extreme ease of use—come wrapped in the same package.

Appropriate ownership of tasks is a key element of both greenability and usability. If you divide up tasks, and provide each part where it's most appropriate, you can get amazingly green and easy results.

## 4.15 The Philosophical Implications of Green Computing

As part of forming a vision of computing, it's worth considering what one might learn from philosophy. The 20th century German philosopher Martin Heidegger was one of the leading contributors to the theory behind how humans use tools, including computers.

Heidegger is controversial today because he was a supporter of Hitler and Nazism during World War II. His reputation was largely rehabilitated after World War II by a group of supporters led by Hannah Arendt, a student of Heidegger's and a famous political theorist in her own right. However, Heidegger's work remains controversial today.

Heidegger's key philosophical insight was that a human being who learns how to use a tool becomes a somewhat different creature from before. For instance, a business consultant with a mobile phone can stay in touch to a much greater extent than before. The consultant with a mobile phone is said to be "constituted" differently from one without. (Imagine a business consultant today without a mobile phone. He or she would be very different from the others.)

Tools are not just extensions of people and their intentions; instead, a person and their tools form something new, a kind of meta-person with much greater capabilities than the "naked ape" that each of us is born as.

In this view, the computing tools and services that IT provides to users and supports are not just provided to users for accomplishing their goals. We are actually helping to create somewhat different people—more capable, but also with new problems and concerns they wouldn't have otherwise.

This is a useful lens for understanding our work in IT better and differently. Why are people's devices and software tools so important to them? In this view, it's because the devices and software become part of a toolkit that is inseparable from how the people define themselves. Why are people so slow to adopt many tools that are recommended to them, even tools that they are told they are required to use? Because adopting the tool is a big change; if it doesn't fit with a person's needs, and if it doesn't fit with a person's (current or imagined) view of themselves, it may well be rejected.

This viewpoint helps us understand how emotional people become about losing the use of key tools, such as losing one's mobile phone or having a laptop stolen. A serious software bug can be nearly intolerable, not just an inconvenience. It's almost like not having your brain work as you expect it to.

Heidegger also emphasized the role of emotion in how people engage with the world. It is only through emotion, he asserted, that we care about anything, so there is no such thing as a wholly rational person; indeed, there can't be. Only through emotion does a person engage with the world.

Heidegger asserted that a computer system could never attain consciousness, for instance, no matter how powerful it became; lacking emotion, it could never begin the learning process that makes humans reasoning beings.

How do Heidegger's insights help us understand green computing? The good news is that computer-based tools can be deeply meaningful to people. A successful green computing effort can, therefore, not only gain people's support but also help them view themselves as different and better than they were before. The bad news is that any computing effort, green or not, can stumble on deeply held self-beliefs and emotional factors that are very hard to get onto a spreadsheet and analyze in advance.

The word or approach that someone "should" do what you want them to do won't get you nearly as far as you might hope—whether you're attempting to order people to do what you want, lest they lose their jobs, or to shame them into doing what's right for the environment. No matter how righteous your green computing cause, or how much money your organization might save by moving to a given green computing solution, you have to do a tremendous amount of work before, during, and after any new computing effort to help make it fully successful.

Green computing, along with the new, complementary vision of computing that I've set out here, is powerfully engaging for many people. Even those who resist the green cause as such are often supportive of many of the values embodied in it, such as leaving a better world for future generations. This kind of appeal, however—or the resistance that may arise among some of the people who you need to support your efforts—is a long way from assessing the areal density (the density per square inch) of a hard disk platter or the megahertz rating of a microprocessor. You want to hurry your green computing efforts, both to get their benefits and to contribute to saving the world; but never rush them.

## 4.16 The Zen of Green Computing

There's a certain tone to activist approaches to problems that is usually different from the approach used by people in corporations. It just feels different to be in an activist group than in a company. Nonprofits often straddle the divide, with some feeling quite stuffy and straight-laced, whereas others manage to bring the feel of the street or the demonstration into their offices.

This begs the question, What is an activist? A good working definition is someone who has social causes or political activities that they engage in a significant part of their time, either in addition to nonactivist, paid work, or as their main occupation or avocation. The Tea Party has activists, as does Greenpeace. Someone who Occupied Wall Street is an activist as well.

More and more organizations, wanting to better understand and connect to all the communities they serve, seek to hire people from the nonprofit world—sometimes more activist, sometimes less so. And the people hired can go into certain jobs that are particularly suitable, such as community relations roles, or into jobs that don't have any specific activist slant.

You can hire activists yourself, in order to better connect with the green and sustainability agendas. You can also—and this is not a mutually exclusive option—seek to connect with what drives green activists yourself.

Getting involved is not only a good way to broaden your intellectual horizons. Many of the sustainability challenges facing people, such as extreme weather, rising sea levels, and food security relating to climate change, get quite frightening as you understand them better (so frightening that fear seems to be a major reason why some people can't accept the conclusions of climate science). Taking action, even if it seems quite small in comparison to the problems involved, can be quite helpful.

Getting involved doesn't just mean sending in a contribution each month or receiving a recommended voting list. Look for organizations in which you can actively participate, not only in attending events, joining a march, and so forth, but in planning, doing logistical work, and more.

Following are a few organizations or movements that I've been involved in that you might want to consider getting involved with yourself, as a way of understanding what "green" means outside the corporate and IT perspectives.

**Transition** is a worldwide movement of people interested in and involved in sustainability. The home page for the Transition Network website is shown in Figure 4.6.

Transition originally began in England as a loose coalition of local initiatives called Transition Towns. The Transition organization is still a loose network of local initiatives. The key concerns for most Transition initiatives are climate change and peak oil. Peak oil is the idea, widely accepted even by oil companies, that oil production worldwide will start to gradually decline as the huge reserves found in the 20th century run out.

**Figure 4.6**   Transition Towns make up a global sustainability movement. (*Source*: http://www.transitionnetwork.org)

The date at which "peak oil" will be reached is a matter of controversy; oil companies tend to say something like 2020, whereas activists and independent analysts often say it already occurred, in 2010 or so. Recent oil development in the United States, for instance, doesn't disprove the idea of peak oil; instead, it shows how harder-to-reach, dirtier, higher-priced reserves will be tapped as the easier, less expensive ones run out.

The key word for Transition initiatives is relocalization—for people to get more of their food, clothing, entertainment, and all the necessities of life from their local area. Transition people talk about "food sheds"—defined by the size of the circle of farmland around a city necessary to feed both the urban and rural people within it. Transitioners also like to raise chickens, plant fruit trees and vegetables in one another's backyards, keep bees, make their own—well, you name it—and promote bike riding.

Some Transition initiatives, especially in the United Kingdom, have gotten strongly involved with local government. After all, promoting local business, and sourcing materials locally, is a huge boost to a local economy, civic involvement, neighborliness, and more. It might even contribute to reducing crime!

I was involved in Transition initiatives in the United Kingdom, when I lived there, and in the San Francisco Bay Area as well. I was one of the founding members of the Initiating Committee for Transition San Francisco, and I stay involved in Transition meetings and activities. I've met some of my favorite people through Transition, and being involved has been a big help in responding to the many concerns that come up in learning about, and trying to act on, climate change.

Transition initiatives are entirely locally organized and run. You can start looking for a nearby initiative, Transition training, and other vital information at www.transitionnetworks.org.

**Permaculture** is an approach to farming—and, really, to everything—that's particularly valuable in improving sustainability. Permaculture is farming in such a way that everything the farm is involved in—the local environment, the local community, people who work on the farm, even the soil itself—are improved by the farm and its way of operating. It would be like organic farming on steroids, except that any organic farmer or permaculture activist would shudder at the thought of taking a growth hormone.

Going to a meeting of "permies" feels a bit like attending a Jedi Council meeting in Star Wars. Many people involved in permaculture seem preternaturally calm and are almost unfailingly positive, albeit quietly so.

The Transition movement, described above, was started by Rob Hopkins, a permaculture instructor. Many people who farm very little, or not at all, take permaculture courses as a way to learn sustainability at a deep level. They then go on to get involved in many activist efforts, including Transition. You can look for a permaculture course locally, go to a get-acquainted meeting or similar activity, and consider signing up.

**Nonviolent Communication**, or **NVC**, is a new way of interacting with others begun by Marshall Rosenberg about 25 years ago. The name and the idea come from Mahatma Gandhi, who said that violent actions often have their roots in communication mistakes and misunderstandings. Poor communications lead to (or exacerbate) tensions, which can then lead to actual or metaphorical violence.

The website for the Center for Nonviolent Communication is shown in Figure 4.7.

One of the key ideas of NVC is not being overly attached to what one communicates to others. For instance, it's common for someone to ask a friend or work colleague to go out to lunch or attend an event. Both parties may get quite caught up in whether the other person says yes right away, asks for details before deciding, or changes their mind about attending at the last minute.

NVC practitioners will wait to make the request until they're comfortable with any answer the other person gives. That way, the invitation is heartfelt,

**Figure 4.7** Nonviolent Communication helps people connect better. (*Source:* http://www.cnvc.org)

and there's no offense taken if the person asked chooses not to go—whether the reason is a dentist's appointment or just preferring to do something else.

NVC approaches can be very helpful in the workplace. I'm sometimes asked by colleagues how I stay calm in the stressful environment of various jobs, and NVC is a big part of the answer.

NVC approaches are very helpful in any kind of change initiative, including sustainability initiatives, in general, and green computing, in particular. That's because they help you look at a problem from a wide variety of angles and to better understand what really matters to people in making an initiative successful.

You can take NVC telecourses, find books and recordings, and much more. You may also be able to find relevant courses locally. Try www.cnvc.org as a starting point.

**Buddhism.** The Buddhist ideal is nonattachment—that is, not being invested in outcomes, while living deeply immersed in the present moment. Buddhist meditation helps focus and calm one's mind. Buddhist approaches show up in surprising places in a wide variety of activist settings. NVC, for instance (mentioned above), strongly applies the principle of nonattachment to interpersonal communications.

Yoga is a common form of exercise and, yes, meditation among sustainability activists. It promotes calm and focus as well as flexibility, core strength, and overall good health.

All of the aforementioned are helpful in pursuing green computing because they open up the mind to new approaches and reduce stress in otherwise tense situations. You can find Buddhist meeting groups—called sanghas—all over the world, and meditation groups, yoga classes, and related activities can be found in schools, churches, community centers, and workplaces.

**"Radical" groups.** In addition to these corporate-friendly activities, there are some activist groups that actively question or oppose what is seen as the "corporate agenda." Being involved in such groups may be NSFW (Not Safe For Work)—but, maximum points if you can pull it off! A few of these include:

- **The Ruckus Society.** The Ruckus Society seeks to disrupt things—to raise a ruckus—in support of a variety of activist causes, often environmental in nature. The Ruckus Society has been involved in Occupy, in the Tar Sands protests at the White House in 2012, in demonstrations for migrant rights, and much more. Visit www.ruckus.org to find out more.
- **Deep Green Resistance.** Deep Green Resistance sees mainstream environmental groups as ineffective and industrial civilization as a plague upon the Earth, with environmental destruction as a logical result of its normal operations. People involved in Deep Green Resistance seek to "deprive the powerful of their ability to destroy the planet." The book, *Deep Green Resistance*,[1] is the best starting point.

- **Anarchist groups.** Anarchist groups have often been the locus for violent protest throughout their long and, in some ways, troubled history. Anarchism is both a tool and a metaphor, as well as a training ground for people who often go on to do quite impactful things. The Occupy movement, leaderless and without any actual demands, was strongly anarchist influenced. Due to the nature of anarchism, I can't really tell you how to get involved, but anarchist approaches are useful as a counterpoint to top-down, hierarchical corporate structures.

There are even groups that explicitly seek to meld a corporate or business-like approach with activism. I had the privilege of attending the Greenermind Summit with people from across the San Francisco Bay Area. Held in the Mendocino woods, it brought together corporate people and a few independent activists to network and discuss sustainability issues. Greenermind Summit is associated with Net Impact, a professional organization for people interested in business and sustainability.

The organizations mentioned here are just a small slice through a vast array of different ways you can get involved, developing fresh perspectives for green computing initiatives and for your whole life. Use the Internet and your personal or professional connections to see if there are opportunities to get involved where you live and work.

## 4.17 Summary

This chapter described a new, greener vision for computing. It discussed the importance of simplicity in workers' lives and how climate change fits in the new, greener IT agenda. It also showed how cloud computing helps advance the cause of green computing. The next chapter shows you how to build up a portfolio of green devices.

# Chapter 5

# Building a Green
# Device Portfolio

## Key Concepts

This chapter presents ideas for planning your purchases of servers, computers, and other IT devices so that your devices are as green as possible:

- Using green ideas to drive device purchases
- Making small devices do the job of larger ones
- Assessing embodied energy
- Assessing running costs
- Using the Greenpeace Guide

## 5.1 Introduction

As humans, we like bright, shiny objects. IT devices—from the latest iPhone to the newest, greenest server—are some of the brightest, shiniest objects ever invented.

As an IT leader, though, you get to think big—you can plan for big purchases, not just one device at a time. In this chapter, I describe how you can purchase and build an entire portfolio of thoughtfully chosen, powerful, capable, and useful green devices. And they'll be bright and shiny, too!

At the end of the day, a company is trying to make the most money possible with the smallest investment. Non-profit organizations are trying to get the biggest return from their investment as well, although the return may not be as easy to measure, in monetary terms.

Investments in hardware are particularly troublesome because they're sunk costs—you can't undo them. You can only recover a fraction of the cost of hardware, once you've made the purchase. So the idea behind this chapter is to step back and look at your entire panoply of devices, not just one device or one type of device at a time. That way, your purchases make sense as a group, not just individually.

Hardware costs are also only the tip of the iceberg; there are further expenditures necessary to run, maintain, and service these devices. You have to buy, maintain, upgrade, and replace software for them, as well. A few years ago, who would have thought mobile phones would need a software budget and a software development team? But today, they do.

So look at your hardware portfolio as part of a combined cost and capability center that includes many different elements. You can talk to users and peers about specific hardware devices. You and your close colleagues in IT can be aware, as you have the hardware conversation, that there's a long tail of other decisions and costs trailing after every piece of hardware that you buy.

One could easily write a whole book, not just a chapter, about building a green device portfolio. This book gives you the big picture for the entire green computing landscape. Other resources are available to help you dig deeper as you make your purchasing decisions.

In this chapter, I'll introduce the big picture considerations you need to take into account as you make green computing device purchasing considerations. In Chapter 6, I'll take a close look at green servers and data centers.

## 5.2  Why Green Works for Device Purchases

Your purchases of devices for IT are a huge commitment—for your IT department and for your organization as a whole. There are many needs that devices need to meet, many agendas being carried out, and a lot of history contributing to every new decision. So suggesting that you "green" your device purchases may seem to be a big and, perhaps, unnecessary burden.

Of course, green is only one desirable goal for your device purchases. Luckily, following a green computing strategy for your IT devices will also result in improvements in how you meet your other purchasing drivers. These other drivers include, but are not limited to, the following:

- **Purchase price.** What's the up-front cost of getting devices in the door? Viewed narrowly, a focus on price often militates against green solutions. However, a holistic green approach is likely to lead to less spending on devices overall—rendering the per-device purchase price a bit moot.

- **Maintenance and replacement costs.** Once you agree to support a type of device through IT, you have to think through how to maintain all the devices of that type, how to replace and expand the pool of devices, and how to eventually move on to a newer generation.

- **Software costs.** Most devices have software costs, and software costs can easily exceed hardware costs. Software can be installed on a device, licensed per device but delivered online, or site licensed in a more or less device-independent manner.

- **Complementary devices.** PCs and other computing devices need printers and routers; all sorts of computer devices that run software need servers in-house to support the software. You can develop ratios that help you assign, say, a fraction of a printer, a piece of a router, and part of an internal server to each PC that you own.

- **Life-cycle cost.** Many people who don't consciously "think green" end up doing something quite similar by considering the life-cycle cost of their devices. The broader the range of considerations included in the life-cycle cost, the closer this analysis gets to a green computing approach.

- **Compatibility.** Your purchases need to be compatible with the existing infrastructure. If your IT people are used to supporting and repairing HP laptops, for example, purchasing any other type is likely to cost you money in retraining, stocking different spare parts and accessories, delays in getting components in, and general confusion and inefficiency. (If you do move off of a particular supplier, you may well want to make a planned and long-term move to the new one, not just make a series of one-off purchases from different manufacturers.)

- **Comfort level.** Purchasing people and the many stakeholders in IT purchase decisions tend to have a comfort level with certain suppliers and types of devices. Part of your job in introducing a green computing agenda in your company is gradually changing your organization's culture so that green choices feel more comfortable than the choices you made previously.

There are many other criteria to be considered in making device purchases, not all of them pretty. Personal relationships between your organization and a supplier, for instance, can affect your purchases, and not necessarily in a good way. But purchase price, life-cycle cost, compatibility, and comfort level are the factors that you should include as you drive toward greener computing.

## 5.3 Pushing Computing Down the Device Pyramid

When you need to buy a certain kind of device, you should look for the greenest product that meets your needs. Further details are presented later in this chapter and in Chapter 6. However, there's a powerful strategy for green computing that goes beyond finding relatively green devices. This approach also strongly complements making each device purchase as green as possible. I call this approach pushing computing tasks down the device pyramid. To fully understand it requires a much different and more powerful way of looking at how computing gets done.

Individuals and organizations now have many more device choices than before. The smaller the device is, the less expensive it is likely to be. The smaller device is also more convenient to carry and keep handy. In general, the smaller device is also greener: Less energy is used to make it (it has less embodied energy), it takes less energy to run, and it's easier and less environmentally damaging to recycle, reuse, or dispose of. So pushing computing down the device pyramid means using these smaller devices for more and more of our work.

Software for smaller devices is greener, too. Less data is being supplied, and processing is pushed into the cloud, where it can be handled more efficiently than on a larger device. (And, for software as a service on a supplier's servers, the resources used are not counted on your books at all.) An entire program for a smaller device and its working data set can be loaded into RAM or flash memory, with much less energy-intensive swapping to disk.

A simple example of pushing computing down the device pyramid is that some organizations are now replacing salespeople's laptops with tablet computers. This takes considerable software development, including custom tablet app development, so that all of the user's tasks—including the organization-specific ones—can get done on the tablet.

But the benefits are tremendous. Tablets are far simpler and easier to use for the tasks that they're suited for than a laptop or desktop PC. IT's job is to refactor and revise tasks so that even complex tasks, from the organization's point of view, are decomposed into simple tasks for the salespeople.

The green benefits are enormous. Laptops are replaced with tablets that are about one-third the weight—so, roughly one-third the embodied energy—and use about one-tenth the energy per hour of operation. At the same time, salespeople become more productive.

The device pyramid approach, as represented in Figure 5.1, has two components: usage and purchasing. You first get people using the smaller-footprint devices for an increasing number of tasks. The idea is to have the smaller devices bear more of the load. When a smaller device is used for a task, the impact of that task is lessened. Larger devices, which are more expensive (in every sense) to replace, then last longer because they're used less.

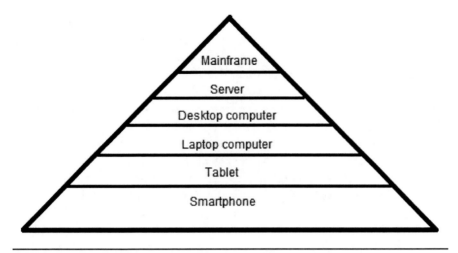

**Figure 5.1** Drive tasks down the device pyramid.

The second component, purchasing, follows. At a certain point, the needs of a given user (or group of users) are mostly being met by smaller devices. You can then identify how to move the remaining tasks off the larger devices, so that users no longer need to have the larger devices at all. This saves on the cost and, from a green point of view, the embodied energy of the larger device. It also "leads the user not into temptation" to spend time using the larger, less-efficient device.

Of course, things don't just evolve. You mix experimentation and planning. Observing what happens when you experiment makes it easier to shift tasks and groups of users down the device pyramid. Here's the formula:

1. Break computing usage down to the tasks that are getting accomplished.
2. Push each task down to the simplest possible combination of device(s) and software that will get it done.
3. Develop software to support task completion on smaller devices.
4. Support task completion lower on the device pyramid.
5. Identify groups who can move off larger devices and migrate them.
6. Reduce provision and purchasing of larger devices.
7. Review.
8. Repeat.

## 5.4 Another Dimension of Device Pyramid Greenness

The hard benefits of moving tasks, and groups of users, to smaller devices are obvious and easily measurable. There are soft benefits, as well, to identifying and promoting a different style of computer use.

Using a smaller device can provide more focus and greater flexibility than is possible when using a personal computer. For instance, to move an app to the iPad—as a company recently did—you really have to think through what the software is doing and what the user needs.

A mouse and a high-resolution monitor can allow—or force—the user to choose from among dozens of alternatives at a time. But a touchscreen, such as the one on a tablet, only works well if the user has far fewer choices. So software developers have to really think through what they're offering the user, and what they ask the user to do in order to complete his or her tasks.

The combination of simplified software and easier to use hardware actually changes the user's relationship to the computing experience. A tablet or smartphone goes easily with the user and can be picked up, used for a quick task, and then set aside.

A laptop or desktop computer, on the other hand, engages much more of the user's attention and focus.

Smaller devices and simpler software make it easier to use a device in the flow of other activities—participating in a meeting, having a conversation, or walking from place to place. (This multitasking, of course, can be distracting or dangerous, if overdone.)

At the same time, smaller devices can support a broader mode of interaction than is typically available on larger devices. Two great examples are Apple's voice-activated Siri service and the speech recognition capabilities built into Google's mobile Android operating system. Both of these capabilities allow fairly free-form verbal inquiries to be processed and responded to via a mobile phone or tablet.

As mentioned in the previous chapter, with my company's iPad app, we were able to create a very simplified process for the end user. A single, more knowledgeable user enters the names of guests who are expected to attend before the event occurs. At the event, many end users walk around with iPads, quickly checking off the names of the people who actually make it to the event.

Of course, you can apply careful analysis and creativity to come up with novel solutions. For instance, you can support salespeople in the field with a phone-in service. They can call or text in questions and get answers, which are provided by a much smaller number of field support people with full laptop or desktop PCs and multiple large-screen monitors.

By creatively shaping your device portfolio, and the software portfolio that runs on it, you can create a lasting competitive advantage for your organization, while steadily lowering costs.

## 5.5 Green Computing and Embodied Energy

Embodied energy is the amount of energy—and, by extension, the carbon footprint—that is associated with the initial creation of a device. Including embodied energy in your assessments significantly increases the energy usage and carbon footprint associated with some devices, much more so than others. For instance, a car may represent embodied energy equaling two or three years of normal driving usage; accounting for embodied energy greatly increases the car's perceived carbon footprint. Embodied energy also suggests other environmental and social costs that may be associated with a product. These can include the following:

- **Rare earths usage.** Computers and consumer electronics—and, ironically, renewable energy devices like windmills and solar panels—use hard-to-obtain minerals called rare earths. Mining them takes a lot of energy and leaves huge piles of tailings—mining waste, often mildly radioactive.
- **Shipping costs and footprint.** Shipping devices from manufacture to consumer is only part of the shipping costs and footprint, including carbon footprint, of many devices. The various raw materials and components that make up a computer, for instance, may make a total of many trips around the world as the device takes shape. The energy expended should be included in calculating the embodied energy in a product.
- **Packaging.** A computer monitor can come in a big cubical box with lots of cardboard and packing foam, several feet in each dimension—or a slimline box with much less packaging. The same applies to all your devices. iPads come in a slimline box not much bigger than the iPad itself, and Apple switched many of its boxes from high-gloss finishes to plain cardboard years ago. Packaging is part of the embedded impact of a device and a good indicator of the environmental consciousness (and conscience) of a provider.
- **Child labor, minimum wage violations, overtime violations, and other labor problems.** Labor abuses are sometimes included in green concerns, or they can be addressed more or less separately. For instance, some US companies that use overseas suppliers have faced criticism over working conditions—including allegations of child labor—at those suppliers.

As you develop your green computing policies, embodied energy is one of the considerations you can use to make informed "green" purchasing choices. Overall, the size of devices is a good rough indicator of their embodied energy. A smartphone is likely to have less embodied energy than a tablet, a tablet less than a laptop, a laptop less than a desktop computer. A desktop computer may not, however, have less embodied energy than a thoughtfully manufactured server.

I suggest that you begin your device purchasing process by first looking at the smallest, lightest class of devices that can meet your needs. Then use embodied energy and running costs to help choose which device to buy.

## 5.6 Green Computing and Running Costs

The running costs—both financial and environmental—of a device are what happen between the time you buy a device and the time you retire it. The main impacts of using IT devices are as follows:

- **Electricity to run the device.** All IT devices use electricity to run. The cost of the electricity is substantial, and the environmental impact of it depends on the source of your electricity. Coal-fired power plants are the biggest polluters; rooftop solar or hydroelectric power are far less polluting. (Even for solar and wind, there's embodied energy in the generating devices, and waste is generated in building and disposing of them.)
- **Electricity to cool the device's environment.** This is fairly important for offices, where devices can make it expensive to keep both devices and people cool. It's critical for data centers, where it can be very expensive to keep optimum, or even just barely acceptable, operating temperatures.
- **Data center, Internet, and cloud computing services.** Most IT devices use the Internet and cloud computing services, which have considerable environmental footprints—some of which your company "owns," others of which are owned by others.
- **Paper, ink, and toner.** IT operations result in a surprising amount of printing; the "paperless office" promulgated in the 1980s never became real. Ink and toner can have bad health effects for people sitting near printers.

Table 5.1 shows who pays for various parts of IT device usage. This is important in calculating the direct financial cost–benefit analysis of any green computing initiative.

No matter where the device is used, you want it to use as little power as possible. This will cut costs (when the device is used or recharged in the office) and reduce the environmental impact (all the time). In the next chapter, I'll discuss power usage for different types of devices.

What makes a device use less power? Here are a few key features:

- **Smaller screen.** The screen is usually the biggest power hog on a computing device. A smaller screen cuts power usage. So does the ability to manually dim the screen, to auto-dim the screen, and to shut the screen off after brief periods of nonuse.
- **Smaller size.** Smaller devices generally use less power. (It's possible for a small device to punch well above its weight and overuse power, but with increasing buyer concerns about power costs and environmental impact for devices, this is rare.) There's just less circuitry to keep warm in a smaller device.

**Table 5.1 – Who Pays for IT Device Use:
By Type and Location of Usage**

| Location | Cost | Who pays |
|---|---|---|
| Outside the office | Electricity | Third party or user |
| | Cooling | Third party or user |
| | Internet access | Varies |
| Inside the office | Electricity | IT or the business |
| | Cooling | IT or the business |
| | Internet access | IT or the business |
| Anywhere | Data center services | IT |
| | Cloud computing services | IT or the business |

- **Battery use.** Manufacturers want battery-powered devices to be as light as possible while running as long as possible, so they optimize for low power usage. This benefits all concerned, even when the device is run plugged-in, as most laptops usually are.
- **No moving parts.** Hard disks are so small and quiet today that it's easy to ignore them, but they're power hogs. Smartphones, tablets, and even some laptops use solid state storage that uses much less power. (Apple has led the way in offering solid state storage for some of its high-end laptops.)

The most incisive comparison here is between a tablet and a laptop. Table 5.2 sums up the differences.

Note that Apple has introduced a very high-resolution display with the third version of the iPad. The new display is 2048 × 1536 (3M pixels) versus 1024 × 768 (0.75 million pixels) for the previous versions. By doubling both the horizontal and vertical resolution, the new screen has four times the pixels. It doesn't use four times the power: The pixels in the new screen are smaller than previously, and high overall brightness can be achieved with less power per pixel. However, Apple had to make the device thicker to include bigger batteries and maintain the iPad's famous ten-hour battery life.

The display is really cool-looking, especially for games and high-resolution photographs. However, it uses significantly more power than the former models—about 4 watts per hour versus 3 watts per hour. A laptop typically uses about 50 watts per hour, and a desktop machine with a large screen uses nearly 300 watts per hour (www.energysavers.gov).

Tablet computers are also used differently—carried around and not hooked up to an external monitor. One trend that increases usability for laptop and desktop computers, but greatly increases energy usage, is the tendency for

**Table 5.2 – Green Assessment of Device Specifications**

| | Screen size (diagonal) | Resolution | Volume | Weight | Mass storage |
|---|---|---|---|---|---|
| iPad 1 and 2 | 9.7" | 1024 × 768 (0.75Mp) | 23.6 cu. in | 1.35 lbs. | Solid state |
| iPad 3 and 4 | 9.7" | 2048 × 1536 (3M) | 25 cu. in. | 1.45 lbs | Solid state |
| Dell XPS 15 laptop | 15" | 1366 × 768 (1M) | 151 cu. in | 5.54 lbs | Hard disk + DVD |
| Greener option = : | iPads (1.5×) | #1: iPad 1&2 (4×) #2: Laptop (3×) #3: iPad 3 and 4 | iPads (6×) | iPads (3–4×) | iPads |

users to run two or more screens at a time. Using multiple screens does tend to increase productivity, but it can be overdone. At one company, many users have a laptop screen and two widescreen external monitors turned on simultaneously. No one can pay attention to that much screen space at once, and the effort to "monitor" email, instant messaging, Facebook, and so forth, while "working" has been shown to drastically reduce productivity.

Consider balancing user desires with efficiency. For instance, you might consider limiting most users to a laptop and one external monitor. Encourage users to turn off the external monitor while quickly checking email and more focused tasks, and to turn it on again when needed. You might also consider encouraging periods of single-tasking, for productivity and effectiveness as well as lower cost and greener computer use.

You may also consider providing employees with tablets that you approve, or offering tablets for both work and personal use at a sharp discount. Every hour of usage on the tablet, rather than a laptop or desktop, results in sharply lower energy usage (especially if laptops and any external monitors are turned off, not left running).

## 5.7  Planned Obsolescence Isn't Green

One of the greenest things anyone can do is use things for a long time. Each item we buy has considerable embodied energy consumed in assembling its raw materials, making it, and getting it through distribution to the consumer. And each additional device will have energy requirements for its disposal. So the longer each item lasts, the better.

Our economy seems to work the opposite way. "Planned obsolescence" is the doctrine of increasing product sales by making sure that each product doesn't last very long. The quicker a device wears out, or otherwise goes out of date—even by simply becoming "uncool"—the faster the industry that created it can sell you another one.

The early days of the automobile give us a revealing story. The early leader in automobile sales was Ford, whose Model T was not particularly stylish but was reliable and fairly indestructible. General Motors—a company built by acquiring disparate car companies—had to find a way to compete.

GM introduced the idea of the "model year," introducing new cars every year. It actually takes four or five years to create a substantially new car, so the "new" cars introduced each year were often fairly minor updates on the previous model. No matter; the idea was a hit, and customers would rush out to get the latest and greatest. GM sales gradually pulled ahead of Ford's. Older cars, perfectly serviceable, were considered undesirable and were pushed down the value chain and junked, well before they truly wore out.

It's rumored that a major car company introduced planned obsolescence in its own product lines. A story is often told of an engineer being sent out to tour the junkyards of the country. His mission: Find out which parts on his company's cars had worn out and sent that car to the junk heap. The engineer noted a wide variety of failures, but was also happy to report that one part almost never failed: the U-joint—a mechanical assembly that converts the rotational energy of the drive shaft through a 90° angle to power the car's rear wheels. (No passenger cars had front-wheel drive, back in the day.) The engineer proudly noted that U-joints on the company's cars seemed to last forever. And a memo is rumored to have quickly gone out stating, "Equip all new cars with a cheaper U-joint."

The doctrine of planned obsolescence is even featured in a hit online video, "The Story of Stuff." Led and narrated by Annie Leonard, "The Story of Stuff" describes how the entire industrial world depends on planned obsolescence to keep factories humming and money changing hands. "The Story of Stuff" has spurred a whole series of companion videos, each about five minutes long, making up a steadily growing series:

**Figure 5.2**   The Story of Electronics, available free online. (*Source*: http://www. storyofstuff.org/movies-all/story-of-electronics)

- **The Story of Stuff** (December 2007). Over 15,000,000 views as of mid-2012.
- **The Story of Cap & Trade** (December 2009). Nearly 1 million views.
- **The Story of Bottled Water** (March 2010). Over 2.5 million views.
- **The Story of Cosmetics** (July 2010). Over 1 million views.
- **The Story of Electronics** (November 2010; shown in Figure 5.2). Over 600,000 views.
- **The Story of Citizens United v. FEC** (March 2011). Over 400,000 views.
- **The Story of Broke** (November 2011). Over 210,000 views.

All of these movies are available free online at www.thestoryofstuff.com.

Note that one of the movies is about electronics—and it's very much worth watching. *The Story of Electronics* points out that most electronic devices last about 18 months—and that there are 25 million tons of e-waste generated every year, about six pounds for every person on earth. The movie shows how electronics workers have a higher likelihood of cancer and advocates safe recycling and disposal of electronics products.

*The Story of Electronics* advocates product take back as a practice, and advocates baking it into laws and regulations. The movie points out that this will give manufacturers incentives to make better, longer-lasting devices with fewer toxic chemicals.

Ironically, the planned obsolescence model for cars has largely broken down. (Sorry—pun intended.) Books such as Ralph Nader's *Unsafe at Any Speed*[1] took Detroit to task for the unreliability, including unsafe operation, of its cars.

In the 1970s, small, reliable, fuel-efficient cars—initially introduced by Japanese motorcycle makers—became more and more popular. It's taken many years, but US carmakers are gradually catching up to the standards for safety, reliability, and longevity that were first set by the Japanese (using American ideas, ironically).

Today, a well-made new car—including the plentiful electronics inside it—easily lasts ten years or more. There's no reason that electronics can't steadily work toward the same kind of longevity. Your purchasing decisions, and your feedback to device manufacturers, can help make this happen faster.

## 5.8 Green Computing and Device Disposal

Disposing of electronic devices is a large and growing issue. With each individual often using multiple devices, and with useful lifetimes of only a year or two for many devices, there's bound to be a lot of waste.

There are huge dumps in China and other countries where electronic devices—e-waste—from all over the world are sent. Very poor people take the devices apart looking for valuable components and metals. They suffer diseases from exposure to toxic materials. Even when it doesn't go to China or other developing countries, e-waste is a big problem.

Here are some of the factors that make e-waste so important:

- **Landfill space.** Space in the world's landfills is limited, and e-waste takes up a lot of space. Packaging for e-devices is also a big contributor.
- **Toxic runoff.** Toxics in e-waste seep down and out from landfills into streams, rivers, lakes, and down to the water table. They then make their way into water used in homes, businesses, and for farming.
- **Impact on workers.** As mentioned above, people who work with e-waste are exposed to dangerous chemicals.
- **Use and reuse of landfill space.** When a landfill has relatively benign contents, it can be compacted, then covered with dirt or paved over. The top of the landfill can then be used like any other space. Landfill space with e-waste (and other hazardous wastes) has to be remediated, which is expensive, dangerous to those doing the work, and of uncertain effectiveness.

The way a manufacturer handles e-waste is also highly visible, with great symbolic value, positive or negative. A manufacturer that takes care of its products all the way through their lifecycle engenders trust—in all its green efforts, in particular, and in its products, overall. Manufacturers that avoid, or minimally meet, their obligations are much harder to trust, in green assessments or as business partners overall.

A smaller device has a big advantage in terms of generating less waste. A cell phone versus a tablet, a tablet versus a laptop, and a laptop versus a desktop are hugely advantaged in their impact as waste.

Devices can also be made with reduced use or nonuse of the most toxic metals and chemicals. This helps worker safety in assembling the devices as well as reducing toxicity at disposal time.

Ideally, the same level of care will be taken when disassembling e-devices and disposing of the contents as was used in assembling them. The party best qualified to do this is the manufacturer, who can best supervise employees, contractors, or a third party who take the device apart and reuse components, where possible, and then dispose of the rest in the most environmentally effective way.

Taken as a whole, an entire laptop computer has to be treated as toxic. Taken apart, however, only a small part of the device needs to be handled carefully; the rest can be reused or recycled.

Under the European Union Waste Electrical and Electronic Equipment Directive (the EU WEEE Directive) of 2005, electronics makers are required to accept used equipment and recycle it properly, at no cost to the customer.

However, there's a huge difference between a manufacturer being willing to do this, if asked, and actively seeking to take responsibility for the devices one has made and sold, all the way to recycling and reuse.

Here are key best practices for e-waste:

- **Reduced use of toxics.** Look for claims, backed up with details, of how devices are made with reduced use of toxics.
- **Clearly stated take-back policies.** The manufacturer should state, in clear English, what they are and aren't willing to take back. The more, the better.
- **Promotion of take-back policies.** Ideally, the take-back policy is prominently promoted as part of the purchase process, and in customer communications after purchase.
- **High penetration of take back.** What percentage of the devices a manufacturer makes does it end up taking back?
- **Nonexclusive policy.** Is the manufacturer willing to take back stuff they didn't make, in at least some cases (i.e., commonly purchased accessories for a computer)?
- **"Highest reuse."** Does the take-back policy include the reuse of entire devices, for instance donations of products to charities, or donations of major components, as well as breakdown and recycling where needed?
- **Transparency around the process.** Is information about recycling and reuse after take back made available?
- **Tone.** Is the tone of the information presented positive and extensive (best); businesslike and relatively complete (acceptable); or limited, defensive, and evasive (unhelpful)?
- **External validation.** Is there external recognition and endorsement of the manufacturer's efforts?

If you are comparing manufacturers, you can make a scorecard to record key points. If you use this assessment as part of your supplier selection—and let your actual and aspiring suppliers know you're doing it—you'll be making a big contribution.

## 5.9 The Greenpeace Guide to Greener Electronics

Before assessing suppliers and specific devices for cost savings and other green goodness, it's highly instructive to look at the Greenpeace Guide to Greener Electronics; an example is shown in Figure 5.3.

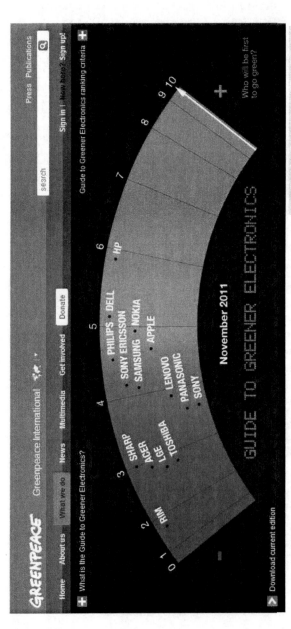

**Figure 5.3** The Greenpeace Guide to Greener Electronics, November 2011 Edition. (Source: http://www.greenpeace.org/international/en/campaigns/toxics/electronics/Guide-to-Greener-Electronics/Previous-editions/how-the-companies-line-up-17/)

The Greenpeace Guide is highly influential. Companies try hard to place well, and they engage in feedback with Greenpeace after each new edition comes out.

Greenpeace uses tight, and ever-rising, standards as to what makes up a green device and a green company. This produces a virtuous cycle of aspiration and competition among companies to make Greenpeace's good list.

The Guide is very useful to green consumers. I consulted the Guide before recommending a computer to a friend a couple of years ago. Having reassurance that we were buying from a relatively green company—HP, which has consistently done well in the Greenpeace rankings—made the purchase a lot easier.

You don't have to use the same criteria as Greenpeace in your own purchasing decisions, but the Guide represents an excellent case study as to how one reputable group has refined and applied the green criteria I've discussed so far in this chapter.

Greenpeace has come up with a ranking system for electronics companies based on the following criteria (as of late 2011). (Note that the Guide uses British English.)

"The primary goals of the Guide are to get companies to:

- Measure and reduce emissions with energy efficiency, renewable energy and energy policy advocacy
- Make greener, efficient, longer lasting products that are free of hazardous substances
- Reduce environmental impacts throughout company operations, from materials and energy used to make products right through to global take-back programs for old products."[2]

There are several things that jump out here:

- The focus on energy usage
- The focus on obsolescence, planned or not
- The emphasis on hazardous substances
- A holistic look at a company's internal operations
- Concluding with a focus on device disposal

It's worth looking at the report cards for individual companies in detail. In the report shown in Figure 5.3, Apple places fourth. Here are Apple's high and low points:

1. **Disclose own operational GHG emissions.** Medium
2. **GHG emissions reductions and targets.** Low

3. **Clean Electricity Plan (CEP).** Low
4. **Clean energy policy advocacy.** Zero
5. **Product energy efficiency.** High
6. **Avoidance of hazardous substances in products.** Medium
7. **Use of recycled plastic in products.** Zero
8. **Product life-cycle.** Low
9. **Measure and reduce energy consumption in the supply chain.** Low
10. **Chemicals management and advocacy.** Medium
11. **Policy and practice on sustainable sourcing of fibers for paper.** Zero
12. **Policy and practice on avoidance of conflict minerals.** Medium
13. **Provides effective voluntary take back where no EPR laws.** High

## Apple Prepping 100 Percent Green Data Center

By Angela Moscaritolo   May 18, 2012 03:17pm EST   4 Comments   Email   Print

+1  8      Share  21      Tweet  35      Share  14      0  Digg      Submit

Apple says that its new $1 billion data center in Maiden, North Carolina will be powered entirely with renewable energy by the end of the year.

On a new Web page announcing its renewable energy plans, the Cupertino tech giant said an "unprecedented" 60 percent of the power at Maiden will be produced onsite from renewable sources. Apple says it will purchase the other 40 percent of power from local and regional renewable energy sources.

The company is currently building two massive solar array installations near its core data center in Maiden. Once finished, the solar farms, which will cover a total of 250 acres, will supply 84 million kWh of clean, renewable energy annually. Later this year, Apple also plans to build a smaller bio-gas-powered fuel cell plant that will provide more than 40 million kWh of renewable energy annually.

**Figure 5.4**   *PC Magazine* described Apple's green data center in detail. (*Source:* http://www.pcmag.com/article2/0,2817,2404618,00.asp)

Apple got right to work after the Greenpeace report, especially since Greenpeace and others loudly focused on #3 (Clean Energy Plan [low]) and #4 (Clean Energy Policy Advocacy [zero]).

Apple has reversed this policy and recently announced the first major 100% green data center, powered entirely by renewable energy. As *PC Magazine* reported in May 2012 (http://www.pcmag.com/article2/0,2817,2404618,00.asp), the center will produce 60% of its renewable power onsite and procure the remaining 40% from local renewable sources. Figure 5.4 shows the article in *PC Magazine*.

You can use Apple's woes—and its effective response—as a cautionary tale for your own green computing efforts. If you use Greenpeace-type standards yourself, you're likely to get praise, rather than criticism, from stakeholders inside as well as outside your company.

## 5.10  Support Employees' Device Choices

When it comes to fun things to do, people vote with their feet. When it comes to showing what they value in IT devices, people vote with their pocketbooks.

Consumers—including your employees—are pushing the IT world in a very green-friendly direction. Consumers are often driving the market in an almost opposite direction to what corporations would prefer:

- **Smartphones.** The corporate favorite, RIM and its BlackBerry phones, is in danger of going out of business. The iPhone, widely disdained by IT for its relative lack of security and lack of a keyboard, and Android phones, which are nothing if not inconsistent, are the clear winners. Consumers seem to prefer typing on glass to hardware keyboards for their phones.
- **Tablets.** Tablets are deeply unpopular with IT departments, who lack the skills to develop software for them. Yet tablets are becoming ubiquitous—in people's homes and in more and more workplaces. In the United States, Christmas 2011 saw tablet penetration—mostly the iPad—go from about 20% of households to more than 30%. It's common now to see business-people bring two notebooks to meetings—a paper notebook and an iPad.
- **Laptops.** Consumers pushed laptops ahead of desktop computers, despite their greater security risks and expense. Widescreen laptops are designed first and foremost for watching DVDs and are not all that well-suited for business tasks such as, well, writing a book.
- **Desktops.** While a great bargain, desktop machines are now unpopular with most users except gamers, who fill them with accelerator boards and connect up a variety of joysticks, airplane yokes, and other exotic input devices.

Supporting employees' device choices allows you to follow consumers toward ever-smaller—and, therefore, ever-greener—devices.

The biggest lag for companies is in software development for tablets and smartphones—that is, apps. Moving software to the tablet is not a simple port. And having a tablet mirror a PC desktop is not a good experience from either the tablet nor the desktop point of view, although such software can be helpful in a pinch.

The challenge is to refactor desktop applications so they can work on tablets and, increasingly, on smartphones. This challenges the very notion of how you develop software. It makes you carefully rethink what you want from your users, and what they want from IT services.

You can't support every device that an employee might buy and want to bring to work. But the major trends—including the increasing use of smartphones and tablets—are good, green ones, and they should continue, if not accelerate, in years to come. Find ways of supporting these trends, and much of your green computing effort, will take care of itself.

## 5.11 Publicizing Your Process

If you really want the cost savings and sustainability benefits that come from green computing, you have to put your organization's own stamp on it. That means setting out a process and publicizing it within the organization. Your company's marketing arm may choose to publicize it beyond the organization as well. These extra benefits help drive further green efforts.

Consider providing the following for other departments and your company's management and employees to use:

1. **A statement of purpose.** A succinct statement that your IT effort is going green, and why.
2. **A checklist of desiderata.** Make a checklist of what you look for when making a strategy decision, choosing a supplier, or choosing a device. Don't try to make it comprehensive; just indicate the major things you look at.
3. **A shortlist of preferred suppliers.** Make a shortlist of suppliers that you've evaluated and are ready to buy from.
4. **Examples of compliant devices.** List half a dozen devices—from smartphones to servers—that fit your criteria.
5. **Examples of initiatives.** Describe, and show, how you'll move the organization to a greener device portfolio.
6. **Benefits for the business.** Describe the benefits that choosing green computing devices will have for the company.

7. **Benefits for employees.** Find ways to make sure the process benefits employees directly. For instance, consider making it easy for employees to get a favored smartphone or tablet computer for work use; the money you save in energy costs alone will help pay for the new devices.

8. **Invite feedback.** We all buy IT devices, and a lively discussion will only improve acceptance of the initiative.

This kind of comprehensive approach will put your green computing effort on a solid footing—very tangibly, as devices are what all concerned see as the most visible reflection of your efforts.

## 5.12 Summary

This chapter covered ideas for planning your purchases of servers, computers, and other IT devices so that your devices are as green as possible. It included using green ideas to drive device purchases, making small devices do the job of larger ones, assessing embodied energy, assessing running costs, and using the Greenpeace Guide to Consumer Electronics. The next chapter discusses green servers and data centers.

# Chapter 6

# Finding Green Devices

## Key Concepts

This chapter describes what to look for from specific kinds of devices:

- Summarizing green buying criteria for devices
- Reviewing green buying criteria for suppliers
- Comparing HP and Dell
- Giving feedback to suppliers and vendors
- Looking at purchase considerations for desktops, laptops, and tablets

## 6.1 What Makes a Device Green?

The last chapter introduced some of the key points that make a device green. In that chapter, I emphasized using the smallest class of device that could do a job; in this chapter, I'll look at specific types of devices. This chapter will help you answer questions, such as: Once you've decided you need to buy a bunch of laptops, how to pick the greenest model?

The buying criteria for a device are mixed up with the selection criteria for suppliers. I've provided buying criteria for devices in this section and selection criteria for suppliers in the next section. If you have a formal supplier selection and approval process, use the criteria for choosing suppliers first; then use the device-specific criteria for choosing devices. The greenest suppliers will, of course, usually produce the greenest devices.

If your purchasing process is a mix of supplier and device selection, use both lists at once. A lot of what a supplier does in making a device green is infrastructure work that's unlikely to happen just for one isolated device. For instance, a supplier is more likely to have product take back at the end of a device's useful life for all of their products (or for most of them), than for just one or two.

There are exceptions, of course. I have a Samsung Replenish cell phone that's largely made with recycled plastics—a very green choice. But Samsung only ranks in the middle of the pack in the latest Greenpeace Guide to Greener Electronics, below Sony Ericsson and Nokia, among others (http://www. greenpeace.org/international/en/Guide-to-Greener-Electronics/18th-Edition/). And Samsung ranks 22nd among technology companies in the latest Newsweek Green 500 rankings (http://www.thedailybeast.com/newsweek/2012/10/22/ newsweek-green-rankings-2012-u-s-500-list.html).

With all this in mind, you need to look at the supplier as well as specific devices every time you make a purchasing decision. Let's sum up green buying criteria in a checklist:

- **Smallest class of device** that will do the job. (Be creative!)
- **Smaller size** for a device of its class.
- **Lower weight** for a device of its class.
- **Longer battery life** (especially where the battery size is the same as a competing device; that means the device itself runs lean).
- **Lower power usage per hour.** (Criteria on this can vary, so don't decide based on manufacturer's assertions alone.)
- **Green packaging**—for instance, plain cardboard printed with bio-friendly black ink, rather than plastic-sheathed cardboard in multiple colors.
- **Slimline packaging**—standard, or as an option.
- **Slimline or electronic documentation**—standard, or as an option.
- **Volume purchase options** for minimal packaging, documentation per shipment rather than per device, etc.
- Meets or exceeds **Energy Star** standards. (This is almost de rigeur these days.)
- Products **free of hazardous substances**: polyvinyl chloride (PVC) plastic, brominated flame retardants (BFRs), antimony, beryllium and phthalates.
- **Use of recycled plastics.** Evaluate this for specific products, and as a percentage of plastics in all products from a given manufacturer.
- **Durability.** Look for statements about, and evidence of, a product being more durable than competitors.

- **Ease of repair.** Look for evidence of, and statements about, a product being easier to repair than competitors. Are spare parts available? Will a manufacturer support on-site repair against large purchases of a specific device?
- **Product take back.** Is the manufacturer willing to cheerfully take back anything they've sold you at the end of its life cycle? Do they publicize this energetically? Do they share how they put returned devices back to use, either as complete devices or as components? Does the manufacturer sell previously used—and, hopefully, refurbished—devices?
- **Reusability.** Look for efforts by the manufacturer to put returned devices back to use—through refurbished product sales, donations, and donations of refurbished components.
- **Supplier green goodness.** Even if you're considering a purchase on device-specific grounds, sum up supplier goodness and add it to the criteria for the specific device.

For additional criteria, and specifics on these criteria, see the Greenpeace ranking guide. The latest version can be found at the following: www.greenpeace. org/rankingguide.

Take these criteria, Greenpeace's criteria, and your own concerns and create your own evaluation ranking system. Include standard business concerns, such as cost, supplier reliability, and past performance of a device and/or supplier.

When in doubt, keep it simple; a few criteria can stand in for a longer list (as with the "supplier green goodness" bullet above).

Apply the system to all device purchases. It will quickly become second nature and will contribute strongly to your green computing efforts.

## 6.2 What Makes a Supplier Green?

The first thing that makes a supplier green is making green products, as per the criteria above. Avoid suppliers who make "feel-good" statements about the environment, or one-off efforts such as product donations to environmental groups. (This is a notorious practice by software vendors who make donations valued at millions of dollars when the product cost to them for CDs and manuals might be pennies on the dollar.)

A positive example of a financial donation is an effort a few years ago by leading global bank HSBC. One year, HSBC donated $50 million (!) to a coalition of green groups, such as the World Wildlife Federation. The partnership was called Investing in Nature, and it focused on environmental research (http://www.hsbcusa.com/ourcompany/bankarchives/bk2002/news_hbarch022102.html).

This is, of course, impressive. But by itself, it might have been merely a particularly expensive form of greenwashing. HSBC, however, has a strong commitment to green causes and sustainability. HSBC is "the world's first carbon-neutral bank" and has made reasonably strong efforts to introduce green and sustainability criteria into its lending policies as well (http://news. bbc.co.uk/2/hi/business/4071503.stm).

All this makes for a good example of what is, and isn't, greenwashing. Bold statements about what a company is going to do, or exaggerated descriptions of what a company has done, fall into the greenwashing bucket. Reasoned descriptions and case studies of what a company has already done tend to be taken as evidence of a serious commitment, especially when supported by third-party verification, such as the Greenpeace Guide and the Newsweek Green 500.

You need to be especially careful to not give the appearance of greenwashing if you're a "sinner" by nature of the business you're in. Tobacco companies, arms dealers, and furriers are going to suffer disapproval from most of the activist community, and many from the public at large. Such companies can recoup somewhat by "going green," but strong efforts with measurable results have to lead, and exceed, generic statements about your commitment to the environment.

So look out for greenwashing when evaluating suppliers—and apply the same criteria to your own green efforts and the way that you talk about them in public.

Here are key criteria for selecting green suppliers:

1. **Leadership commitment.** "The fish rots from the head," as the saying goes, and the opposite is true as well. You want to hear from the top about a company's green commitment—and, hopefully, see signs in leaders' resumes that they've been onto this for a while. (The long-time Chairman of the Board of HSBC Bank was also a part-time pastor and had been speaking out about corporate social responsibility for decades.)

2. **Company-wide commitment.** As you'll find in implementing green computing, you need the commitment of the whole company to get very far. Look first for a company-wide commitment to sustainability and low environmental impact.

3. **Long-standing commitment.** Pressure to go green is increasing, so recent commitments might be more reactive than sincere. Companies that made the commitment earlier, saw the problem earlier, and have had more opportunity to get at least some things right.

4. **Green supply chain.** You can't go very green all by yourself. A company that's greening its supply chain—not just its upstream suppliers, but its partners, distributors, and customers—is starting to do the hard work of becoming green for the long term.

5. **Leading point in marketing.** Marketing green credentials before you have any is a huge problem, and not marketing them once you do have them is a problem as well. Truly sustainable sustainability efforts make up a virtuous circle, including innovative efforts, cost savings, promotion, and ongoing improvements in the organization's efforts.

6. **Promotion to employees, new hires, and other audiences.** College graduates are a discerning audience. A company that can, and does, credibly market its green efforts to the most exciting college graduates has accomplished something and is hiring the very people who will help it accomplish more. Look for the use of sustainability in the company's hiring efforts.

7. **Case studies.** Look for published case studies of sustainability efforts that are spaced out over a period of time, described in detail, and build on each other. Few companies get this right; those that do are highly likely to be reflecting a sustained commitment.

8. **Carbon footprint assessment.** "That which gets measured gets done," management guru Peter Drucker says, yet there are few hard measures for green computing and overall sustainability. For example, a carbon footprint assessment is hard to do, so doing it is a sign of seriousness. Tracking and improving the numbers over time is a strong validation of long-term commitment.

9. **Industry leadership.** Look for an organization to assert industry leadership on sustainability in groups of like-minded organizations, professional bodies, at trade shows and conferences, and in other venues. If there's truly good news here, it will be repeated to small, focused groups as well as to the public at large.

10. **External verification.** Look for awards earned by the company. Two excellent resources are the Newsweek Green 500, shown in Figure 6.1, which ranks the Fortune 500 by green-related criteria, and the aforementioned Greenpeace Guide to Greener Electronics. These are two resources that cut through the blather by clearly stating their criteria, stack ranking the companies involved—not everyone gets to be above average—and repeating the exercise over and over again. If a given supplier isn't included in the published rankings, use the same criteria that Greenpeace and Newsweek use to assess the company yourself.

I don't mean to suggest that you are going to build the perfect green supply chain, green company, or green computing effort. The supply chain effort, for instance, is generally referred to as "greening the supply chain," suggesting an ongoing process. You do want to achieve steady improvement.

Use other criteria to narrow down the list before applying green criteria. Your company has external commitments that require it to meet many specifications, while seeking out the lowest cost (even if the lowest-cost supplier

**GREEN RANKINGS**

From Newsweek

## Global Companies

Oct 16, 2011 11:15 PM EDT

**Here's a look at our environmental ranking of the biggest companies in developed and emerging world markets.**

Print    Email    Comments (5)    +1    Tweet ⟨408⟩    Like ⟨839⟩

Because a global ranking includes U.S. companies, some appear on both the U.S. and the global lists. Newsweek's Green Rankings cut through the green chatter and compare the actual environmental footprints, management (policies, programs, initiatives, controversies), and reporting practices of big companies. We teamed up with two leading research organizations to create the most comprehensive rankings available. View our full methodology.

See more on the top 15 Global companies.

See our U.S. 500 Rankings

SEARCH:

Search by Company        SEARCH

e.g. Hewlett-Packard        reset search

INDUSTRY SECTOR:
Any

COUNTRY:
Any

Showing Results **1 to 25** of **500** Global Companies - Green Rankings 2011

View: **25  50  100  ALL**        ◀  Next ▶

**Figure 6.1** Newsweek Green 500. (*Source*: http://www.thedailybeast.com/newsweek/2011/10/16/green-rankings-2011.html)

doesn't always win). Use green criteria to reward potential suppliers who get all the basics right—and manage to meet green criteria as well.

Of course, these are not mutually exclusive. Greener companies tend to be better suppliers for three major reasons:

1. **The peacock effect.** Male peacocks with dramatic tail feather arrays are attractive to females because only a healthy male can afford the resources to grow such a striking display. Only a healthy company can meet green criteria while also being fully competitive on traditional criteria as well. HP, for instance, is the world's largest vendor of PCs—and a perennial leader in green assessments.

2. **The serendipity effect.** Green efforts are costly at first, taking up time, effort, and management attention. However, they often yield surprising savings while also helping attract and retain top employees, executives, business partners, and supply chain partners. So the green company gradually finds it easier to excel on traditional criteria as well (not the least of which is price competitiveness).

3. **Longer-term orientation.** Green concerns reflect an interest in the longevity of an organization and the systems in which it plays a part. These concerns suggest that the company will also take its relationship with you as a customer more seriously, investing the extra effort needed to create a sustainable "win-win."

As you implement green computing, and green your own supply chain, you'll benefit from these effects as well.

Create a supplier checklist for all aspects of your selection criteria, non-green as well as green. Then rank suppliers on it. Build and deepen relationships with the best of them, entering into long-term supply contracts, seeking large volume discounts, and helping them understand your business. For other purchasing decisions, use the supplier checklist as a short-term tool. You'll steadily green your supply chain.

## 6.3 Case Study: HP vs. Dell

Two of the biggest suppliers of personal computers are HP and Dell. Let's take a quick look at some of the supplier-level considerations for choosing one over another. The following comparison holds as of mid-2012:

- **Greenpeace Guide rating.** The Greenpeace Guide to Greener Electronics currently ranks HP #1 overall, with a ranking of nearly 6 out of 10; Dell is #2, with a ranking of just over 5 out of 10. (Apple is third among computer vendors, with a ranking somewhat below 5 out of 10.) It's no accident that the leading vendors are also green leaders (http://www.greenpeace.org/international/en/Guide-to-Greener-Electronics/18th-Edition/).

- **Newsweek Green 500 ranking.** The Newsweek Green 500 ranking ranks HP #2 in its segment, Technology Equipment, and Dell #5. Apple, by contrast, is #50 (!) (http://www.thedailybeast.com/newsweek/2012/10/22/newsweek-green-rankings-2012-u-s-500-list.html).

- **Website review.** HP has a simplistic website (see Figure 6.2). Searching in the About section yields an Environment mini-site, including information on recycling, carbon footprint, and more. Dell has a much richer site, but Environment is pushed down a level to a heading under Corporate

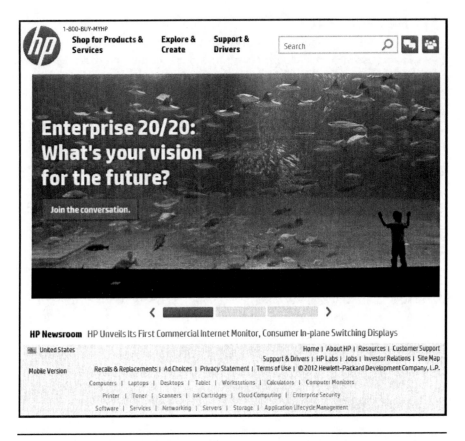

**Figure 6.2**   HP's current website is sparse, but dramatic. (*Source*: www.hp.com)

---

Responsibility in the About Dell section of the site. The Dell Environment area is somewhat richer, with areas of focus including recycling, energy efficiency, and green IT, with case studies. Both seem representative of a solid green commitment.

- **Classes of devices.** Both companies offer a full range of desktop and laptop computers. Both are weaker in tablets (neither offers the leading device, the iPad), and neither offers much in the smartphone arena.

Clearly, both companies are leaders; and clearly, HP has the overall edge on green criteria. You would, of course, complement the company-level study with a look at specific computers that meet your criteria, and Dell might win at that level. You'd then have to compare the vendors on having the products you want, support, price, and other factors.

If you go through this process, make the purchase decision, and let the vendors know why, you'll contribute quite a bit to the green computing cause.

## 6.4  Giving Suppliers and Vendors Feedback

Choosing green suppliers helps green your own organization. Giving feedback to suppliers helps green every organization.

When you buy a green or greener device, no one knows why you did it—unless you tell them. Not only do you need to tell them, you need to make sure you're heard. There are two main ways to do that. The first is to use the old model that speakers use to organize their talks:

1. Tell them what you're going to tell them.
2. Tell them.
3. Tell them what you've told them.

This means a lot of repetition. Here's one way to implement this model:

1. **Tell them what you're going to tell them.** Create a statement of principles as to how you buy, including green principles that you rely on. Put it on your website. Vendors research potential customers; they're likely to see this statement. If not, direct them to it.
2. **Tell them.** When you create a request for quotation, include your principles. Raise them in conversations with vendors. Note what they tell you and use it in your buying decision.
3. **Tell them what you've told them.** When you make a purchase, let the winning and losing vendors know why, at the same time as you tell each vendor "yes" or "no." Refer back to your statement of principles. You'll give your vendors powerful incentives to do better with the next customer—and with you, the next time around.

Another way to make sure you're heard is to ask vendors to repeat back what you've told them. You can do this literally, and in person: Describe your buying criteria and ask vendors to repeat the key points back to you. Also, in quotations, ask vendors to spell out how they meet—or don't meet—each of your key criteria.

This can be an eye-opening experience for vendors. I know from experience that there's not much worse than having nothing to say when a potential customer asks you about one of their key criteria. If several of your key points have to do with green computing, you'll make a powerful and lasting impression on vendors.

Even when you say "no" to most vendors, that may not be the end of the story. Don't be surprised if vendors who lose out on one purchasing decision start keeping you up to date on their green efforts, with their eyes on your next request.

You can also take advantage of the dynamic summed up in the old expression, "A rising tide lifts all boats." Share your approach with other companies—even competitors. If your industry segment gets a strong reputation with vendors for using green criteria, you'll all get better offers. If your industry segment gets a strong reputation with customers for using green criteria, you'll all get more sales.

Ironically, your communications around your green buying principles may make as much, or more, of a difference than the simple fact of having and using them, because good examples can resonate far and wide. So pay attention to all parts of the process.

## 6.5 Publicizing Your Selection Process and the Winner

You have many degrees of freedom in how much you publicize all your green computing efforts, and device purchases are part of it. There are some special considerations around device purchases, though, that are worth thinking about.

You can actually do marketing and PR around a purchasing process, especially if (1) it's a relatively large purchase (or a supplier review), and (2) there's a "hook" that the public at large can get interested in—like, say, green computing!

The normal urge is to go through the purchase process and then share the results, not only with internal audiences and vendors, but with the world. However, doing your first publicity at the end of the process is likely to come across as self-congratulatory. Green marketing about an event like this is likely to work better if it ties into an ongoing story. And you can create that story yourself. Consider publicizing the entire process, creating an arc of interesting and engaging communications along the way.

What might be the benefits of such a process? Here are a few:

- **Enhanced vendor participation.** Your business might be valued more highly by suppliers if they're going to get good publicity as well as money from a win. And suppliers who see you being thoughtful will also conclude that they might be able to build a longer-term relationship, not just make a one-off sale.
- **A greener offer.** Highly motivated vendors will go the extra mile to win your business. For instance, they might offer you specialized packaging options and product take back that might not otherwise have been forthcoming.
- **Better financial terms.** Vendors will sharpen their pencils while creating your quote if there's a lot at stake for them in a win. Not only lower prices but better financing terms and "extras" included for free might be part of a deal.

- **Better support.** You may well receive better support after the completion of the deal if the vendor perceives that there's benefit in keeping you saying good things about them.
- **Better products.** A vendor might offer you early access to products after development, or give you early input into an upcoming generation of devices that you might consider in a future deal.

Note that I'm not recommending you pursue green devices just to get these benefits; it's unlikely to work. But if you are making a sincere effort, which will cost some money (at least up front) and management time, you might as well get all the benefits you can from it. The benefits you create for yourself will serve as an incentive to do even more on later rounds of purchases, and on other parts of your green computing effort.

Here's an example of how to publicize a major purchasing event. Let's assume that you're going to take a year to go through the whole purchasing cycle, for a purchase process that starts in the spring and needs to be budgeted in the fall, for delivery in January of the following year:

- **Spring:** Decide what you need. Do you want to buy specific equipment, create a flexible master purchase agreement, create an approved vendors list? Decide on your overall goal. Share what you're doing—including the use of green criteria—internally. You might consider a small, low-key press release describing the overall process you're entering into, just to lay the groundwork.
- **Early summer:** Get details for the initial purchase. Survey affected departments about their needs. Work with them to meet needs with a smaller class of devices, where possible. For example, some departments might get inspired about having fewer support costs and hassles by having some employees use smartphones or tablets instead of full computers.
- **Late summer:** Send out a Request for Proposal. Now's the time to kick the publicity machine into gear. Consider creating a news release, with supporting Web content, about your green computing focus. Include early wins, such as choosing smaller-footprint devices. Publicize your criteria. Don't be surprised if a better class of vendors than usual responds!
- **Fall:** Get proposals and quotations back from vendors. Have vendors come in to present. Stick with all your criteria—cost and other suitability requirements, as well as green requirements. Without naming names, you can challenge each vendor to match the best aspects of other vendors' proposals. You can also rough out your budget for the purchase using the information you've gathered.
- **Winter:** Winnow quotations down to finalists and decide. Consider having you and the winning vendor issue separate, but complementary, press

releases. (Joint press releases raise too many issues for most companies.) Highlight traditional criteria—cost, performance, etc.—as well as green criteria. You can also include the process as a case study in your annual report or other communications.

- **January:** Receive the shipment—or the initial, partial shipment of devices. Consider a small press release to mark the occasion and finish your messaging.

Here are a few suggestions to follow in publicity efforts of this sort:

- **Keep it low key.** It might have taken a lot of effort for your organization to start adopting green computing, but that's "inside baseball" that no one outside cares about (or needs to know about). Be businesslike and matter-of-fact in your announcements and statements.
- **Keep it positive**. Don't say anything bad about anyone in your communications. Talk about how you want to "improve" the environment and "reduce" negative side effects. Focus on the good qualities of the winning vendor; don't mention the bad qualities of the losing ones. (Keep in mind that you may be buying from one or more of them at a later date.)
- **Measure success.** Note the public impact of your announcements—Web page hits, media mentions, and so on. Write an after-action report describing the positives and negatives of the effort. This will prove invaluable for colleagues in your organization seeking to make similar efforts of their own.

## 6.6 A Sample Statement of Green Buying Principles

It's much easier to create any kind of marketing or purchasing wording if you have an example to work from, so I'm providing one here. You don't have to use the example as is—heck, you might go in an entirely different direction. But having something to start with will save you a lot of time, even if it only serves as a model of what you don't want to do.

So the following is an example statement, incorporating the major points from the Greenpeace Guide to Greener Electronics:

We at Bud Smith Consulting have incorporated green computing principles into our IT buying process. We have made a commitment to pursue green computing, and that includes buying the lowest-impact devices that meet our needs.

Our criteria reflect a wide variety of business needs as well as green-specific requirements. They include the following eight points:

1. **Supplier commitment.** We want to buy from suppliers who have made an ongoing, visible, and longstanding commitment to green computing, in their own operations and in their products. We particularly value efforts suppliers make to measure, publicize, and reduce their carbon footprint.

2. **Smaller classes of devices.** We use the smallest class of device that will do the job. We won't buy a laptop if a tablet can do the job, and we won't buy a tablet if a smartphone can do the job.

3. **Smaller devices within a class; recycled materials.** When we do buy a laptop, for example, we lean toward smaller and lighter ones. And we lean toward devices that include recycled materials.

4. **Battery life.** Other things being equal, we prefer devices with longer battery life.

5. **Rare earth and other hazardous materials usage.** We ask that you avoid or minimize use of rare earth minerals and other materials that are hazardous, or that generate hazardous waste in their production.

6. **Light packaging and documentation.** We prefer that standard packaging and documentation be as small and low-impact as possible, and that lighter packaging and documentation options be available, especially for bulk purchases.

7. **Labor and legal issues.** We prefer that suppliers treat workers fairly and well within the bounds of locally applicable laws and internationally accepted principles.

8. **Take-back policy.** Please include product take back in your proposal for our purchase requirements. This should include take back for complementary products, such as additional batteries or power cords for laptops, even if not made by you. We prefer that you have a uniform product take-back policy for all your customers.

For a much more detailed plan that we use as a model in our purchasing decisions, please see the Greenpeace Guide to Greener Electronics ranking criteria. The latest version of the ranking criteria is available as a PDF, which you can access at the following URL: http://www.greenpeace.org/international/en/campaigns/toxics/electronics/Guide-to-Greener-Electronics/

## 6.7 Desktop Computers

Desktop computers are now a minority of computer purchases; laptops sales comprise more than half of computer sales worldwide.

Desktop computers can, however, be workhorses. A desktop computer typically has a larger power supply, more slots for add-in cards, and connectors for multiple monitors. It's not by accident that many of the remaining customers for desktop computers are hard-core computer game players.

Desktop computers can also be inherently more secure: A computer that doesn't leave the premises is far easier to protect from loss or theft than one that does.

One problem with buying desktop computers, however, is that employees will then ask for a laptop to complement the desktop machine. If you don't give them one, they'll keep sensitive company data on their own computer, or on several of their own computers. All the cost, support, and security problems you solved by getting a desktop machine in the first place open up again if the desktop computer doesn't really meet employees' needs.

Another problem with buying desktop computers is that the advantages of a desktop machine militate against green computing principles. A desktop machine has more capacity and is more flexible—that's because it has more electronic and physical "stuff" in it. Vendors who are creating a machine that never has to run on battery power can waste power freely without anyone noticing.

There are several steps you can take in "greening" your desktop computing purchases:

- **Get your specs right.** Take the time up front to understand the likely needs of each computer user you're buying for. This will give you far more flexibility in planning your purchases.
- **Look at laptops first.** Try to downsize your desktop computing purchases to laptops, where possible.
- **Look at specialized "green" desktops.** Many vendors now make specialized "green" desktops. These are small and boast reduced power consumption. Some include recycled materials. They are almost as portable as laptops, making it easier to work at home, for instance.

The Planet Green website, shown in Figure 6.3, highlights several green desktop computers. HP, Dell, Apple, and Lenovo are among the companies represented. One featured computer, the Zonbu Desktop Mini, from specialty maker Zonbu, is entirely cloud based and comes with carbon offsets to make the whole operation carbon neutral.

The Mac Mini is the most senior of major green desktop computers; Apple's made them since 2005. That means you can get really good at buying and supporting them. It's worth reading the history of the Mac Mini on Wikipedia (see Figure 6.4) to get a sense of how general computer trends, as well as green computer trends, have shifted in the last decade or so. Along with standard computer uses, Mac Minis are often used as media servers in homes and as Web servers by businesses.

A Discovery Company

By Jaymi Heimbuch
San Francisco, CA | Mon Nov 3, 2008 13:12

## Buy Green: Desktop Computers

Your old desktop computer is upgraded to the max and still processing at a snail's pace: time for a new, mean green machine. Technology is one place where sustainable design is growing by leaps and bounds. You may want to do your own research, as often the folks at the local big-box computer store don?t know much about the environmental features, other than what trims your electric bill: energy efficiency. While energy efficiency is certainly something to keep in mind, a green computer is the sum of its eco-friendly parts. Some desktops with excellent energy savings include the Fulwood from VeryPC, Shuttle's X27, and CherryPal's C114. However, there are manufacturers who are doing far more to make sure that their desktops have the smallest footprints possible. That includes packaging, materials, energy efficiency, and more.

It should also be noted that desktop computers, when compared to laptops, are generally cheaper with a longer shelf life.

We've taken the bigger picture into account with the five desktop computers listed here.

### Studio Hybrid From Dell

**Why We Like It:** The Studio Hybrid uses about 70% less energy than a standard desktop computer, meets Energy Star 4.0 standards, and is practically pocket-sized, at about 80% smaller than typical desktops. Packaging is made of 95% recycled materials and options include a sleek bamboo shell.
**Nice Touch:** With your purchase, you can plant a tree. Plus, Dell as a company has very high green standards.
**Where:** Dell Computers
**How Much:** Starts at $500
**Read More:** TreeHugger

---

**Figure 6.3**  Planet Green highlights green desktop computers. (*Source*: http://planetgreen.discovery.com/buying-guides/buy-green-desktop-computers.html)

## 6.8  Laptops

Laptops are becoming the workhorse computers for most businesses. Many of them, ironically, rarely leave the desktop. Others travel regularly to meetings, to employees' homes, and on business trips.

In my current workplace, most people have laptops in docking stations with at least one large-screen monitor attached. Some laptops are Macs (most of which also run Windows, using special software as a bridge); the rest are Windows laptops. The laptops often accompany people to meetings and out of the office. There's hardly a desktop computer in the building of this five-year-old company.

# Mac Mini

From Wikipedia, the free encyclopedia

The **Mac Mini** (marketed as **Mac mini**) is a small form factor desktop computer manufactured by Apple Inc. Like earlier mini-ITX PC designs, it is quite small for a desktop computer. 7.7 inches (20 cm) square and 1.4 inches (3.6 cm) tall. It weighs 2.7 pounds (1.2 kg). Before the mid-2011 revision, all models, except the mid-2010 server model, came with an internal optical disc drive. Models pre-2010 used an external power supply and were narrower but taller at 2.0×6.5×6.5 inches (5.1×17×17 cm). The Mac Mini is one of three desktop computers in the current Macintosh lineup, the other two being the iMac and Mac Pro, although it generally uses components usually featured in laptops, hence its small size.

The Mac Mini was the first consumer level Macintosh desktop to ship without a display, keyboard, or mouse since Apple's success following the release of the iMac, with Apple marketing it as *BYODKM* (Bring Your Own Display, Keyboard, and Mouse) to reinforce this fact. The primary intended market for the Mac Mini was users switching from a traditional Windows PC to a Mac who might already own a compatible display, keyboard and mouse, though these could be easily purchased if needed.[5] A special Server version of the computer is also intended for use as a server in a small network, and starting with the mid-2010 revision, all Server models include the Server edition of the OS X operating system.

The updated unibody Mac Mini is notable as Apple's first computer to include an HDMI video port to connect to a television or other display, more readily positioning the unit as a home theater device alternative to the Apple TV.[6]

Main page
Contents
Featured content
Current events
Random article
Donate to Wikipedia
Wikimedia Shop

▼ Interaction
  Help
  About Wikipedia
  Community portal
  Recent changes
  Contact Wikipedia

▶ Toolbox

▶ Print/export

▼ Languages
  العربية
  Català
  Česky
  Dansk
  Deutsch

2011 Unibody Mac mini

**Mac mini**

| | |
|---|---|
| Manufacturer | Apple Inc. |
| Type | Desktop[1] & Server[2] |
| Release date | July 20, 2011 (current release) January 22, 2005 (original release) |
| Introductory price | US$599 |
| Media | CD/DVD drive (pre-July 2011 models) |
| Operating system | OS X[3][4] |
| Power | 84 W PSU (7 A@12 V) |
| CPU | Intel Core i5[3] & Core i7[4] (current release) PowerPC G4 (original release) |
| Storage capacity | 500 GB[3] 1 TB[4] (server) |

**Figure 6.4** Wikipedia goes deep on the Mac Mini. (Source: http://en.wikipedia.org/wiki/Mac_Mini)

Many employees, at my workplace and in many others, have their laptops in a holder that puts them in a strange-looking, wide-open, upright position, so the screen is at eye level, but the keyboard is nearly unusable. A separate keyboard is plugged into the base station for desktop use; some people also use a mouse. When the laptop goes with the employee, the laptop keyboard and trackpad are used.

Before you buy a laptop, consider several other possibilities:

- **Desktops.** A green desktop may do the job and can be greener (and cheaper) than some laptops. This is especially true for employees who can use tablets for meetings and short trips. Get in a few green desktops as examples, then ask employees to compare before deciding.
- **Tablets.** A tablet can replace a desktop or laptop, but you may need custom software development to make company-specific applications run on the tablet. A tablet's footprint is far less than a laptop's. Even using a tablet part-time results in savings, as hours of very low-power usage of the tablet replace hours of higher-power usage of the laptop or desktop.
- **"Dumb" terminals and stripped-down PCs.** If everything is in the cloud, a bare-bones machine may do the job. Many companies offer ways to run Windows on a server and mirror it on a tablet or dumb terminal. A stripped-down PC running Windows, or a Mac, may do the job if software and data are all, or almost all, in the cloud.

These many uses give rise to many needs for laptops, including specific twists on the green-related needs shared by all IT devices:

- **Low power use.** Laptops have to be efficient in their power use because they have to be able to run a long time on batteries—and battery life is one of the most-watched laptop specifications. So it's easy to compare power use and weight of laptops.
- **Small screen size.** Check with your users as to what screen size they prefer; they might like a smaller model, as it's easier to carry. When the laptop is used on the desktop, external monitors can carry the load for display power when needed.
- **Sufficiency.** Today's laptops have to do a lot. They should be as small and as low-powered as possible, but not offer less capability than needed.
- **Durability.** A laptop that lasts twice as long means a lot less embedded energy gets thrown away. Use external reviews and other sources to identify makers and models of laptops that are more likely to last a long time.
- **Maintainability.** A laptop that's easy to clean up after spills and easy to repair after, say, a drop may serve you better than a more disposable model.

- **Connectivity.** Laptops serve as hubs for numerous other devices. They need a strong assortment of ports and an excellent connection to a durable dock. The laptop and dock need to survive and thrive through potentially thousands of docking/undocking repetitions (some of which might be rough).
- **Safety.** Engineers push the limits of technology to make laptops work, and some laptops develop dangerous "hot spots" on the bottom or edges, or even burst into flames occasionally. Pay close attention to problem reports, and to whether manufacturers respond effectively to problems that do arise. (Safety is also green, as having to suddenly replace a bunch of new-ish laptops, among other problems, is not very sustainable.)
- **Home office and road usability.** Consider whether a laptop can easily support work-at-home days and travel. Consider making additional peripherals, such as docks and monitors, available to employees, so they can create consistent work and home-working environments while carrying the laptop back and forth.

Put a lot of time and energy into deciding when a laptop is the right choice and picking the right suppliers and models. Keep buying the same model, where possible, so as to negotiate a lower purchase price and keep accessory, maintenance, and support costs under control.

## 6.9 Sustainability and Failure to Supply

"Failure to supply" is a way of describing a surprisingly persistent phenomenon: Customers often don't leave suppliers; instead, suppliers, in effect, leave their customers. That is, customers, out of habit or laziness, will often stick with a supplier, or at least a type of solution, for a very long time indeed. But if the supplier ever—even briefly—fails to supply the expected product, the customer can quickly, and permanently, go away.

A version of "failure to supply" is that the market can subtly shift away from a vendor or a type of solution. For instance, customers have gradually moved sustainability from a nice extra to a necessity. Their definition of an acceptable product has changed. (Laptops used to have red on black or green on black displays, and color screens became a necessity, in a similar shift.) Any vendor who wasn't ready with reasonably sustainable products as this shift is occurring will have been caught out, and replaced by vendors who are ready.

Look out for this phenomenon with vendors, especially with regard to sustainability. It's no accident that the two biggest Windows PC makers worldwide, HP and Dell, are the top two in the Greenpeace Guide to Greener Electronics. They see that the definition of a "standard" PC is changing, and that the new definition includes sustainability, so they're leading the charge.

Actually, a similar definitional shift is happening to you with regard to your organization's upper management and stakeholders. The definition of what an IT department provides an organization is changing to include at least a reasonable effort towards green computing. The definition of "reasonable" depends on many factors, including your competitors' actions and the predilections of your upper management and Board of Directors. Exceeding these steadily rising expectations is likely to be rewarded; falling short of them, not so much.

## 6.10 The Case of Windows 8

A potential future business school case study around "failure to supply" seems to be germinating in the market for Windows-compatible computers.

Since its launch in January 2010, the iPad has taken the tablet market by storm. Competitors have tried, and largely failed, to establish viable alternatives. At this writing, in mid-2012, the iPad is on its third generation—and Microsoft has just announced its first tablet—the Surface, and Windows 8—a new version of Windows for tablets and personal computers. For the first time, Microsoft was selling a tablet—the Surface—directly. According to *ComputerWorld*'s Preston Gralla, after the first few months, Windows 8 sales were said to be sluggish. Partners were said to be concerned about the situation (http://blogs.computerworld.com/windows/21721/new-report-shows-windows-8-sales-remain-sluggish-no-significant-growth-sight).

Windows 8 offers a new interface, called the Metro UI, based on tiles (see Figure 6.5). For Microsoft's new Surface tablet, it's an attractive interface, and a first-time tablet buyer might consider it over an iPad. (The initial Windows 8 tablet, though, is behind the current iPad on important specifications, such as screen resolution.)

Except for Microsoft and Windows 8, no other major vendor tries to have the same interface from the smartphone all the way up to the desktop. Apple has one OS for personal computers—OS X, and one for tablets and smartphones—iOS; Google offers Android for smartphones and tablets and doesn't have a strong personal computer entry. Unix is available for personal computers, but not for smartphones or tablets.

In fact, no other vendor differentiates the UI from the underlying operating system the way Microsoft is trying to do. All the other vendors have a different UI for different operating systems. (While it's true that there's some blurring between current versions of Apple's OS X and iOS, that's "blurring," not "the same as," and Apple users are far more used to change than Microsoft users.)

Let me summarize the "use case" for the Metro UI, on two different OS's, on different platforms:

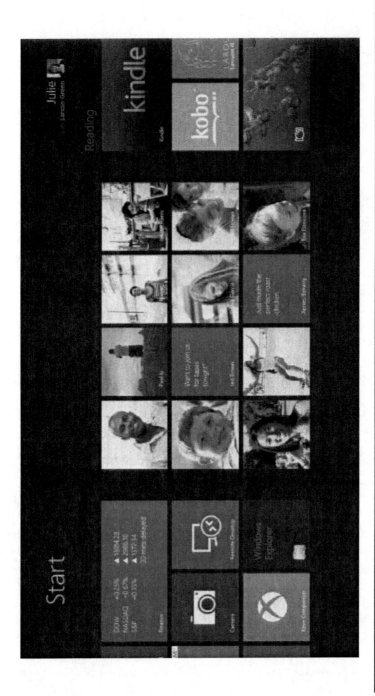

**Figure 6.5** Microsoft Windows 8 in action. (Source: http://www.microsoft.com/en-us/news/presskits/windows/videogallery2.aspx)

- **Smartphones** (Windows Phone OS plus Metro): Strong entry, almost no one uses it.
- **Microsoft's Surface tablet** (Windows 8 for tablets plus Metro): The Surface line of tablets has received mixed reviews and is not yet a rival to the iPad, the market leader.
- **Laptops and desktops** (Windows 8 with Metro): Windows 8 is a big change from Windows 7 and earlier versions of Windows, presenting challenges for adoption.

## 6.11 Tablets

Buying tablets is a Good Thing. They cost much less than personal computers and are easier to use, more portable, and far less impactful environmentally. It's worth buying tablets instead of personal computers, where you can. It's even worth buying tablets in addition to personal computers, because they cost less to buy, less to get software for, and much less per hour to run (environmentally and in terms of power usage).

There are a few things to look out for, though, with tablets:

- **Obsolescence.** A tablet's battery(ies) may wear out after as little as 18 months of heavy use. Look for longevity in the product descriptions and reviews of tablets you're considering.
- **Durability.** The iPad, the industry standard, seems pretty rough and tough. I've almost managed to break my iPad 1: It developed an ugly bulge around the volume rocker after I dropped it, and steam got in there while I was taking a bath and shorted it out for a while. It still works, though. So durability is an important issue.
- **Scrubbing and finding.** It's very easy for tablets to be lost or stolen; make sure a tablet can be easily "wiped" and locked remotely, and that it has a remote findability service. The iPad has all of this; if you consider competing tablets, they should, too.
- **Connectivity.** Tablets are very low on connection options, both for physically plugging things in, and software drivers for making them work once you do. One of the main advantages of a non-iPad solution may be enhanced connectivity.
- **Accessories.** Carefully consider tablet accessories. I'm one of the millions of people, for instance, who bought a Bluetooth keyboard for my iPad, and now rarely use it.
- **Custom software development.** Employees are going to want to use their iPad to get through short trips. Make certain they can access email and

their calendar, and be aggressive about giving them at least partial access to other applications as well.

An example of partial access to an application is the development by cloud marketing software vendor Marketo of a check-in app for the iPad. You can't, at this writing, run the Marketo interface on an iPad; what you can do is run a special iPad app that helps check people into an event, such as a tradeshow. The app then synchronizes with Marketo software in the cloud to update the records of these current and potential customers with their check-in status.

Salesforce, which makes cloud software for salespeople, offers more—a version of their software with fairly full capability for the iPhone and iPad. Use these considerations in your hardware as well as your software choices.

## 6.12 "Less Computer" and "Computer-less" Solutions

It sounds radical, but some employees won't need a computer at all—and some won't even need a tablet. A smartphone can be used as a PDA (Personal Digital Assistant) to automate many tasks.

Also consider a smartphone capability that many people overlook—the phone part. If you can avoid giving tablets and/or laptops to 20 or 40 field employees by having them call into or text one or two internal phone support people for updates, you're ahead of the game. (And, you can train the phone support people to use your full array of software.)

There are also exciting options around using "dumb" terminals and accessing a Windows interface from an iPad or Android tablet.

Be creative. People weren't created to use computers and consumer electronics devices; computers and consumer electronics devices are there to help people. Helping people help themselves using a minimal device, or even no additional device, has the potential to be the greenest solution of all.

## 6.13 Summary

This chapter described what to look for from specific kinds of devices. It summarized green buying criteria for devices; suggested green buying criteria for suppliers; showcased HP and Dell's green claims; described how to give feedback to suppliers; and discussed purchase considerations for desktops, laptops, and tablets. The next chapter discusses green servers and data centers.

# Chapter 7

# Green Servers and Data Centers

## Key Concepts

This chapter describes how to green your data center(s) and servers:

- Choosing green suppliers when you buy in data center services
- Why you should start now
- Planning buildings
- Planning power supplies
- Servers, storage, and networking

## 7.1 Choosing and Creating Green Data Centers

More and more of the intelligence and information used by a computing system is housed away from the primary device itself. This is simply a return to a past reality, and perhaps the future will see another swing of the pendulum.

In the mainframe computer era, computing took place on large computers—mainframes. As computer technology grew more powerful and less expensive, minicomputers became another option. Users interacted with dumb termi-nals—dumb because they had no processing power nor storage of their own.

Some of us will remember the IBM 3270 series of terminals, with green-on-black, text-only screens, as a standard.

The microcomputer era, beginning in the 1980s, placed computer processing power and storage directly on the user's desktop (oftentimes alongside a 3270 or other terminal). Early data sharing took place by carrying floppy disks from one PC to another, which was called "sneakernet." The rise of personal computer networking began the process of easier sharing of work and messages among microcomputers.

Now, we are turning nearly full circle. More and more computing work is done on servers—some located inside an organization, others outside, in what is now known as cloud computing or Software as a Service (Saas). In many cases, the user's device—whether a smartphone, tablet, or personal computer—just provides the user interface for processing and data that happen in the cloud.

But "the cloud" is really a collection of a whole bunch of clouds. Companies such as Google, Facebook, and Apple compete on the basis of the power, low cost—and, increasingly, green credentials—of their data centers. Even mainframe computers are now sold as particularly large and capable servers.

Google, in particular, has become known for its unique server and data center design, which saves energy and expense. This has been said to give Google a cost advantage of perhaps 30% per processing operation, compared to competitors. The accompanying power savings are inherently green, and Google is pressing its advantage in this area.

Google, going much further than its competitors, is even a significant investor in renewable energy. Google also pioneers potentially green technologies, such as the Google Car. (Cars would be far more efficient if driven by computers.)

Given the emerging nature of distributed computing, your first opportunity to green your data center(s) is to outsource as much data center–type processing as possible. For example, if you use Google Apps heavily in your organization, you've just chosen to have much of your data center work done outside your company. The same goes for every SaaS application that you buy (e.g., Salesforce.com).

Some vendors even give you a choice. Microsoft's competing Customer Resource Management, or CRM, application is called Microsoft Dynamics CRM. It comes in both an internally hosted version and a cloud-based version, called Microsoft Dynamics CRM Online.

Use green criteria to help determine what software services to buy in from outside and which ones to perform in house. Give preference to green vendors, using criteria similar to those described for green devices in the previous chapter. This is the easiest way to green much of your data center efforts—by outsourcing them. Outside vendors will usually be "greener" than you can easily manage, because they have such large efficiencies of scale compared to you. You can also use additional green criteria in choosing SaaS software vendors.

Amazon is famous for selling books, but savvy IT managers know that it is also the leading provider of scalable computing services. These services are called Amazon Web Services, or AWS for short. AWS is as close as you can come to getting your processing and storage services in a way that is similar to buying electricity. AWS is flexible and reasonably priced, for most purposes.

Google is working hard to catch up. With either of these providers, computing power becomes a utility, like electrical power: you just plug into it as needed; then you pay a bill at the end of the month, depending on how much you use. (The Amazon approach comes closest to this, as it's more flexible in terms of the tools you can use in crafting solutions.)

To green your entire operation, follow the same approach for computing services that you use with computing devices: move services to the greenest, least impactful approach first (someone else's green data center); then to the next most impactful one (your own green data center); and, only as a last resort, to the most impactful one—your own non-green data center, or local processing on the users' own devices.

Even if you decide to run servers yourself, they don't need to be servers you own, nor do the servers need to run in space you own and operate directly. Rackspace (see Figure 7.1) is one of the best-known of many companies providing

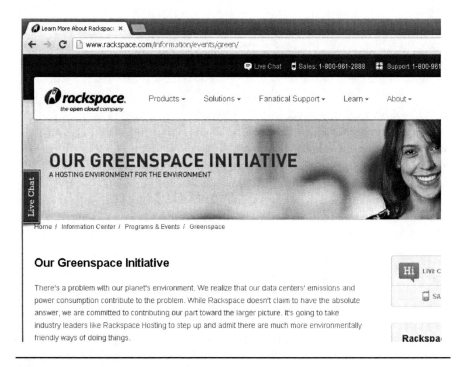

**Figure 7.1**    Rackspace is a leader in Green Data Center Hosting.

server facilities for hire, and they have a robust green program. Consider using offsite hosting for your services where possible.

## 7.2 Green Data Centers as a Model

Data centers have been estimated to use between 1% and 1.5% of the world's total energy, according to an article in the IEEE's *IT Professional*.[1] Data center facilities use more than 100 times the energy than standard office buildings, according to the US Department of Energy.[2]

Your internally owned and operated data center, or centers, are the most visible and most expensive physical investment your IT department will make. Hardware costs are usually only a part of the total, and may be less than the associated software, management, facilities, and cooling costs. However, they still represent a large investment all by themselves. Hardware investments also set the terms and direction of all the related investments you make.

Data centers also take time to plan, build (if you build your own), and equip. Launching a new data center can be a big event, if you choose to make it one.

Adding green considerations to your data center planning, or implementing green efforts for existing data centers, are expensive efforts up front and may seem like distracting ones as well. But they're at the core of what you do as an IT manager. They're also likely to save money, not cost money, over the lifetime of a data center.

I mentioned in the previous chapter that "failure to supply" is a chief failing of many businesses, and a service organization such as an IT department can also "fail to supply" services that meet the shifting needs of internal customers. These internal customers and other stakeholders are increasingly expecting "greening" of the IT services they depend on. You may be asked to lead this move, follow others' efforts, or get out of the way.

*The Green and Virtual Data Center*, by Greg Schulz,[3] goes into a great deal of useful detail about what it takes to create and run a data center that's, well, green and virtual. I'll introduce some of the key concerns in this chapter; please use the Schulz book for greater detail.

## 7.3 The Last Shall Be First . . .

Because data centers represent such a large investment, it's tempting to defer greening them until you get some experience with, say, buying green laptops. I recommend that you start right away. Individual computing devices come and go, with a useful life of, at least, a few years. But data center–related decisions are serious infrastructure decisions. You'll be living with them for years, even decades to come. Green decision making also takes place on a learning curve. Many more possibilities open up as you gain momentum. The longer you wait to start, the fewer possibilities you'll have in the years ahead.

Even a decision to outsource computing capability has long-term effects. Let's say you decide to use Salesforce.com instead of an on-premise solution. Once you make that commitment, it's highly likely that people at your company will be using Salesforce 10, 20, even 30 years down the road.

If you choose a data center architecture that's as green as possible now, and keep greening it, you open up a lot of possibilities for progress. If you proceed without working green considerations into your plans, though, you cut off all sorts of opportunities for improvement. At the same time, be careful not to overinvest in data center infrastructure. Look at your likely needs many years down the road, especially with SaaS and outside hosting as more and more important players in the computing landscape.

Rightsize your "hard" investments so that your use of traditional "green"— money, that is—can be as effective and farsighted as your support for green computing efforts.

## 7.4  What Makes a Data Center Green?

For a data center, green means two fairly different things:

1. Mainstream environmental and sustainability issues, such as those on which most of this book is based
2. Power, cooling, floor space, and environmental health and safety issues, abbreviated as PCFE

Mainstream environmental issues and PCFE concerns often lead to the same destination. However, you can pursue PCFE goals without any concern for the environment as a whole. PCFE is more about efficient use of resources and worker safety, which are more traditional organizational concerns than environmental and sustainability issues.

PCFE arises from the fact that demands on IT, and therefore on data centers, seem to always only escalate. Without PCFE, a data center could become extraordinarily large, need impractical amounts of power or cooling, and constitute an unsafe environment—and still face demands to grow further. PCFE is an effort to keep data centers manageable, in both the colloquial and business senses of the term.

To make a green data center, combine PCFE concerns with mainstream environmental and sustainability efforts, as described throughout this book.

That way you get all the benefits of both approaches, without that much additional effort from just using one or the other.

Another factor that makes a data center green is virtualization. Virtualization separates what you do to manage computing resources from the actual physical resources at hand. For instance, a software-based virtual machine allows you to host several application servers and/or Web servers on a single physical machine—or to host a single application server on several physical machines, if demand requires it.

Virtualization seeks to enable you to view your computing resources as a single pool, ready to serve your software, storage, and processing demands as needed. This avoids duplication of equipment and waste. Although technical in its details, the effects of virtualization are very green indeed.

## 7.5 Building and Power Supply Considerations

Let's consider the exercise of building a new data center from scratch, with nothing determined up front except the likely needs of your company. You may actually be making decisions in a more constrained environment; for instance, you may be looking at taking up another floor in an existing office building, rather than doing a new build. Even so, looking at how to build up the data center from a clean slate will inform your overall approach.

In planning a building, you're going to juggle half a dozen factors:

- **Floor space.** What's the most floor space you can expect to use?
- **Power.** How much power can you get from the local utility in an area without paying exorbitant rates?
- **Cooling.** How much cooling will you need for a given amount of power consumption on a given amount of floor space?
- **Health and safety.** What are key health and safety concerns for your data center, such as exhaust from servers or printers? Are there particular sensitivities in a given local area, for instance, due to recent problems of a specific kind?
- **Device power consumption.** Given a certain budget of floor space, power availability, and/or cooling capacity, how many of what kind of devices can you have?
- **Organizational computing needs.** How much of your organization's needs will the data center be able to meet? How can you meet any needs over that limit?
- **Tripwires.** How can you set up early warning systems when you start approaching a data center's limits, so you have plans in place to prevent running up against them?

Now the model doesn't exist that allows you to simply treat all these numbers as unlimited, then juggle combinations of them. You have to start assuming some factors, then see how others are affected. You can pick a geographic location, for instance, and find out what the local utility can do for you in terms of power supply. You can assess cooling needs based on that area's weather and some assumed amount of floor space and mix of devices on that space.

One useful exercise is to plan initially for a one-story building, running all the numbers for a given amount of floor space on a single floor. Figure out cooling, device mix, and so on. Then make sure you can add more floors, as needed, to meet growth in your needs.

Even more valuable is to find existing data centers, either within your organization or outside it, that you can use as models. The mix of needs served, software applications used, and so on should be as similar to your own as possible. (And the task of finding a comparison site will be easier, the more up-to-date your own approach is.)

## 7.6 Servers, Storage, and Networking

In planning your data center, you need to plan for servers (for application and Web processing), storage, and networking—among your servers and storage devices, and to connect with the world outside the data center.

The storage and networking components depend on the decisions you make for servers, so I'll primarily focus here on server options. For more on all three of these elements, and much else besides, see *The Green and Virtual Data Center*.[3]

The first (and greenest) option to consider for servers is to use someone else's. When you do need to buy servers, though, you can help yourself with careful planning.

Servers are typically the largest single user of power in a data center, directly or indirectly. (The biggest power bill will be for cooling, but an outsize part of the cooling needs are generated by the servers.)

Servers stop working when they get too hot. Server manufacturers will give you a recommended temperature range that you have to stay within.

The biggest problem for your servers and your costs is the same problem utilities have: what to do on the very hottest days of the year, when air conditioning loads—and, often, electricity rates—go through the roof. Many utilities will pay you good money to take demand offline during these peaks, but taking your data center down is hard to explain to your stakeholders. If you have two data centers in widely different locations, though, you can juggle demand between them during peaks.

Here are tradeoffs you make when choosing a server at a given performance level:

- Physical size—small is good.
- Power usage—less is good.
- Heat output—less is good.
- Flexibility—the more one type of server can do, the fewer different types of equipment you need to support. The more different ways a server can be "racked" in different cabinet configurations, the more you can do with scores or even hundreds of servers.

While "less is more" for size, power, and heat output, the priority of each depends on your circumstances. If you have a facility in a cold place—some data centers are placed underground, cheek by jowl with icebergs—heat output may not be your biggest problem. You might have an air-cooled facility that can only take away so much heat, but plenty of floor space for devices. Power usage should always be minimized, though; it helps with cooling as well as direct power bills, and also reduces risk from potential increases in energy costs.

Flexibility is crucial. Virtualization and green solutions are both easier to implement if you have a well-understood hardware base. Using fewer different types of devices makes it easier to understand and manage your hardware base.

Along with servers themselves, consider clustering software. Clusters can be managed more easily than single servers, and clusters can serve specialized purposes, such as high-performance computing or heavy input/output (I/O). A cluster can be active, or placed on standby for use when needed. A grid is quite similar to a cluster, and any difference may be more marketing spin than substance.

Once you make progress on server and grid/clustering solutions, you can see how those decisions affect storage needs. Solutions range from solid-state storage, through hard disks, tape, optical, and more. Within each type of storage, and across the different types, you're trading off read speeds, write speeds, capacity, and expense.

Be aware that storage needs are increasing exponentially. Regulatory requirements are one reason. It's increasingly important that you keep, for instance, many years' worth of email exchanges for regulatory purposes.

Another problem—oops, I mean opportunity—is deep data. This means, for instance, storing every action each user takes on your website for months and years at a time, then analyzing the traces for insights. Often, management wants data stored just in case they want to do a data dive later—but doesn't like seeing the resulting bills.

A crucial differentiator for organizations today is their ability to mine vast archives of data for information that contributes to sales and marketing, even product development and support effectiveness. However, you can't mine vast archives of data if you've thrown it away. Keeping this information cost-effectively, for either planned or unknown future uses, is a bit of an art form.

Storing huge amounts of data that you would otherwise just delete, then churning through it repeatedly in the hope that something interesting turns up, is not inherently very green. Nor is it very efficient; one company I work with throws away "trivial" data after 90 days to save server space and speed up processing. Clearly, there are a lot of choices to make here.

Storage can be divided into tiers: very fast, very expensive; fairly fast, fairly expensive; slow and inexpensive. Each technology type can be used in one or more of these tiers. Data compression can optimize your usage within a tier, or across tiers. You also need to consider remote backup of all of your data, all of the time, and whether additional compression is risky for archived data. With all this, you need to consider PCFE and mainstream green concerns as well.

Networking capabilities are similar in structure to data storage: You have very fast networking for interconnections among servers, then a grid of fast networking within the data center, then slower connections to and from the outside world.

## 7.7 Data Center Suppliers

You can use all kinds of suppliers for data centers. (I continue to refer to actual, physical data centers that you own or lease directly.) Suppliers will do all of the work for you, and you only need to approve a Request for Proposal and write a check. Or, you can own and manage as much or little of the process as you'd like.

If you choose a green-oriented supplier, you may be able to get a lot of benefits without too much work—including, again, risk reduction from reduced exposure to energy price increases. You can let a supplier do a great deal of the work on one data center, then use what you learn to do more of the job yourself in additional data centers later.

As with end-user computing devices, you need to consider the green credentials of data center device suppliers as well. A simple comparison is to use relatively green devices from highly rated suppliers in the end-user world as a benchmark for devices from more specialized makers. At this writing, HP is the leader in the Greenpeace Guide to Greener Electronics, and they certainly make servers. You can thus use HP servers as a "green" reference comparison for competing bids. (Tell the other vendors that you're doing this, and why; it will drive them nuts, but you'll get better bids.)

And, as your data center specifications firm up, you can compare one last time to outsourced approaches. These include outsourced processing and storage capabilities from the likes of Amazon and Google. Odds are, you can't handle all your needs via outsourcing. However, you may be able to do a lot.

In fact, for a medium or large organization, you probably always want to use a mix of solutions—SaaS and internally hosted software; data centers you own and computing capability that you rent. That way you can flexibly shift your assets around as opportunities present themselves. If you don't use a modicum of, say, Amazon services for anything at all, you won't be ready to use them for a big project when an otherwise suitable opportunity presents itself.

Building, owning, managing, and improving data center resources is a huge challenge, and doing so in a green computing–savvy manner that also meets PCFE concerns makes things even more complex. The rewards, though, are commensurate with the challenge.

## 7.8 Summary

This chapter described how to green your data center(s) and servers: choosing green suppliers; planning buildings; planning power supplies; choosing servers, storage, and networking; and understanding why you should start now. The next chapter discusses the hardware life cycle and reducing hardware impact in depth.

# Chapter 8

# Saving Energy

## Key Concepts

This chapter describes how to save energy through green computing:

- Reducing costs, risk, and carbon footprint
- Improving your reputation and building your brand
- Analyzing energy usage
- Using solar power as part of the solution

## 8.1 Saving Energy Serves Many Masters

Saving energy is the *sine qua non* of green computing—the core element at the heart of most green computing efforts. That's because saving energy meets several core needs at once. We can briefly summarize them as:

- Saving money
- Reducing risk
- Reducing carbon footprint
- Improving your reputation and brand

In pursuing energy-saving efforts, you need to keep each of these four elements in mind at once: "Less money. Less risk. Smaller footprint. Better reputation."

There are two main reasons for keeping all the points in mind at once. As you talk to different audiences, each audience will care about these elements in a different way. And, by continually drawing attention to all the elements, you keep reminding people that you are solving several problems at once.

Another reason for calling attention to all four elements is that things change. For instance, electricity costs are dropping—or at least unlikely to rise—in some regions because of fracking, or hydraulic fracturing of underground rocks to extract natural gas. This environmentally dubious practice is all the rage in the United States, whereas European countries, among others, are going slow or considering outright bans.

If you base your strategy on only one element—for instance, saving money, while ignoring risk reduction, reducing your carbon footprint, and branding—then small shifts in that one element can undermine your entire approach. A more holistic view is more resilient to shifts in the various constituent elements over time.

Take the time to justify your efforts carefully up front, then follow through and show what was actually achieved. This builds up credibility and lays the groundwork for bigger, more complex efforts in the future.

In this chapter, I'll focus on identifying where energy is being used and on bringing in renewable energy. The other big component of energy savings is choosing energy-saving devices and software, which I'll cover in the next two chapters.

## 8.2  Cost Savings through Energy Savings

The number one driver for many green projects is direct financial savings by cutting electricity and gas bills. There are three main components to these savings:

- **Reduced energy use by devices.** Savings can be achieved by managing devices differently or shifting usage to new, less energy-intensive devices. Turning off monitors that are not in use is a relatively quick fix; replacing energy-hungry servers with energy-efficient ones is a slower fix; getting your entire sales force off laptops and onto tablet computers is slower still.
- **Reduced heating and (especially) air conditioning costs.** Devices take space, and that space has to be kept warm enough for both the devices, and the people who use them and look after them, to operate effectively. Devices also give off heat, and this is a bigger and bigger concern, especially for data centers. The cost of air conditioning for electronic devices is increasing, not least because global warming is slowly increasing average ambient temperatures.
- **Reducing other facilities costs.** Besides costs due to HVAC—heating, ventilation, and air conditioning, facilities cost a lot of money for

purchasing or renting floor space, cleaning, security, and so on. Although these costs are not energy costs per se, projects that reduce energy use often reduce related facility costs as well.

Saving money by saving energy is a hugely neglected source of cost savings around the world. Experts refer to "negawatts"—saving megawatts of energy through energy efficiency, hugely reducing energy bills.

In fact, energy efficiency is so neglected that it's somewhat of a mystery why organizations don't do more in this area. Return on investment (ROI)—even when focusing only on dollar costs, not risk, carbon footprint, and reputation—is often huge for energy-efficiency projects. Organizations spend a lot of time and energy pursuing much more difficult projects, with a much smaller and more uncertain payoff than these.

What this means to you in the here and now is that there's likely to be some low-hanging fruit for energy-efficiency projects, with big payoffs, in your organization. Even if you've plucked some of that low-hanging fruit in previous projects, you shouldn't have too much trouble finding more worthwhile efforts to make.

## 8.3  Risk Reduction through Energy Savings

Cost is, of course, a huge driver of business decision making. But, increasingly, so is risk.

Energy prices are a huge source of risk exposure for organizations because they vary so much. Figure 8.1 shows the world oil prices for the first decade of the new millennium, 2001–2010. Prices varied by a factor of nearly 10! This is amazing for such an important driver of business costs, and of the world's economy as well.

Electricity is the main source of energy for air conditioning and, of course, for powering devices. Electricity prices are less volatile than oil prices because electricity is more often supplied by natural gas or coal, where prices are less volatile (and, where utilities have some ability to switch among power sources to keep their costs lower). In fact, as mentioned above, fracking is driving natural gas prices down in some areas. Heating is more often provided by oil; about one-sixth of the United States' oil consumption is for heating.

Energy costs are only somewhat fungible. If the utility you use for a given facility is smart, they'll be able to move flexibly among different energy sources for electricity as availability and cost considerations change—ideally, a mix of renewable power and natural gas, with oil or coal only, perhaps, for occasional peaks in demand. (In the most populated areas, these tend to be a dozen or two hot summer afternoons and evenings.)

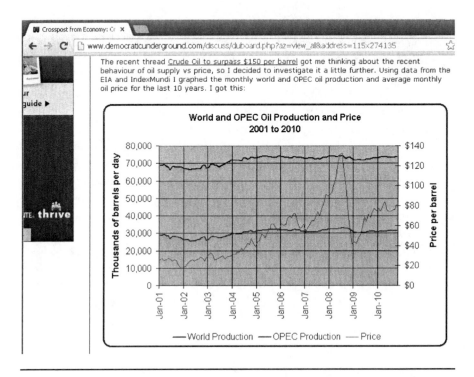

**Figure 8.1** World energy prices, 2001–2010. (*Source*: http://www.democratic underground.com/discuss/duboard.php?az=view_all&address=115x274135)

Energy prices are not very fungible between utility-provided power and oil. Oil is so useful for transport, as a feedstock for chemicals and other products, and for other purposes that it can't easily be substituted for electricity. You can take advantage of this; for instance, you can use telecommuting and teleconferencing to help cut expensive car trips and air travel (which use oil) in favor of using IT facilities (which use electricity).

Organizations have little control over what they pay for a given kilowatt-hour or other measure of energy. Prices are set regionally (for natural gas and coal) or on the world market (for oil). You can enter into long-term contracts for energy needs, but this only helps dampen monthly fluctuations, without affecting long-term trends.

You can also help yourself with renewable power. Solar panels are a perfect fit for facilities—such as data centers—with strong air conditioning needs. As the sun shines brighter on a warm afternoon, air conditioning needs go up—and solar panels deliver maximum power. You can size solar installations to greatly reduce peaks in electricity costs when the weather warms.

Storage for renewable energy sources is never as cheap or efficient as you might want, but storage of solar power for just a few hours is relatively cheap and effective. This is great for continuing to cool a facility on a hot summer afternoon and evening as the sun is going down, but enthalpy—latent heat—is keeping temperatures uncomfortably high.

Unlike solar panel output for powering air conditioning, energy costs are anticyclical—they tend to increase in good times (when demand is up) and decrease in bad times. This is, ironically, good for risk reduction: Energy costs will rise in time to help stop you from becoming rich, but they may not contribute as much to the problem when you're experiencing a financial downturn.

However, explaining to your peers and upper management that your over-exposure to energy costs is actually good for the organization, in the really big picture, is not a winning strategy. You want to contribute to maximizing profits, when profits are there to be had, and to minimizing negative exposures when losses loom.

Find out who handles risk management in your organization. If no one has the responsibility formally, the Chief Financial Officer (CFO) and the Chief Executive Officer (CEO) are likely to be strongly concerned with risk management. Find out how to plug into your organization's approaches, whether formal or informal, for managing risk.

The most direct way to reduce your exposure to energy price fluctuations—your risk—is to reduce the amount of energy you use. Radical reductions in energy costs are also likely to be radical reductions in risk.

## 8.4 Carbon Footprint Reduction through Energy Savings

When discussing green computing, "carbon footprint" has both a narrow and a broad meaning.

The narrow meaning is fairly well understood. Energy use usually requires the burning of fossil fuels. Your carbon footprint is the amount of carbon dioxide ($CO_2$) and equivalents that go into the air from the fossil fuels burned to produce the needed energy.

The impact of your energy use depends on where the energy comes from. If your local utility burns coal exclusively, for instance, your carbon footprint for using electricity will be quite high; each kilowatt-hour requires the burning of a lot of coal. If your local utility uses solar power when it's available—or if you use your own solar power—the footprint may vary depending on the time of day that you use the energy. You can research what your local utility does, or use regional or national average figures to calculate the carbon footprint for a given activity.

If people have to drive or fly to an event—or if teleconferencing or telecommuting prevents the need to drive or fly—the carbon footprint impact will depend on the vehicles involved. Again, you can come up with precise figures, or figure out averages that you use on an ongoing basis. (The important things to look out for in using averages are clarity and consistency.)

You can look at the carbon footprint of an activity narrowly or broadly. Running a laptop will use a certain amount of energy per hour—30 watts is a typical figure, about half the energy use of a 60W light bulb (which is on the low end of a bulb that people use for, say, residential lighting). So, narrowly speaking, the carbon footprint of the laptop is whatever's needed to generate 30 watts per hour of electricity.

More holistically, though, the user in an office has to get there, and his or her presence in the office will cause a certain amount of energy usage. For tele-commuting, you can compare this to the impact of the worker's staying home.

In the beginning of carbon footprint assessment, consider using narrow measures for specific activities or changes you're considering. Over time, you're likely to end up estimating the impact of most of what your company does, so you can easily assess the reductions from various efforts that you make to save energy.

Your carbon footprint also reflects a lot of other aspects of the green computing efforts that you make. As you reduce your carbon footprint, you also reduce:

- **Pollution.** Power generation is a huge source of pollution. Some pollutants are obvious and tend to wash out of the air with the rain, such as soot; others, such as mercury emissions from burning coal, remain in the environment for a long time. Although emissions are regulated, the cumulative effect of many sources of pollution still contributes hugely to pollution on a local, regional, and worldwide basis.
- **Collateral damage from resource extraction.** Coal is mined by lopping the tops off mountains; oil is extracted from risky deep-sea drilling and highly polluting tar sands mining in Canada; natural gas is wrenched from the surrounding rock by fracturing, using high-pressure water injections with dangerous chemicals. As you reduce your carbon footprint, you reduce your contribution to the damage caused by resource extraction.
- **The need for new power plants.** It takes a lot of energy to build a power plant, and each new one is likely to generate a lot of $CO_2$ and other pollutants during its lifetime. (Forty years is a typical estimate for energy infrastructure.) Reducing your carbon footprint reduces your contribution to the demand for new power plants.
- **The energy intensity of the economy.** One of the features of advanced economies is that they're able to wring more and more productivity (measured, in the end, in company revenues and profits) from less and less energy. For instance, through clever regulation, California has managed to maintain flat electricity usage for decades while growing strongly in population and economic output. Your efforts to reduce your carbon footprint increase your efficiency and decrease the energy intensity of your operations.

## 8.5 Improving Your Reputation and Brand

The fourth reason for energy-saving efforts is the hardest to measure objectively and, perhaps, the most important: the opportunity to improve your reputation and brand.

The US Small Business Administration has a Green Guide for New Businesses, shown in Figure 8.2, which directly addresses the positive branding impact of green efforts, including green computing.

Although reputations belong to individuals as well as organizations, "brand" is usually used to refer to the name and the visible symbols of an organization. Reputation is part of brand, but there's also an almost mystical quality to how people see brands. Reputation is more prosaic and easier to talk about. (Some people talk about a "personal brand" and so on, but the mainstream uses the term at the organizational level.)

Your energy-saving efforts will only have a strong, direct impact on your organization's brand if one of two things is true:

**Figure 8.2**   The SBA's Green Guide for New Businesses. (*Source*: http://www.sba.gov/content/green-guide-new-businesses)

- Your energy-saving efforts are part of an organization-wide energy-saving or green effort.
- The organization is highlighting your energy-saving successes—most likely, as a precursor to an organization-wide greening effort.

In this section, and this book, we'll mostly, therefore, talk about reputation. The impact of your efforts on your organization's brand depends on how the organization uses, or doesn't use, your efforts in its communications, hiring, partnering, and so forth.

Even at the level of IT, though, energy-saving efforts have a powerful effect on reputation, which the organization can roll up to the branding level whenever desired. There are certain core attributes that green computing efforts speak to:

- **Trust.** People want to trust organizations to operate responsibly. An energy-saving effort in IT says, "Not only does our organization run its operations effectively, we look at the bigger picture and work to improve at that level as well." An efficiency effort that's perceived as successful builds trust.
- **Safety.** People worry about the impacts of pollution, the future of a warming planet, and how workers in global supply chains are treated. An energy-saving effort helps people feel safer. Although you may not address every possible issue at any given point in your efforts, people generally feel that your organization is looking out for them if it can mount a successful green computing effort.
- **Forward-thinking.** People want organizations to take a long view—this is part of trust and feeling safe. There's huge criticism of the quarterly profits focus shown by so many organizations. An energy conservation effort demonstrates a lively concern for the future.
- **Efficiency.** Customers like to think an organization handles money effectively; stockholders may be even more impressed than customers are by a healthy concern for efficiency. Your energy-saving effort shows that your organization as a whole is savvy in its use of resources.
- **Green.** Being green, in and of itself, is valued much more by some audiences than others. If you emphasize cost savings, you'll get a little credit from green-oriented stakeholders; if you prominently include carbon footprint calculations in your communications, the green quotient of your efforts increases.

One potential immediate impact of an energy-saving effort, especially if you emphasize its green aspects, is on hiring and retention. People want to work for smart, savvy organizations; among young people, in particular, "green" is considered a key value. Many young people don't want to work for an organization that isn't green.

## 8.6 Why Energy Prices Will Stay High

The variability of energy prices might seem as much a hopeful sign as an ominous one. What goes up must come down, right? There might seem to be just as much of a chance of energy prices dropping as of rising.

First, consider that oscillating energy prices are not nearly as business friendly as stable prices. Shareholders and other financial stakeholders value steadily increasing profits more than just about anything. It's very, very difficult to keep profits on a steady, stable growth path if large costs such as energy prices are rocketing upward and downward—especially if the underlying trend is toward higher prices, so the lows never quite compensate for the highs.

Cash flow is also a big concern for many businesses. Businesses like to invest cash, rather than hoard it, but oscillating energy prices push businesses to keep big cash cushions. So variable energy prices are a bad thing in and of themselves; minimizing your exposure to them, by cutting energy usage, helps your organization even if prices don't move upward.

But move upward is what they are likely to do. There are separate reasons why each kind of energy is likely to stay expensive. The riskiest energy play is oil. Oil production is, at best, stable, whereas global demand is skyrocketing. The inrush to world energy markets of hundreds of millions of people in steadily improving economies is causing rising demand for gasoline and other oil products, even as supplies remain the same. Oil prices are likely to go nowhere but up.

New reserves, such as the Alberta tar sands or the Bakken shale in North Dakota, are often cited as evidence that more reserves can come online. However, these "reserves" are very expensive to develop and are subject to legal challenges and political pressure, as demonstrated by President Obama's decision to delay the Keystone XL pipeline in November 2011.

The reason for the delay is that these new reserves are very damaging environmentally. Climate change campaigner Bill McKibben has stated that developing the Alberta tar sands means "game over" for climate change. So, resistance to tapping them is understandably intense.

Equally important is that these reserves are very expensive to develop, even if allowed. They only make economic sense if oil prices are around $100 a barrel or higher. If the price starts to fall below that level, production in these expensive regions slows, and then stops. That creates a shortage that tends to push prices back toward the level needed for more development and delivery—and that's only if environmentalists like myself (and perhaps you), who protest and vote against such development, can't stop it from happening.

So the development of expensive reserves tends to put a floor under oil prices, while ever-increasing demand means that there's not really a ceiling on them. The price that the market will bear seems to be gradually going up, with $4 a gallon gasoline in the United States—once seen as disastrous, now seen as merely distasteful.

Coal is also likely to increase in price. Coal companies are using a despicable technique called mountaintop removal to get at coal seams, literally blowing the tops off more than 500 mountains in the United States alone; many other countries would never allow such a practice. Entire regions in the backcountry of various American states are devastated, and streams stopped or loaded with poisonous runoff (http://wvgazette.com/News/201112120118).

Activists are scoring more and more victories against coal mining and against the construction of new coal-fired power plants in the United States. The price of coal is likely to increase, and the availability of coal-fired power to decrease.

The only energy source that is more likely to stay low in price, in countries that have shale deposits of the stuff, is natural gas. Hydraulic fracturing of underground deposits of oil and gas, or "fracking," is a harsh process that risks chemical contamination of groundwater and causes earthquakes, albeit small ones so far. The United States is the "leader," if that's the right term, in the use of fracking, and it's seeing a big increase in natural gas reserves and a decrease in natural gas prices.

Fracking is uneconomical below a certain price for gas, and export facilities are being built for liquefied natural gas (LNG). Both developments tend to put a floor under natural gas prices, so they are unlikely to drop much from today's low levels, and may gradually rise.

Coal, oil, and gas are also all fossil fuels, and all therefore contribute to climate change. Coal is the "dirtiest" fuel, about three times as polluting as traditional natural gas, whereas oil is twice as polluting as natural gas. However, tar sands oil is roughly as polluting as coal, and fracking for natural gas and oil causes methane emissions that put both fuels into coal-type categories as well.

Even minimal regulation of $CO_2$ emissions—a process which the EPA is introducing in the United States as I write this book—will cause prices for all fossil fuels to rise. International agreements, regional agreements, and national, state, and local laws are all potential sources of regulation. As fossil fuels get dirtier, and climate change grows worse, pressure to "do something" continues—and it takes very little "doing something" to make fossil fuel prices rise steadily.

The prospect of regulation is not only a negative when it actually happens. The risk of stronger regulations is another source of risk to your organization— one that can most easily be mitigated by reducing your use of energy. (This includes your organization's supply and distribution networks' use of energy, as price increases there will hurt you as well.)

With all of this going on, it's very unlikely that energy prices will drop, and, conversely, it is probable that they will rise steadily, if not sharply. The only serious potentially mitigating circumstance is the arrival of another big recession, similar to the 2008 credit crunch, and there is a good case to be made that very high oil prices at the time were a major contributor. You don't want to be the one to tell the rest of your organization that your IT department can keep using lots of energy because more credit crunch–type recessions are likely to come along and impose a cap on the price.

## 8.7 Embodied Energy

One important area to pay attention to in your energy-saving efforts is "embodied energy." You may not want or need to track it carefully, especially when you're just getting going; however, you need to at least be aware of it, and be ready to track it if you escalate to a fully holistic view of your energy usage.

Embodied energy is the energy needed to create a device or an infrastructure before you ever start using it. For a device, the embodied energy is the energy (and accompanying carbon footprint) needed to mine the raw materials, transport them to the manufacturing plant, make the device, and ship it to your facility.

Embodied energy calculations are subject to lots of variation. A spate of newspaper stories in 2012 described the embodied energy of a car as greater than the energy the car would use in its lifetime; later analysis indicated that embodied energy was more like one-fourth the lifetime operational energy usage of the car.

Embodied energy has little to do with the direct cost of a device to you, nor does it affect your energy-cost-related risk. The costs and risk are all incurred before you buy the device.

Where embodied energy affects you is in the carbon footprint of a device, and in the reputational impact of your energy-saving efforts, when you consider these aspects broadly. If part of the advantage of a green computing strategy is to assure your stakeholders that you're forward-looking and green, knowing about the embodied energy of the devices you select is a wise move.

Smaller, lighter devices that use less energy to operate tend to have proportionally lower embodied energy than larger, heavier devices that use more energy to operate. However, you may want to research embodied energy specifically when making recommendations for your energy-saving efforts. It may be enough simply to note cases where the embodied energy for a device is unusually high (bad) or low (good) compared to the lifetime energy expenditure of operating the device.

Computer services also have embodied energy. A service delivered via the cloud, for instance, requires that a lot of infrastructure be "lit up" as you use the service. The direct energy usage by you is only whatever's required to run the device while it's connected to the service, plus what's needed to keep the user comfortable. But a lot happens before the service can show up on the user's screen, even though the energy costs and risks of the energy use are buried in the price you pay for the service.

The great thing about cloud computing is that you can shop for these aspects of a purchase just as you can shop for other desired or undesired aspects. A well-run cloud computing vendor is going to be carefully managing their energy costs anyway, just so they can have a healthy bottom line. The smart ones will take these efforts further in a green direction, and then publicize them. This not only makes that provider a more desirable choice, but users of their services can use the information to show that they have a green supply chain.

Rackspace is one of the major providers of server space to cloud computing companies. They have a fairly strong green effort, operating under the name Greenspace, as described in Chapter 6. Rackspace customers—and their customers' customers—can include Rackspace's efforts as part of their own green initiatives.

## 8.8  Analyzing Your Energy Usage

The old saying says, "That which gets measured gets done." You can only get the full benefits of pursuing energy savings by having a baseline of usage before your conservation efforts begin.

Here's an outline for analyzing your energy usage:

- **Overview or detailed audit?** Decide whether you're going to do an overview or a detailed audit. In most cases, you'll want to start with an overview. Then "drill down," as needed, to help make specific energy-saving decisions.
- **Site-based, service-based, or organizationally based?** You will want to decide whether you want figures that total up by site; by the type of service provided (heating, cooling, lighting, etc.); or by which organizational customers you're serving. You may have other ways of slicing the pie in mind. I recommend that you consider choosing a site-based approach, plus one other approach. Site-based energy information makes inherent sense to decision makers and aligns well with solutions, such as adding renewable energy capability.
- **Look at your bills.** Your organization's finance people are going to be very aware of your energy spending in the form of various bills that you

receive and pay for. Be sure to align your energy audit with your firm's bills, so each helps to explain the other.

- **Get information from manufacturers.** Manufacturers of devices that use lots of energy—either per device, or in aggregate—provide energy information. If you have a facility full of servers, and you have your energy bills in hand, you can compare your bills to the manufacturer's information about power usage and understand a great deal about how that facility uses energy.
- **Get energy cost information.** Find out how much energy you're using—in dollars per kilowatt hour ($/kWh) for electricity and cost per gigajoule, cubic meter, or liter for natural gas. Take peak usage rates into account. Consider converting your natural gas figures into equivalent kWh for easy comparison.
- **Get historical trends.** Find a way to compare to historical trends and account for obvious changes, such as a merger or acquisition or a major new facility opening. Figure out how much comparative history you're going to research, then present the results briefly and at a high level.
- **Get comparative information.** Nothing gets a senior manager's attention like hearing how far ahead or behind your organization is with competitors and comparable organizations. Look hard for such information, including industry averages and initiatives by competitors.
- **Find three key drivers.** Find three areas for effective medium-term or long-term savings. Relate the best opportunities you find to the organization's key initiatives. For instance, if increasing revenues is a key organizational driver, software development efforts that move salespeople to iPads and save them time might be a win-win.
- **Find three quick fixes.** This should not be your main focus, but you shouldn't ignore it, either. Look to save enough money in one-year fixes to at least pay for the analysis effort, if not much more. Switching to energy-efficient light bulbs, adding insulation to cut heating and cooling costs, moving some operations to non-peak hours, and outsourcing a major software package or service are some potential wins.
- **Risk management.** Include risk management as you share your results. For instance, take current costs and show how much they would increase or decrease with reasonably possible or historical changes in energy costs. Participants will automatically "get" the need to reduce your exposure by reducing usage.

## 8.9  A Recipe for Energy Savings

There are lots of quick fixes for energy savings, and these can produce short-term improvements. They can also be a trap.

Let's say you buy software that helps your current servers run more efficiently. Such software might produce savings of, say, 20% in your direct energy costs for the servers, and a similar decrease in your air conditioning costs. (The air conditioning savings might even be larger, since these costs tend to be disproportionately affected by peak needs. Cutting peaks, even by a moderate amount, can save a lot of money.)

But the software you buy to save money does so *on your current servers*. If you would have been better off replacing your servers with inherently more energy-efficient models, your software investment might have actually cost you money. The good, in this case, would be the enemy of the best.

That's why I recommend that you take a holistic look at your energy costs; figure out where you're going, and what's a realistic mix of devices, software, and services over a three- to five-year period. Then figure out a plan to get there.

Once your plan is in place, you can be as opportunistic as all get-out. You will probably find, once you begin, that one improvement leads to another, in a virtuous circle.

But you'll only get the best results if this takes place in the context of an overall plan. So let's look at the elements of serious medium- and long-term energy savings. Then, in the rest of this chapter, we'll look at energy itself. In later chapters, we'll look at devices, software, and support.

Here are the interacting elements to look at for serious energy savings:

- **Letting someone else do it.** Look at outsourcing as an option for all your computing needs and services. This is a two-step process. First, consider the benefit of getting energy usage off your premises and onto someone else's. This tends to be inherently energy-efficient overall because suppliers will be able to centralize efficiencies, and because they're far more motivated than you are to save energy. (It's a much higher proportion of their costs.) Then, include reduced energy usage and "green" considerations in your buying decisions.
- **Energy itself.** Look hard at your sources of energy. You may have the ability to enter into long-term contracts, for instance, for solar power for a data center. (The source could be your own solar panels, a contract for solar power from a utility, or a combination of the two.) This may only provide, say, 20% of the total power for the data center, at current usage. But once you have, in effect, prepaid for 20% of your power—and made it green—you'll be surprised at how motivated you'll be to cut the rest of your energy usage. These cuts will make the green component a much bigger share of your power usage.
- **Servers.** In this day and age, you should be reducing your ownership of servers. Computing is becoming more like electricity, with the heavy

lifting done offsite. Where you do need to keep using (and owning) servers, buy the most energy-efficient models you can. This saves money immediately and opens up greater opportunities for supplying all of the energy for a data center, for instance, through green power.

- **End-user devices.** Rethink your use of devices; think tablets. Then, think smartphones. Don't forget to consider having people call a help desk for answers instead of undertaking complex computer tasks themselves.

    How many people can you liberate from the drudgery of interacting with a personal computer? Many organizations are moving their entire sales forces, for instance, onto tablets and smartphones. This requires new software development to provide all the needed functionality on smaller devices. But the result should be not only energy savings, but savings of thousands of hours of end-user time, of support hassles, and of customer hassles as well.

- **Software.** Yes, software is a good "fix" for saving energy. Much of this, though, is really a hardware decision—doing more of the processing centrally and doing more of the processing offsite. Some software "quick fixes" are worthwhile, including utilities that idle unused computers and dim unused monitors. But using software to reduce energy usage for an inherently inefficient data processing architecture is, to quote an old saying, "like putting lipstick on a pig."

- **End-user habits.** Users are a big part of the picture, but you'll get further by making the right thing easier than by gathering pledges to stop doing the wrong thing. Users who check their email on the go on a smartphone are saving energy already; they're also less likely to print, or to forget to turn off their monitor. If you standardize on an energy-efficient laptop model, you no longer have to go through complex decision making between desktops and laptops. Still, end-user habits can make a difference. Consider getting ideas from users themselves, then getting users' help in implementing the best ideas.

- **Get buy-in.** Start early on getting support for changes from the people who are going to be affected. There's nothing to engender resistance like making people feel something is being forced on them—and like you're getting all of the credit for a change they have to implement and live with.

- **Keep a narrow focus.** At least in your initial efforts, consider focusing only on your organization's direct, paid-for energy usage. Use additional considerations, such as embodied energy, commuting, and travel-energy usage, and so on, for efforts that directly affect these supporting areas. (These additional areas are valuable but risk distracting from your main focus and things you control more directly.)

## 8.10 Understanding the Unique Energy Needs of IT

Using renewable energy for IT is different than for just about any other major organizational activity. That's because IT is so much about heat.

All the devices that are part of IT generate heat. End-user devices—smartphones, tablets, laptops, desktops, and monitors—all generate heat. So do the transformers that help power them.

This heat adds to heat from lighting and body heat, as well as heat trapped in a building's materials and air spaces, to significantly increase the cooling needs of a typical office. So end-user devices contribute a great deal to air conditioning costs in typical offices.

The real villain, though, from an energy-use perspective, is the racks of servers, routers, and other internetworking equipment that today's IT departments major in. In smaller companies—or larger companies that get much of their work done via cloud-based, offsite services—this equipment fits in a large closet or a small room. Often, for security reasons, this closet is right in the middle of an office, far from access to outside air that could otherwise be used to cool it.

An IT closet or room generates a great deal of heat, yet operates best when kept cool. This means big air conditioning costs, even on cold days. In fact, it's very hard to balance the A/C blasting in the data area with the heating or cooling needs of the people in the office, which vary throughout the day—and to which people, cooped up as they are, can be exquisitely sensitive. A couple of degrees too cool, and people grumble and put on sweaters; a couple degrees too warm, and people start falling asleep at their desks!

This whole setup—an office full of people, end-user devices, servers, and routers, all generating heat at different levels of intensity—is extremely expensive to try to keep at a moderate temperature, whether the outside temperature is warm or cool.

The big, expensive expenditures, though, come in two areas:

- **Air conditioning for offices when it's hot.** In a poorly insulated building, it can be almost impossible for the A/C to keep up with the combined effect of high temperatures outside, body heat, and IT devices of all sorts. Add peak pricing for energy, and costs can be exorbitant. You're a lucky IT manager indeed if your bosses haven't yet figured out to assign a lot of your organization's energy costs to the IT budget.
- **Air conditioning for data centers, especially when it's hot.** Data centers are likely to need air conditioning most or all of the time, but—as with offices—this gets worse the hotter it gets. If you run data centers, the energy costs to keep them heated (a little bit) and cooled (a lot) are almost certainly part of your budget.

Luckily for all concerned, there's a very green solution to the high energy costs of IT devices and data centers.

## 8.11 Focusing on Solar Power

Using renewable energy is a huge step in green computing. It's generally not easy, but it really is the mark of a fully serious green computing effort.

Even if your green computing effort is just beginning, incorporating renewable energy is a great idea. The benefits that you gain, and the lessons you learn, will serve as models for your green computing effort and your "green" efforts in the organization as a whole.

It's hard to give useful, global advice about using renewable energy, though, because the availability and usefulness of different types of green energy are very much site specific. You can solve the whole problem by locating any and all data centers in an area served by hydro-electric power, or you can innovate by being among the first to use solar energy in Canada.

So as an example, I'm going to focus on one of the best "hand in glove" fits between renewable energy and business energy needs around: the fit between solar energy and air conditioning for data centers and offices.

A quick caveat: Always, before buying in energy, do at least an overview assessment of your current energy costs, and gain at least an initial understanding of where you may be able to save energy. Your request to spend money is unlikely to be positively received if you aren't already working on saving money as well. This is especially true with solar power because it works so well with energy-saving opportunities. Insulation, turning off unused and excess equipment, and other straightforward steps can greatly reduce your energy needs, especially at peak usage times, so that even a small solar installation can meet a very high percentage of your remaining requirements.

Why is solar energy perfect for meeting the air conditioning needs of offices and (especially) data centers? Here are several key reasons:

- **Solar energy peaks when cooling needs are highest.** A major problem with solar power, wind power, and some other renewables is intermittency; renewable sources have peaks and valleys, whereas utilities want power generation they can switch on and off as needed. However, solar energy's peaks occur, almost by definition, exactly when the need for cooling—provided by air conditioning—is greatest. Intermittency works for you, instead of against you.
- **Solar energy peaks when energy prices are highest.** More and more utilities are instituting peak-time pricing. The biggest price peaks tend to be when it's hottest, and again, this is when solar energy is at its best.

- **Solar energy for A/C is excellent risk management.** A hot year and lots or peak-time pricing is a big risk exposure—and ever more likely to pinch as climate change kicks in. "Smart solar"—solar sited and sized to take the top off of peak usage periods—is brilliant risk management.
- **Small amounts of solar are cheap or free.** Solar installations that only seek to round off peaks are cheap. You can use your very best solar site and not pay for too many panels while getting the most bang for your buck. In many cases, solar installation companies will put up the panels, contract with you for their output at a reasonable price, and save you money year over year—with no cost to you, ever.
- **Smart solar is a great way to start.** You and your organization may have great potential for solar—or, you may be in a site or sites where it's truly borderline. This kind of high-payoff installation is just the opportunity you need to get on the learning curve for discovering how best to use solar, then apply the lessons learned to other renewables.
- **Solar panels speak for themselves.** "Half of life is showing up," the saying goes. When people see solar panels on your facilities, you are definitely "showing up" in the move to green computing. The fact that you're starting out in a focused manner just makes the story better for investors and other stakeholders.
- **A little storage goes a long way.** One solution to solar energy's intermittency is battery storage. This is perfect for offices and data centers, where heat can build up, then persist for a few hours after the sun starts to slide down in the sky. You can use a reasonably sized bank of low-persistence batteries—the cheapest kind—to give you the extra few hours of energy storage that you need.
- **Solar is scalable.** There's no real barrier to doing a small solar installation first, then expanding it if it's successful. Just add panels . . . and steadily develop skills in site selection, forecasting costs and savings, and other areas of expertise for using solar effectively.
- **No solar = no job?** When the right thing to do is painfully obvious, not doing it has downsides. If you don't jump on the renewable energy bandwagon, your management might hire someone who has experience doing this at another organization, while you were leaving money on the table. If you're seeing solar installations sprouting up around your facility, it may be time to, in the harsh Silicon Valley saying, "get on the train or die."

Solar energy is not only good for you and your company. Believe it or not, your local utility is not really enjoying charging you top dollar for energy on the hottest day of the year. For political and fairness reasons, they can't really charge as much as they sensibly should. That's because many utilities have entire power-generation facilities—a mix of coal, oil, and natural gas units—that are only used a few days a year, when it gets hot and air conditioning needs go off the charts. On the hottest days, especially hot weekdays, utilities are frantically cranking up little-used generating facilities, buying and selling energy among themselves, calling industrial customers to ask them to stand down for a few hours, staving off brownouts, fixing things that break when they overheat, and generally tearing out their hair.

If your organization and others can meet some of your own peak energy needs with on-site solar power, this takes a tremendous burden off the local utility. It also reduces the need for new power plants and is quite likely to keep old, dirty coal-fired power plants, in many locations, from having to be fired up as peak times approach.

It might occur to you that utilities could make your life much easier by doing all this for you, then offering clean and green power at a small premium. They could even partner with organizations like yours to site, develop, and pre-sell power from renewable sources. Unfortunately, utilities are usually paid for the amount of energy they sell, not for being efficient. So they're not really motivated to take these forward-looking steps.

You can also look into other types of renewable energy. Solar thermal is an overlooked champion in terms of "bang for the buck" for many needs, but it doesn't do much for the key green computing need of cooling data centers and office buildings. (Yes, some clever people manage to get cooling out of solar thermal, but that's not as straightforward as solar panels.) Wind power's intermittency probably works against the needs of green computing—the hottest days tend to be still, so wind is least available when you need it most.

## 8.12  Saving Energy and the Supply Chain

You may be meeting a growing part of your computing needs through cloud computing, also known as Software as a Service (SaaS). Often, these decisions are made without a detailed analysis of the energy costs involved. The analysis would be likely to end up in favor of cloud computing, though: You're taking energy usage off your premises and onto someone else's.

This isn't just a cheap and easy shifting of energy use off your books and onto someone else's, either. You would probably use one or more servers for each separate service you provide internally. Even if you mix services on a single server, you're not going to do it as efficiently as a cloud computing provider, for whom this is their only business. Cloud computing providers are far more efficient than internally provided IT services. So using cloud computing reduces energy usage *and* shifts it off your books. That's a true win-win.

You can also use green criteria in choosing providers. Several SaaS companies use hosting providers that are committed to green initiatives of varying extent

**Figure 8.3**   Apple is "going green" at its main data center. (*Source*: http://www.
reuters.com/article/2012/05/18/us-apple-idUSBRE84G0YW20120518)

and depth. Expect these to continue, and for SaaS companies to compete on just
how green they are (and, by extension, how green you become as their customer).

Apple plans to power its main United States data center entirely from renewable energy, as shown in Figure 8.3, and is building the solar arrays that will
provide most of the power needed. You can use the good efforts of your suppliers as part of your own green computing effort. You can do this in a general
way, simply by highlighting them, or in detail, by giving kilowatt-by-kilowatt
comparisons of internally hosted services to cloud computing services.

## 8.13  Energy-Saving Pilot Projects

It's easy to find lots of good ideas for green computing, in general, and savings
on energy costs, in particular, at conferences, in articles, and in books—not
excluding this one. But how best to get started with renewable energy and saving energy?

A pilot project is a really good approach—especially in a low-commitment
environment (by which I mean an organization where you're not finding a lot

of support for investments in green computing). You're going to need to prove the benefits to get the support you need for a wider effort, and a pilot project is a great way to do it.

For a pilot project, you can do everything right: First, do a detailed analysis, not just an overview, of the "before" situation. Evangelize the people involved about what you're trying to do. Show them how they can help, and keep checking back with them during the project.

If you have two or more data centers, there's an obvious target for a pilot project: one data center. Find your worse energy hog and fix it. Get greener servers, add software to better balance loads and save energy, arrange them better, and put in small amounts of solar power to reduce the intensity of peak energy demand periods. (The ROI on this should be off the charts.)

Even if you have just one data center, use it for a pilot effort that you can then apply to the rest of your organization. It's easier to measure the before, after, and improvement in a standalone, all-IT facility like a data center than anywhere else.

Greg Schulz's book, *The Green and Virtual Data Center*,[1] is a great resource for this kind of work.

If you lack data centers, or if they aren't good candidates for a pilot project, use of energy in the office is the next logical option. If your offices are on multiple floors, pick one. If you have several departments with lots of users, pick one of those. (Often, you can find a single floor where all the employees are, say, engineers, combining your areas of focus.) Being part of a pilot project can make people feel special, eliciting more effort and more ideas to help save even more energy.

Try to do your pilot project quickly and inexpensively. What you're going for is not so much total savings as high return on investment and a fast time to savings. Return on investment is measured by dividing savings by cost; the smaller the cost number, the larger the ROI.

Keep it simple in other ways, too. Reducing commuting, for instance, is a good way to save energy, but it doesn't show up immediately on your company's income statement. Use your pilot project to generate hard numbers that help you increase your credibility around green computing efforts; you'll be able to do more with "soft" factors over time if you build up your credibility using "hard" results first.

## 8.14 Selling Energy Savings

IT professionals are often not comfortable with selling their efforts—internally or externally. Green computing can be particularly challenging to IT pros, because it touches on social and political issues that IT traditionally stays away from.

Energy savings, however, are first and foremost about a language every businessperson understands: money. So it's important to learn to position and promote your energy-saving efforts. In doing so, you'll not only learn to "speak green," you'll learn to speak dollars and cents, which is the language of love in business.

I suggest the following seven-point plan for selling your energy-saving efforts. You may not use all of the steps for every green computing effort you make, but you should use all of them over time.

1. **Measure twice, cut once.** You can't solve a problem until you define it, to everyone's satisfaction. When it comes to energy savings, the problem is the higher-than-needed energy usage, carbon footprint, and spending of your current approach. So I recommend an overview-type assessment of your overall energy usage, but a detailed assessment of each specific area that you want to change. You need to be able to show a convincing before and after picture for your efforts.

2. **Think ROI.** Return on investment is the measuring stick of a great many efforts in business. You may already routinely use ROI in your project selection, but if not, your green computing efforts are a great place to start. Don't be afraid to cherry-pick and execute the highest-ROI projects first, even if they aren't particularly glamorous; if you execute these successfully, you'll establish a track record that will make it easier to keep winning.

3. **Get backing from your boss(es).** Your immediate boss needs to be a firm supporter of your efforts—ready not only to defend them, but to promote them. Also get support from your key peers, and consider getting a mentor high up on the org chart. All of this ensures visibility for your efforts and support for bigger initiatives down the road. Just be sure your boss mentions your name occasionally in what will otherwise be understood as his or her own accomplishments.

4. **Tie your efforts to your organization's priorities.** Find out the top three priorities of your organization and tie your green computing efforts to them. Making employees happier? Green computing does that. So gather anecdotal or detailed, survey-based evidence to support it. Cutting costs? That's an easy one for energy-saving efforts.

5. **Keep the bigger green picture in mind.** Don't just talk money when you describe energy-saving efforts. Fully justify them in financial terms, but also work on broader issues about risk management, employee satisfaction, sustainability, and "future-proofing" your company. This helps your financial success extend to support for other efforts with softer payoffs.

6. **Publicize your efforts internally.** Let people know what you're going to do, what you're doing, and what you've done. Set goals for who should

know about your efforts and figure out ways to reach them. Give a lunchtime talk for anyone interested; do a presentation at your team or company meeting. Don't be afraid to promote yourself a bit in the bargain;
there are worse things to be in an organization today, or in the job market, than an authority on green computing.

7. **Publicize your efforts externally.** With your boss's support, look for
opportunities to give talks, speak at conferences; write articles; speak to
college classes; and make other, similar efforts. You're not trying to get on
Oprah (which is good, because she stopped doing her show), just to build
skills and expertise and make connections. At the same time, you'll be
creating great PR for your organization, which should help in areas such
as hiring and marketing.

## 8.15 Summary

This chapter described how to save energy through green computing—reducing
costs, risks, and your carbon footprint; improving your reputation and building
your brand; analyzing energy usage; and using solar power as part of the solution.
The next chapter discusses reducing greenhouse gas emissions in depth.

# Chapter 9

# Reducing Greenhouse Gas Emissions

## Key Concepts

This chapter describes the importance of greenhouse gas emissions in green computing:

- The role of greenhouse gas emissions in global warming
- Cutting embodied energy
- Changing energy sources
- Sweating your supply chain

## 9.1 Why Greenhouse Gas Emissions Are Important

We discussed energy use in Chapter 8, as well as elsewhere in this book.

Resource use, discussed in the next chapter, may be the most visible issue in green computing; wasted "stuff" is very visible. Greenhouse gas emissions, by contrast, are the least visible.

Electricity, while literally invisible (unless it starts a fire or explosion), costs money, and that has its own kind of visibility. Greenhouse gas emissions are invisible in the literal sense, and also free, in most of the world. (Many European countries and the state of California are among the places with functioning carbon markets that charge for some greenhouse gas emissions.) Emissions are not very expensive, to the emitter, even where they do cost money.

So why are greenhouse gas emissions important? Because they're the leading cause of global warming.

In this chapter, I'll discuss greenhouse gases separately from energy use, and then discuss how they do—and don't—correspond with each other.

Greenhouse gas emissions are actually just a shorthand for a much more complex process. The Earth is kept warm by a small amount of greenhouse gases; the two leading greenhouse gases, by far, are carbon dioxide ($CO_2$) and methane ($CH_4$). Somewhat ironically, carbon dioxide is a byproduct of burning fossil fuels; methane *is* a fossil fuel, which we call natural gas. Natural gas is very often found in conjunction with oil.

The greenhouse gases in the air "thicken" it, in a sense, with relation to ultraviolet rays. Sunlight—visible light, carried by photons—comes from the Sun to the Earth's surface with little absorption by the atmosphere. Ice, ground, foliage, and ocean water are among the major surfaces light hits. Some of these surfaces, such as ice, reflect a lot of light; others absorb most of the light, generating heat. And here's where greenhouse gases kick in.

Light that's reflected back from the Earth's surface as light mostly passes straight through the atmosphere, back out into space. But light that generates heat is another story. If there were no greenhouse gases in the atmosphere, the heat would also mostly pass back out through the atmosphere—more slowly than light, but quickly enough.

However, greenhouse gases—which are transparent to light—trap heat. This heat-trapping effect, called the "greenhouse effect" and discovered in the late 1800s, keeps the Earth about 30°C warmer than it would otherwise be. (If the whole world were 30°C colder, it would almost certainly be mostly or completely covered by ice—as it has been at least once in the planet's history. Look up "snowball Earth" online, if you're curious.)

One of the discoverers of the greenhouse effect, Svante Arrhenius, understood (even in the late 1800s) that industry was adding greenhouse gases to the atmosphere. He was the first one to calculate that a doubling of greenhouse gases in the atmosphere would lead to a global average temperature rise of about 3°C.

Figure 9.1 shows an explanation of climate change from the US National Park Service. It illustrates the difference between the natural greenhouse effect and the human-enhanced greenhouse effect.

The most easy-to-understand resource for understanding climate change remains Al Gore's *An Inconvenient Truth*—released as a book and a movie in 2006.[1,2] Either, or especially both combined, lays out the basic global warming argument in an accessible form that no one smart enough to work with

**Figure 9.1**   The US National Park Service explains how greenhouse gas emissions trap heat in the atmosphere. (*Source*: http://www.nps.gov/goga/naturescience/climate-change-causes.htm)

computers for a living, like yourself, will have any trouble understanding. Events since the book was released have shown that his assessment and prognostications of the problem were actually quite conservative. Gore also reached such a wide audience that understanding the case he makes will make it much easier for you to talk about climate change with a wide range of people.

There are, of course, thousands of articles, books, movies, podcasts, and much more about climate change. Some of them disagree with parts of the case Gore laid out, but that case has only gotten stronger with time, overall. Please refer to the existing body of work for details and arguments on all sides. I will only give brief descriptions in this chapter of my own "take" on it and how it relates to green computing. There's a world of fascinating and contradictory information out there for you to sink your teeth into, if you wish.

So why does all this matter to you? Simple: Making and using electronic devices is a very energy-intensive process, and nearly all of our means of generating energy generate greenhouse gases. These greenhouse gases are what cause global warming.

## 9.2  Sources and Sinks of Greenhouse Gases and Warming

In nature, the major sources of greenhouse gas emissions include:

- **Volcanic eruptions.** Volcanoes emit greenhouse gases that last for decades; they also throw up dust that can block sunlight, causing months or even years of cooling effects.
- **Fires.** Any burning of vegetation or wood releases trapped carbon into the atmosphere. Most of this is $CO_2$.

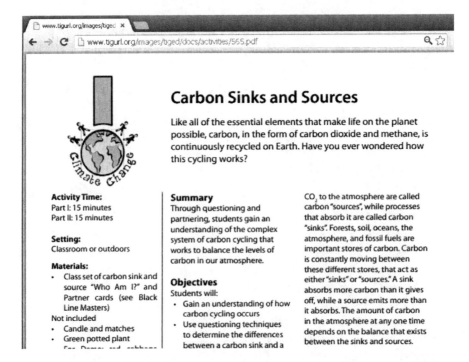

Figure 9.2   The natural carbon cycle is balanced between sources of carbon and sinks that absorb it. (*Source:* http://www.tigurl.org/images/tiged/docs/activities/565.pdf)

- **Decomposition.** Rotting releases greenhouse gases. If it occurs in the open air, most of it is $CO_2$, but if it's within, say, a log, or underwater, it's likely to be mostly methane. Rotting is perhaps the biggest single source of methane.
- **Respiration and digestion.** All animals take in oxygen and emit $CO_2$ through breathing (respiration). Animals also emit a fair amount of methane through the expelling of digestive gases. Ruminants such as cattle, which have complicated internal "distillers" for digesting grasses, emit significant amounts of greenhouse gases as part of their digestive processes.

Figure 9.2 (from a website for students) shows the natural part of the carbon cycle. Humans contribute to all of these processes except volcanoes. We burn firewood and burn down forests (emitting $CO_2$ through burning), or clear them (which emits methane from rotting), dry out wetlands and peat bogs (more rotting), and host huge herds of cattle and other ruminants that we keep penned up, which emit plumes of ruminant digestive gases. We pave over land, so vegetation can't grow and reabsorb some of the greenhouse gases from the atmosphere.

In addition to accelerating and augmenting natural processes that emit greenhouse gases, humans generate lots of greenhouse gas emissions directly:

- **Burning coal.** Coal is the source for a huge proportion of power plants all over the world. Coal is the "dirtiest" fuel, at about four times the greenhouse gas emissions of natural gas, the cleanest fossil fuel.
- **Burning oil, including diesel and gasoline.** Oil is burned in power plants and in engines, from jet planes to ship engines to car engines. Being a liquid, it's the most convenient fossil fuel by far. It's the next dirtiest fossil fuel after coal, ranging from twice the emissions of natural gas (for lighter oil made into gasoline) up to three times, nearly equivalent to coal (for heavier oils made into diesel and other heavy fuels). Oil from the Canadian tar sands, which is in thick, heavy deposits that have to be boiled out of the ground, may equal coal in the total emissions they generate.
- **Burning natural gas.** Natural gas is the cleanest fuel when burned, much less damaging than oil or, especially, coal. However, it's not clean enough; if we were somehow to stop burning coal and oil tomorrow, there's still enough natural gas to cause us to exceed planetary boundaries for "safe" total greenhouse gas emissions. Gas flaring by drillers, which are substantial, plus leaks—ditto—also send unburned methane directly into the atmosphere.
- **Fracking for gas.** Hydraulic fracturing of rock—fracking—is new as a major source of gas, but requires tons of chemicals and water to be

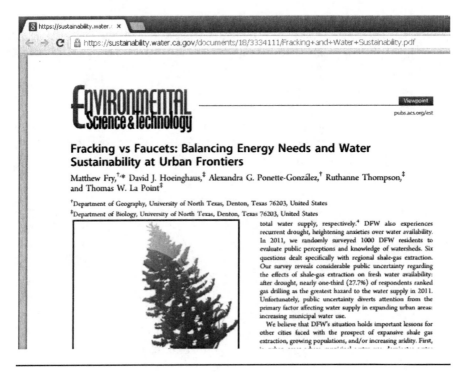

**Figure 9.3** Fracking requires that rock be "cracked" to free natural gas. (*Source*: https://sustainability.water.ca.gov/documents/18/3334111/Fracking+and+Water +Sustainability.pdf)

pumped into the ground, where groundwater can be contaminated. Leaks of natural gas (methane) directly into the atmosphere are common and offset much of the beneficial effect of burning natural gas instead of coal or oil.

Figure 9.3 shows a simplified diagram of how fracking works; it's worth studying, as both critics and supporters of fracking will cite diagrams like this one to support their arguments. Critics bemoan the injection of chemicals that could affect (and have affected) drinking water and cause earthquakes. Supporters point out that fracking takes place well below most aquifers and assert that it's quite safe, if done responsibly (which, as with the huge Gulf of Mexico oil spill of 2010, is always the issue, isn't it?).

## 9.3 Is There Still Doubt About Climate Change?

Yes and no. The mainstream of scientific study, and particularly of "hard" sciences, such as physics and chemistry, overwhelmingly supports that climate change is occurring, and that human greenhouse gas emissions are the leading cause. (Human-caused land use changes, such as clearing forests, are the next largest cause.)

Natural cycles, such as the Earth's distance from the Sun and the multiannual La Niña cycle, affect temperatures, but they seem to be causing the temperature to move up and down around a steadily rising central tendency. That steadily rising average temperature is the signal from global warming.

There are doubters, just as there are for cigarette smoking causing lung cancer, CFCs causing the ozone hole that peaked in the late 1980s, and evolution being responsible for biological diversity. However, in all of these cases, most of the doubters have strong economic or religious reasons driving their doubts. Neutral observers overwhelmingly side with the scientific mainstream in all of these cases.

I personally believe that those of us who work in areas made possible by scientific progress, such as computing, aeronautics, and medicine, have a particular duty to support and give credibility to the scientific process. We help put the results of this work into operation, hopefully to the benefit of humanity; using our (often-considerable) intellectual powers to generate weakly founded doubt and dissension seems disrespectful to the very process that allows us to make a living.

Recent extreme weather events have helped many who only believe what they see with their own eyes, so to speak, to give greater credibility to global warming. And skeptics are gradually crossing over to the mainstream view. In the most notable defection so far, Richard Muller, a University of California at Berkeley scientist, went from doubter to supporter of climate science almost overnight.

Muller had formerly made a sideline in denier-friendly quotes, some of which are hosted on the Skeptical Science site, shown in Figure 9.4. Here's a representative quote from Muller about Al Gore's book, *An Inconvenient Truth*: "80 percent or 90 percent of what's in Inconvenient Truth is wrong or exaggerated or cherry picked." Muller said this in March 2011 (http://www.skepticalscience.com/skeptic_Richard_Muller.htm).

But Muller and several colleagues were funded to revisit existing evidence on climate change, and he came away convinced. Muller was quoted later to state, "Humans are almost entirely the cause" of climate change (http://www.huffingtonpost.com/2012/07/29/richard-muller-climate-change-humans-koch_n_1715887.html). He rendered nearly all his previous criticisms inoperative. Muller's change of heart generated headlines worldwide.

Most doubters are not going to get funding to study climate science themselves, nor do they have the education and experience to fully weigh the available evidence. We choose to believe what the vast majority of experts do, or find reasons—in some cases, rationalizations—to go the other way.

**Figure 9.4**　Richard Muller once made many skeptical statements about climate change. (*Source*: http://www.skepticalscience.com/skeptic_Richard_Muller.htm)

There's room for reasonable people to disagree about what we should do about climate change. And you're entitled to doubts about climate change, but you'll find yourself in a steadily shrinking minority if you do. We can all hope you're right—but the damage you're part of, if people use doubts as a reason to slow action, is likely to be considerable.

## 9.4　Why Are There Still Doubters and Deniers?

There are a lot of climate change doubters and deniers. I believe that the basic reason is similar to the doubts that were so long expressed about cigarette smoking causing cancer: If climate change is really happening, it's likely to lead to uncomfortable consequences.

People do this kind of revisionist thinking all the time. If you tell them most Americans are overweight, they'll sneak a glance at their waistline, then start arguing with you. It's the same with exercise, financial planning, or talking on their cell phones while driving. People don't want to accept facts that reflect badly on their past choices and future freedoms.

In the United States, particularly, this well-known human tendency is aug-mented by a big disinformation campaign around climate change. Campaigns funded by big oil companies and others sow doubt and promote alternative explanations. There's a whole network of institutes and mutually promoting "experts" who serve an industry that manufactures doubt.

A survey has shown that Americans who watch Fox News are more likely to be factually wrong on climate change, and several other issues, than people who don't watch the news at all. This shows just how strong the echo chamber of doubters and deniers can be.

If you're a climate change doubter or denier yourself, I believe that you'll get on board with the reality of global warming at some point. If climate change is indeed real, it will cause ever-escalating problems in the years ahead. One by one, people who currently don't accept climate change will have to yield in the face of increasing evidence that the world is indeed changing.

Public opinion continues to support action on climate change. Figure 9.5 shows the results from a 2012 survey, with almost two-thirds of the US public supporting action on climate change, regardless of what other countries do.

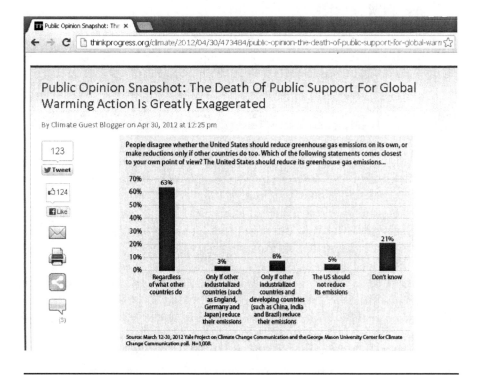

**Figure 9.5** A strong majority of Americans support action on climate change. (*Source*: http://thinkprogress.org/climate/2012/04/30/473484/public-opinion-the-death-of-public-support-for-global-warming-action-is-greatly-exaggerated/)

Only 5% thought the United States should not reduce its emissions, regardless—the "hard" doubter or denier position. Support for action is only likely to increase as the impacts of extreme weather and other climate-change related problems take hold.

I'm a kind of doubter myself—in the opposite direction from most. I notice that most predictions about climate change have been too "nice." Rising emissions, ice melting, and extreme weather are all happening faster and more intensely than mainstream scientists predicted just a few years ago, when Gore wrote *An Inconvenient Truth*.[1] I think we're in a lot more trouble than most nonscientists realize.

In the meantime, whatever your views, what to do? If you're a doubter, should you still pursue green computing initiatives? Should you object to and oppose them on principle?

Well, there are many reasons to "do" green computing, whether you believe in the science behind climate change or not, including these seven key reasons:

1. Saving money
2. Reducing business risk
3. Cutting pollution and waste
4. Treating people better
5. Attracting and retaining customers, employees, and supply chain partners for your company
6. Complying with, and getting in front of, current and likely future regulations
7. Positive publicity for your IT group and for your company as a whole

You don't have to believe anything specific about climate change to want these benefits—and you can sell your plans on these benefits without having to change anyone's mind about anything.

## 9.5 What If I Work for Doubters and Deniers?

In the short term, if you believe climate change is happening—especially if you're an über-believer, like me—working with and for people who doubt or deny climate change can be really uncomfortable. My advice is to just sell the benefits, as described in the previous section. And keep selling them.

In the longer term, climate change will either increase, or fizzle. I pray it fizzles. I'd much rather be wrong than right. But if it does increase, as is much more likely, customers, employees, supply chain partners, and others will vote with their feet—and their wallets.

People in IT usually have more job opportunities than others. Many doubters and deniers will change their minds. If your organization doesn't change fast enough, you can find an opportunity with someone more sympatico—or wait until your employer's business declines and you get a pink slip.

## 9.6  So What's Next with Climate Change?

Understanding what's likely to happen next with climate change is next to impossible—but very valuable, if you can manage it. I can introduce you to some upcoming events and some trends in climate science that will help you stay oriented and proactive (rather than just reacting to changes in the climate over time).

For better and for worse—mostly better, in my opinion—the most important body for public understanding of climate change is the Intergovernmental Panel on Climate Change, or IPCC. I have my own opinions about their work, but will just point out here that it's an inter*governmental* panel. That is, scientists do the work, but governmental representatives sum it up and agree on conclusions. Governments don't want to have to act unless the current state of opinion is very certain indeed. This tends to mean that the IPCC lags somewhat behind the mainstream of climate science and predicts less change, and slower change, than many working in the field.

For instance, at the time of the IPCC's Fourth Assessment Report (2007), the subject of sea level rise was under active discussion. There are two sources of sea level rise: thermal expansion (water takes up more space as it gets warmer) and ice melting. The IPCC was having trouble getting a consensus on ice melting speed at the time of their report, so they just left out ice melting entirely!

The Fourth Assessment Report's estimate of 21st-century sea level rise, one foot to three feet by the end of the century, was based entirely on predictions of thermal expansion. Scientists doing work at that time—though not submitting their newest work in time for the report—called that prediction far too conservative, and it's now predicted that we may see three feet of ocean level rise by 2050, and double that by the end of the century.

It's said that every foot in sea level rise moves the coastline inland by fifty feet or more in most areas, so this is a big deal indeed. (In Florida, for an extreme example, the Everglades is about a foot above sea level; all of the islands in the Florida Keys are less than ten feet above sea level.) The degree of sea level rise to be expected is just one of the many debates around climate science.

The important thing to understand about the public debate on climate change is that the terms of discussion are largely set by the IPCC's reports. These occur every five to seven years. Here's the schedule of reports so far:

- First Assessment Report: 1990.
- Second Assessment Report: 1996.
- Third Assessment Report: 2001.
- Fourth Assessment Report: 2007. Al Gore's *An Inconvenient Truth*[1] was based on an early draft of this one, and the IPCC and Al Gore shared the Nobel Peace Prize for their work on climate change in 2008.
- Fifth Assessment Report: planned for fall 2014, at this writing.

As the IPCC prepares a report, they begin circulating drafts from various working groups. When the report itself comes out, people from all sides respond—attacking, supporting, clarifying. So far, at least, each IPCC report largely sets the parameters for discussion of climate science in the years following—until the next one!

Unless you're a real climate change nerd, I don't suggest you try to read the reports themselves. However, the Summary for Policymakers is written to be understandable by politicians, or at least by the nerdy public policy types that politicians hire to analyze scientific input for them. So the summaries might be worth a try.

When an IPCC report comes out, you'll also find useful descriptions in the mainstream media—as well as many other places—some well-informed and well-intentioned, some not.

This is being written in 2012, just as the Fifth Assessment Report is beginning to be prepared. I expect it to be far more somber and serious than the Fourth Assessment Report—and well behind the cutting edge of climate science at the time the report comes out. But time will tell.

Other important trends you can expect over time:

- **Climate change news tracking weather extremes.** People worry about climate change when heat records or storm records are set, and don't worry when they're not. As I write this, the United States is experiencing a Dust Bowl–type summer of 2012, with drought in more than half of these United States. Hurricane Sandy, which hit the Northeast just before the US Presidential election in November, was widely attributed to global warming. News like this increases discussion of climate change.
- **A steady increase in events related to climate change.** Major news organizations are finally, in mid-2012, getting the story right: extreme weather is not necessarily "caused" by climate change, but each new extreme event is far more likely in a warming world.
- **Gradual decrease in doubt and denial as facts accumulate.** If climate change is indeed real, the accumulation of extreme weather events, plus the machinery of the governments, military, business, and civil society

gearing up to respond, will gradually silence the doubters. Doubt and denial will become harder and harder to support.

- **Climate change becoming "normal."** Preparing for climate change will gradually become normal, without much further discussion as to whether it's "true" or not. The only question will be what an individual or organization is doing to prepare, not whether climate change is happening.
- **Disproportionate rewards to early adopters.** The public will hear a lot of competing claims about businesses taking steps to reduce their greenhouse gas footprint and other environmental impacts. These will be hard to evaluate. The only incontrovertible fact will be, when did a given organization finally start taking steps to reduce their environmental impact? Organizations will have to "wear" the results of decisions made many years previously.

## 9.7 Reducing Emissions I: Embodied Energy

One major way to reduce carbon emissions is to reduce embodied energy in stuff that you buy—in particular, of course, computer and networking gear. However, if you put up a new building to house a data center, that will have embodied energy as well.

Reducing embodied energy has a double benefit. Not only do you reduce emissions directly, but most decisions you might make that reduce embodied emissions will reduce ongoing emissions from use as well.

For instance, if you buy a tablet computer instead of a laptop, the embodied energy will be less. (A thumb on the wall guesstimate is that you'll reduce embodied emissions by about a third, going by the relative weight of the two kinds of devices.) And, not at all coincidentally, the ongoing emissions are far less—in fact, about 90% less (30–40 W/h vs. 3–4 W/h). Not building a new data center avoids new embodied energy and large amounts of ongoing emissions as well.

Of course, sometimes you're looking at tradeoffs as well as savings. A very energy-efficient data center might actually save you energy over whatever you're currently doing, despite the embodied energy in the new building.

It's not that easy to get information on embodied energy, and reasonable people can disagree on just what should be counted. Develop a relatively consistent methodology or find a source that includes estimates for as wide a range of objects as possible. Or, consistently use a rough estimate, such as comparing electronic products by weight. Find an estimate for a relevant device or two to use as benchmarks for comparison.

The US Environmental Protection Agency (EPA) addresses issues such as the relative advantages and disadvantages of sustainably preserving existing

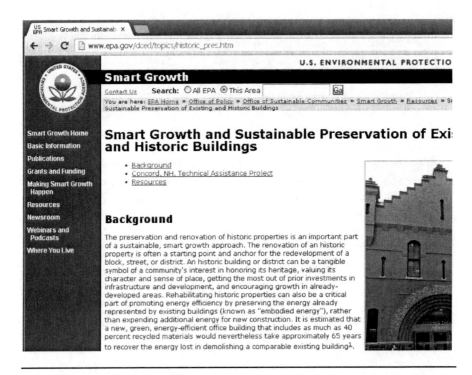

**Figure 9.6**   The EPA is one source of information about embodied energy. (*Source*: http://www.epa.gov/dced/topics/historic_pres.htm)

buildings. Figure 9.6 shows a Web page on the topic, within an overall focus on "smart growth."

## 9.8  Reducing Emissions II: Daily Energy Use

Reducing energy use will certainly reduce your greenhouse gas footprint. However, the degree to which reducing energy use reduces greenhouse gas emissions depends on where you get your power from.

Areas with lots of coal-fired power plants will have energy that's cheap in terms of money (usually the cheapest), but expensive in terms of greenhouse gas emissions (the most expensive). In addition to the carbon footprint, "green" monitoring sites such as Greenpeace and the Newsweek Green 500 will notice if you get a disproportionate amount of your energy from coal. You'll have to decide if the reduced cost (for now) is worth the higher greenhouse gas footprint and the opprobrium, which is likely to only increase in the future.

Coal-fired power is in decline in some places, including the United States. At this writing, near the end of 2012, activists have almost stopped new licenses from being granted for coal-fired power plants, on a variety of grounds. Some existing plants are being challenged, mothballed, or largely kept out of active use by utilities because of regulatory and activist pressure. The low cost of fracked natural gas, which has its own environmental concerns, is quite competitive with coal. Unfortunately, coal mining continues, including mountaintop removal, largely to serve the export market.

Oil-fired plants are a small and declining producer of power. This was always a poor use for oil—it's much more valuable as a transportation fuel and a feedstock for plastics and other petrochemical products. Even more so than coal, oil-fired power plants are vulnerable to competition from natural gas generators.

And natural gas–fired plants are being built quite quickly, in the United States and elsewhere, largely to take advantage of fracked natural gas. The carbon footprint of these plants is quite low in operation, about one-fourth of coal and one-half of oil. Unfortunately, fracked gas has a big environmental impact, as well as considerable methane leakage directly into the atmosphere. As a source of natural gas, fracking is new and may be quite vulnerable; we may be only one or two serious groundwater contamination problems away from much stricter limits on fracking.

Hydroelectric power is a special case. It can be even cheaper than coal-fired power. Some energy-intensive facilities, such as aluminum smelters, are located near dams for just this reason. (Norsk Hydro, originally a hydroelectric power generating company, ended up owning aluminum smelters and fertilizer production because these operations are so dependent on cheap energy to make a profit.) Unfortunately, unused sites for new hydroelectric plants are few and far between, and environmentalists tend to fight new dams (and understandably so; the environmental impact is inarguable).

Other renewables, besides hydroelectric, have much more potential for growth. Solar and wind power are both growing steadily, although fracked natural gas is putting price pressure on both of them. Also, both solar and wind power provide such a small proportion of all energy—a few percentage points, total, depending on what region you're in—that it will be years before they represent a big percentage of very many energy bills.

So as you calculate the greenhouse gas impact of energy reductions, take the sources of power into account. Do the math to understand your actual carbon footprint.

## 9.9 Reducing Emissions III: Taking Steps to Use Different Sources

What can you do? If you're part of a large organization, you may have considerable leverage with your local power company and other energy providers. You may be able to arrange an outsize share of natural gas–fired and renewable energy for your own use. (And don't worry about crowding others out of the pool; this kind of effort encourages all utilities to invest in reducing the carbon footprint of the power they provide.)

Paradoxically, you can also enter into agreements to shut down some operations when demand peaks. It may sound radical, but reducing operations on two or three of the hottest days of the year can be a very big contribution. And imagine how happy your employees would be if you gave many of them an occasional day off when the weather was hottest—almost always in summer, when their kids are out of school as well.

These peak-time reductions are a huge savings for power companies, because they can avoid building power plants that would otherwise be needed only when loads peak. They can also leave their reserve plants—often coal-fired plants that don't operate the rest of the time—offline, again with a disproportionate impact on everyone's carbon footprint. And, they can avoid brownouts, which are extremely unpopular.

Whether you're big or small, you can put in solar panels and solar thermal for water heating on rooftops and parking lots. Putting up solar panels is a powerful symbolic as well as actual commitment to a greener future. Solar panels are "procyclical" for IT, as well as general office building, use: The days when the sun shines are the days you crank up your air conditioning, and also the days when your solar panels deliver the most power. Just start by putting up enough solar panels to lop the peaks off your grid energy purchases.

Solar thermal is brilliant for homes, but most companies simply don't use that much hot water. And IT, at least, needs cooling a lot more than heating. An inverter can help you use solar thermal for cooling, but this is more complicated, more expensive, and less efficient than direct use of solar thermal for hot water and heating.

## 9.10 Reducing Emissions IV: Supply Chain Success

Reducing greenhouse gas emissions from your supply chain is a multistep process:

- **Cut at home.** Cut as many emissions as possible out of your own operations, including by outsourcing them. Yes, outsourcing emissions is just hiding them in the short term, but hang on.
- **Pocket outsourcing savings.** Give yourself credit for the emissions reductions you get where your supplier is more energy-efficient than you are. One study showed that a cloud computing company was seven times more efficient at running server farms than a nonspecialist company with data centers. The company that ran the study went on a massive spending

binge to make its operations nearly as efficient as a cloud computing company's, but you're more likely to just outsource, then "pocket" the automatic savings.

- **Sweat your supply chain.** Make emissions reductions a big part of your selection criteria for suppliers. Keep emphasizing this with them over and over. It's not usually something they can fix overnight, so you can just ask them for a bigger discount until they get around to it. You can also keep checking with competitors who might have a better offer.
- **Consider nonuse.** Companies hate writing checks to suppliers, even when it's fully justified. You won't get much argument from your bosses if you propose to trim your supplier list, reducing less-used and inefficient suppliers.
- **Repeat.** Keep cutting at home. Share best practices with suppliers. And promote your successes: It will help you get more management support for further work.

## 9.11  Summary

This chapter described the importance of greenhouse gas emissions in green computing—the role of greenhouse gas emissions in global warming, how to cut embodied energy, how energy sources are changing, and how to apply pressure for improvement to your supply chain. The next chapter discusses how to reduce resource use.

# Chapter 10

# Reducing Resource Use

## Key Concepts

This chapter goes into depth about resource use and green computing:

- Understanding the importance of resource use
- Reviewing a checklist for resource use
- Avoiding planned obsolescence
- Learning about Apple's practices and the EPEAT registry
- Tying repetitive stress injuries to green computing efforts

## 10.1 Why Resource Use Is Important

Resource use may be the most visible issue in all of green computing. After all, electricity is invisible; even coal-fired power plants don't throw off much visible smoke these days. But electronic waste is highly visible, and familiar to everyone.

Almost every household has experience with extra power chargers that are hard to match with devices; old cell phones; old computers; old televisions; and more, all hanging around in a "junk drawer" and odd corners of someone's room or the garage. This somewhat humorous problem becomes a real issue in a company that may be responsible for thousands of devices at a time.

Your company can stand out strongly by intelligently handling computer "stuff" and all the related issues that go with it, including worker safety in your facilities. Let's look at some aspects of this issue.

The first is that computers are, as the Story of Electronics video eloquently puts it, "designed for the dump." I'll focus here on Windows-based PCs; Apple's products have their own issues, which I'll highlight in the next section.

Windows PCs are assembled out of piece parts from a worldwide marketplace of suppliers. Dell Computer, one of the top computer makers on Earth, is a good example. Their sourcing people are constantly scouring the globe looking for new sources for the components that make up a PC.

A hard disk from here, a motherboard from there, a video card from somewhere else—and you're much of the way to building a Windows PC. Each supplier only has to meet minimum standards, and globalization means those standards depend on the standards of enforcement that are in place in the countries where devices are made.

**Figure 10.1**   Michael Dell has received reams of good press. (*Source*: http://www. amazon.com/Direct-Dell-Strategies-Revolutionized-Essentials/dp/0060845724/ref =sr_1_1?s=books&ie=UTF8&qid=1342418540&sr=1-1&keywords=dell+computer

This is brilliant business strategy; it helps keep costs to an absolute minimum. Much of the job of a company like Dell is making sure that these various parts work well together. Dell, in particular, has done this so expertly, most of the time, that it's been the subject of a stream of laudatory books, magazine articles, and more. Figure 10.1 shows just one of several books about Michael Dell, who founded Dell Computer from his college dorm room decades ago.

When such a computer breaks, what are the odds that a replacement part will work perfectly with the rest of the parts that were put together? Pretty good, but not 100%. Dell is said to be responsive, usually getting someone out to their customers within a couple of days. Of course, you're without the computer until then, and who wants to do that?

In fact, most savvy IT departments—and even savvy end users—will immediately put a new computer through its paces, making sure it "does what it says on the tin." That's because it's important to get any repairs started right away—within the warranty period and before you've loaded software on the computer, imported your Web browser bookmarks, and started to count on the computer to get anything important done.

Dell has overlapping warranty periods of 90 days of complete coverage (United States only), one year of fairly full coverage, and extension periods that you can pay for. If a problem occurs outside of the included coverage, and any extensions you buy, you're out of luck.

And out of luck is a good way of describing what happens; when an out-of-warranty computer fails, it can cost several hundred dollars just to get the problem assessed. This has to be weighed against the cost of buying a new computer that's faster, smaller, potentially greener—and still within its free warranty period.

It's not just hardware that's a problem. Software on a Windows PC is such that performance steadily degrades due to hard disk fragmentation, disk space filling up, and, importantly, the effects of various kinds of malware and viruses. A good antivirus program can help save you a lot of money—it costs several hundred dollars for a consumer to have a computer cleaned up.

There's an old rule of thumb that it's less expensive, overall, to replace any kind of product if the repair cost is more than about a third of the price of buying a new one. If a Windows PC costs $500 to buy (for the system unit only), and it costs $200 to get it assessed for repairs, you've passed the spending threshold before you even think about actually fixing anything.

It's also not unheard of that the process of cleaning debris from your computer's system files will introduce some software incompatibility or data loss that leaves you worse off than before.

Although you, as an IT pro, can handle these issues somewhat more effectively than a consumer, it will still cost an IT department a lot of money to keep a PC in shape—and you have a lower purchase price for a new system than a consumer does. You're about as motivated to replace, rather than repair, a Windows PC as an end user can be.

## 10.2  A Resource Use Checklist

I've mentioned The Story of Electronics as a resource for green computing. Along with the story itself, the video includes a built-in Frequently Asked Questions (FAQ) list. It's made up of convenient links to key topics around responsible resource use for electronics products, as shown in Figure 10.2.

For all its virtues, though, The Story of Electronics is consumer-oriented. Let's take a look at the FAQ topics and expand on how they apply to your purchasing decisions as you pursue green computing:

- **Toxic Stuff.** Computers and related products are full of exotic materials and chemicals. More and more people are sensitive to these materials—

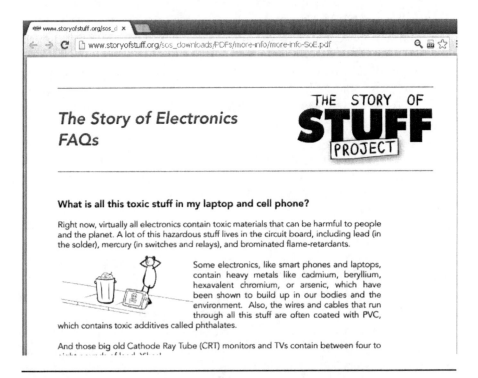

**Figure 10.2**   The Story of Electronics has a convenient FAQ. (*Source:* http://www. storyofstuff.org/sos_downloads/PDFs/more-info/more-info-SoE.pdf)

and, yes, some of them may simply believe that they are. But the materials in computers include known and suspected carcinogens and other pollutants: lead, mercury, and brominated (bromine-containing) flame retardants. Bromine, according to The Free Dictionary online site, is "A heavy, volatile, corrosive, reddish-brown, nonmetallic liquid element, having a highly irritating vapor." Also commonly used are heavy metals like cadmium, hexavalent chromium (the toxic substance featured in the Julia Roberts movie, Erin Brockovich), and arsenic.

Polyvinyl chloride (PVC) coats many wires and cables, along with a toxic additive called phthalates. Old-style monitors include pounds of lead—which is why they're so heavy—and all kinds of monitors can contain mercury.

You'll help the Earth by using smaller, lighter devices where possible, and specifically looking for vendors who reduce, minimize, or eliminate the use of as much of this junk as possible. Your employees will be particularly appreciative of your effort to "green" their work environment as part of your green computing initiative.

- **Exporting e-waste.** More and more of your stakeholders will be aware that exporting e-waste is common, and that it causes serious problems wherever it's shipped. In the United States, CRT-style monitors—the ones that are full of lead—can't be exported as waste, but other electronics can. They end up in garage-style recycling operations where totally unprotected workers—often desperately poor and, as you might imagine, ill—smash up the devices to get at the resellable parts of the materials inside. Children in these areas show high levels of lead, dioxins, and other toxics in their blood. You only need to mention "reducing e-waste" as a headline item in your green computing efforts; your savvier employees and other stakeholders may well educate others about what this means.

- **Extended Producer Responsibility (EPR).** You can fight back against manufacturers' power to inflict disposal responsibility and costs on you. Seek out manufacturers who support Extended Producer Responsibility, also called "producer take back." This means that manufacturers take their products off your hands when you're done with them and see to their safe and sane disposal (which is far easier for them to do than you).

EPR encourages manufacturers to use fewer toxics (to protect themselves), to design for reusability and recyclability, to create recycling capabilities adapted to their own products, to create products that last longer, and to reduce waste.

I mean, think about it—the chances you can make the best use of an old computer are quite low. But Dell, which has embraced EPR, can do much more. Facing hundreds and thousands of taken-back computers, they can resell or donate working computers; reuse working hard disks; safely extract and resell some hazardous chemicals, while safely disposing of the others. So EPR not only shifts a burden off you, it creates the opportunity to make the highest possible reuse of potentially valuable parts of electronic devices.

You can also donate products yourself. The National Christina Foundation and the World Computer Exchange are two organizations that are well regarded in this area.

- **Responsible companies.** Identify companies that are taking these steps. Set a minimum standard; for instance, you can refuse to buy from companies that aren't reducing toxics or embracing EPR. Then give bonus points for additional steps, such as greening entire supply and distribution chains. This will encourage a "race to the top" among suppliers, as well as distributors.

Use this information in making decisions for your green computing efforts—and also in selling the benefits, within your company, to stakeholders,

**Figure 10.3** The Electronics TakeBack Coalition helps you find responsible suppliers. (*Source:* www.electronicstakeback.com)

and externally. Resources such as The Story of Stuff are creating a vocabulary that you can use to help people understand your work. You can use these criteria to give a single grade, or multiple grades, to companies as you make purchasing decisions.

One great resource is the Electronics TakeBack Coalition (ETBC) at www.electronicstakeback.com. They keep a report card for computer, TV, printer, and game console companies. Dell and Apple are among the companies who are currently near the top of their list. Visit their website, shown in Figure 10.3, to learn the latest about electronics take back and related issues.

## 10.3 Planned Obsolescence and Resource Use

Many green computing issues involve complex trade-offs, and planned obsolescence is a good example.

The Story of Electronics evocatively describes most products today as "designed for the dump," and that's a good, catchy phrase. Even a relatively green product will have a much greater footprint if it lasts for one year rather than if it lasts for three.

A product that's easy to expand and upgrade may have more embodied carbon, for instance, but may last longer than a minimal product. You have to know applicable products and your users really well to be able to make intelligent choices about who gets what at computer-purchasing time.

Obsolescence is not only a hardware issue. Windows computers are famous for accumulating debris on their hard disks, noticeably slowing the computer in as little as a year. Some of this is due to malware and virus attacks; some of it is due to the way Windows itself operates.

Part of the problem here is motivation. Computer manufacturers like selling you new stuff. Repair shops like charging you a lot to clean the viruses off your computer. No one's all that motivated to make the whole system last longer.

The simplest way to keep your Windows computer free of viruses is to keep all your software CDs and keep your data backed up. Then you can erase everything on your hard disk, reinstall your software, and restore your data every year or so. This is a hassle, but could help your computer last years longer.

Apple computers, on the other hand, are known to last longer than Windows PCs—and their lower profile with regard to virus attacks may be a big part of the reason. However, my prescription for Windows PCs applies to Macs, too: Keep your software CDs and back up your data. Then erase your hard disk, reinstall your software, and restore your data every year or so.

Better still for manageability are centralized software products like Citrix, which centralize your Windows installation and make it much easier to preserve

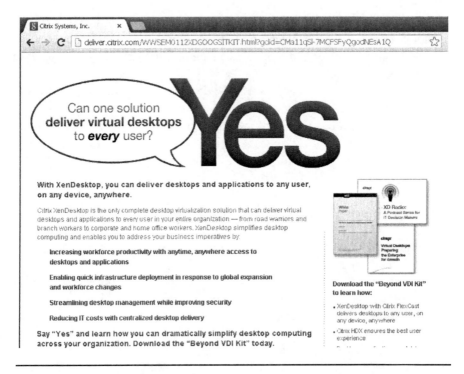

**Figure 10.4** Citrix XenDesktop is a popular desktop virtualization product. (*Source*: http://deliver.citrix.com/WWSEM0112XDGOOGSITKIT.html?gclid=CMa1 1qSl-7MCFSFyQgodNEsA1Q)

individual computers from problems. XenDesktop, shown in Figure 10.4, is a desktop virtualization product that helps your PCs work a lot less.

## 10.4 The Story of Apple and EPEAT

Apple has given us an excellent example of the power of resource use as an issue in green computing. This has to do with Apple's long-standing practice of making relatively closed computers, balanced against the increasing power of green standards–setting organizations.

Apple has long been a member of the green-friendly product registry, the Electronic Product Environmental Assessment Tool, or EPEAT. Companies award themselves Gold, Silver, or Bronze EPEAT designations for each of their products. The EPEAT people then come around and check the product against the claimed award level.

In mid-2012, Apple introduced new products, including the MacBook Pro's Retina versions. (A Retina display is a very high-resolution display, about four times the pixel density of other Macs.) The display, which is power hungry, has its own glued-in battery to keep all those pixels burning brightly.

Well, gluing anything in is an obvious no-no for an environmentally friendly product. Glue is itself prone to including toxic chemicals, and gluing makes recycling much harder. The EPEAT standards require, among much else, that products be capable of disassembly by a single individual with common hand tools; gluing generally makes that impossible. So Apple refused to subject its MacBook Pro Retina versions to assignment at any EPEAT level—and withdrew from the EPEAT registry entirely.

Now this was a big step. Apple has made many strong green efforts and has gotten a lot of good press and credibility for doing so. Abandoning a big green registry was a shocking step. And the ramifications were huge: The city and county of San Francisco, a combined governmental body, was the first organization to tell employees they could no longer have Macs. San Francisco refuses to buy any non-EPEAT-listed products, and every Mac, as well as iPads and iPhones, was suddenly off the list (http://www.huffingtonpost.com/2012/07/11/apple-epat_n_1666438.html).

Well, San Franciscans consider themselves cool, and Macs are often considered the coolest computer, so the employees were nonplussed. More organizations quickly followed San Francisco in banning Mac purchases, with others promising to join in.

Among the organizations that was widely quoted as a critic of the Apple move was the Electronics TakeBack Coalition (ETBC), mentioned in the previous section. Barbara Kyle, the US national coordinator for ETBC, said the MacBook failed the Design for End of Life criterion, among others (http://macnews.gr/how-the-new-macbook-pros-got-epeat-gold-rating).

And Apple, after just a few days, caved in. They returned their products to the EPEAT list, admitting to having made a mistake. Everyone breathed a sigh of relief, and the sun returned to rising in the East and setting in the West. The controversy continued, however. Apple quickly awarded the MacBook Pro Retina a gold star(!). Word circulated that Apple had negotiated an easing in the standard in return for returning to the EPEAT list (http://techcrunch.com/2012/10/15/retina-macbook-pro-found-to-meet-epeat-standards-thanks-to-external-upgradeability-options/).

## 10.5  Case Study: Computer Hardware and RSI

Green computing can cover a wide range of concerns. The health of workers in the electronics industry is now considered a mainstream green computing issue. But what about the health of workers who use the products?

A longstanding and very serious concern about computer use is RSI, or Repetitive Stress Injury. All sorts of physical ills are tied to computer use. The most widely known RSI, because it's so common and otherwise relatively unusual, is carpal tunnel syndrome. This is soreness of tendons in the wrist associated with computer keyboard and mouse use.

Some computing companies make fairly strong efforts to provide information about RSI, and RSI-safer products. Others ignore the issue.

Should you include RSI in your green computing concerns? It's a judgment call. You can address RSI outside of green computing efforts, without necessarily losing effectiveness.

I would argue, though, that RSI is a good fit with green computing. It has to do with the impact of electronics on people, in a similar way to toxics. And your including RSI in green computing criteria shows that you care just as much about the health of your employees as you do about the health of, say, people who disassemble computers, or about saving habitats for polar bears (good causes in their own right).

You may find that some of the recommendations in this book are inherently RSI friendly. For instance, the nature of tablet use may make it less likely to cause RSI than a typical laptop or desktop computer. Just switching between the two types of devices for different tasks not only saves energy (while the tablet use is replacing computer use) but also provides variety that takes some of the "repetitive" out of "repetitive stress injury."

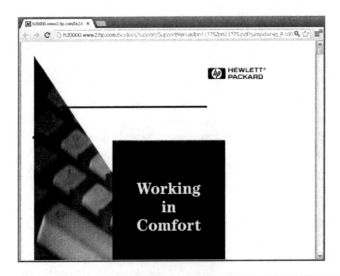

**Figure 10.5**   Repetitive stress injury (RSI) is a valid green computing concern.

HP is among the companies that provides information about using RSI. Figure 10.5 shows a web page from the HP site that addresses RSI concerns (using a picture of an old-fashioned-looking giant CRT screen!).

## 10.6 Summary

This chapter went into depth about resource use and green computing, including understanding the importance of resource use; using a checklist for resource use; avoiding planned obsolescence; encouraging recyclability; and understanding how repetitive stress injuries relate to green computing efforts. The next chapter discusses energy costs and risk management.

# Chapter 11

# Green Computing by Industry Segment

## Key Concepts

In this chapter we discuss the public face of green computing:

- What constitutes "greenness"
- How to use the Newsweek Green 500 for green computing
- Green technology, service companies, and IT departments
- Technology equipment suppliers
- Telecommunications suppliers
- Analyzing your department and your company

## 11.1 Evaluating Greenness

There are a million ways to evaluate how green you are. This book has highlighted many of them. We can categorize the major factors you can look at in relation to how green you are:

- **Energy savings.** Energy usage is perhaps the single biggest factor in "greenness" for computing. Generating electricity and moving things around requires energy, and most of the energy comes from fossil fuels. The less energy you use—in making something, in using it, in getting people to the right places to do their work, and in disposal of "stuff"—the better.

- **Curating "stuff."** Every "thing" has an environmental footprint all its own. Getting raw materials to a factory, making a "thing," and getting it to you have almost innumerable environmental consequences. The reverse journey that a "thing" makes when you're done with it has its own trail and footprint. Electronic "things" have a particularly large footprint, mostly because of the toxic minerals and chemicals involved. Planned obsolescence and people's desire for the "latest and greatest"— not unrelated factors—increase the rate of churn on "stuff."

- **Public credibility.** Getting public credibility for your green computing work has two different, and somewhat discordant, effects. The first is that good press on green issues can help your company with all its stakeholders, including end customers. The second is that the publicity you generate for your green efforts helps encourage all around you—even your competitors—to raise their game, which is a *good thing* for the world as a whole. Your green effort functions to "encourage the others"—"pour encourager les autres," in the words of Voltaire.

Pursuing green computing goals at the expense of actual green accomplishments is greenwashing—putting a green veneer on efforts that are really driven by the same old profit motive as other business. However, a completely ego-less green effort, with no publicity attached, is not nearly as powerful as a solid real-world initiative backed by an appropriately sized reporting effort.

So how on Earth can you decide what to do, and report what you've done, in a way that has the maximum positive impact—internally and externally—and is least subject to charges of greenwashing? I recommend "borrowing credibility."

"Borrowing credibility" means using established frameworks, getting external recognition, and winning awards. When you do this, the people who established the frameworks you use, the people who give you recognition, and the people who give you awards (and past and future winners) all "bless" your efforts.

In this chapter, I'm recommending using the Newsweek Green 500 as a framework you can borrow and apply to your own efforts. If your company is one of the top 500 companies in the United States, or globally, it will already be included in the Fortune 500 or the Global 500, and therefore in the Green 500. All you need to do is take the Green 500 lens and apply it to your efforts in IT, rather than at the level of the entire company.

If you're not in a company listed in the Fortune 500 or the Global 500— and that's the situation for the vast majority of companies—you can still use the Newsweek approach to evaluate your own efforts. That's the approach I describe, and recommend, in this chapter.

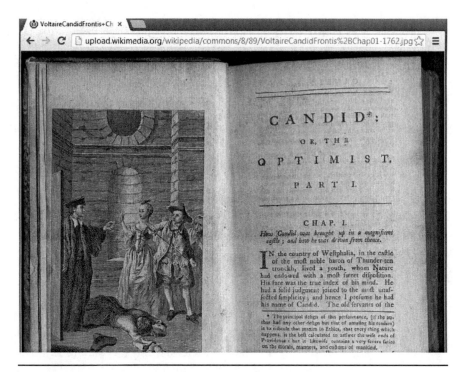

**Figure 11.1**    Voltaire's novel *Candide* describes an admiral who was executed "to encourage the others." (*Source*: http://upload.wikimedia.org/wikipedia/commons/8/89/VoltaireCandidFrontis%2BChap01-1762.jpg)

As a side note, you might be interested in knowing where the phrase "to encourage the others" comes from; it's background that can be useful in business. John Byng, a British admiral, lost the Battle of Minorca in 1756 to the French and failed to relieve an embattled British garrison on the island. Byng was then court-martialed for failing to do all he could to relieve the garrison and executed on board the HMS Monarch.

Byng's execution shows up in Voltaire's famous short novel, *Candide*, shown in Figure 11.1. His death is described with the line "Dans ce pays-ci, il est bon de tuer de temps en temps un amiral pour encourager les autres." The English translation is, "In this country, it is wise to kill an admiral from time to time to encourage the others."

## 11.2 The Newsweek Green 500 Approach

The Newsweek Green 500 is three years old, at this writing. It makes a big splash each year and is likely to continue for many years to come (see http://www.thedailybeast.com/newsweek/features/2012/newsweek-green-rankings.html).

Newsweek has taken on a very different task. Comparing different companies on how "green" they are is very difficult. Different industries—such as making jumbo jets, publishing, and franchising fast-food restaurants—have very different environmental impacts. How do you equitably compare one to another?

The other problem is companies themselves. A Fortune 500 or Global 500 company, which are the ones included in Newsweek's survey, is likely to actually cross several industries, with each company having its own mix of activities. The financial press and analysts, however, lump many fairly different companies into industry segments for purposes of comparison, and to guide investment decisions. This actually does tend to make the companies more and more like each other over time, as they have to keep analysts and investors happy. Still, big differences remain.

So how do they do it? The Green 500 rankings give companies scores in three green-related areas:

- **Environmental Impact.** The Green 500 rankings look at the environmental impact of a company's operations all over the world. Impacts include greenhouse gas emissions, other air and water pollution, use of raw materials, waste disposal, and much more. Impacts are indexed to a company's revenues. The rankings are compared to benchmarks for each industry sector that a company operates in.
- **Environmental Management.** This is where a company's policies and programs, targets it has set, certifications, and awards are considered. If you are "greening" your supply chain, cutting hazardous waste, or protecting biodiversity, it will show up here. These factors are compared to competitors to come up with a score.
- **Environmental Disclosure Score.** This score evaluates how open a company is with information about its environmental efforts. It includes company involvement in transparency initiatives, such as the Global Reporting Initiative and the Carbon Disclosure Project, shown in Figure 11.2.

I find the approach that Newsweek uses fascinating—and reflective of what happens in the real world. Notice that only one of the three scores—the Environmental Impact score—relates to the actual physical impact of a company's actions. The Environmental Management score assesses how you structure your efforts, and the Environmental Disclosure score assesses how you talk about them.

In this book, I've talked a lot about measurement and about the importance of how you organize and publicize your efforts. The Newsweek Green 500 show that these organizational factors may actually outweigh the real-world impact of your actions.

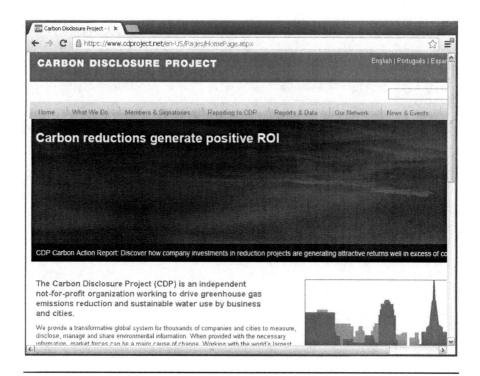

**Figure 11.2**   The Carbon Disclosure Project is a global effort with thousands of companies involved. (*Source*: https://www.cdproject.net)

Should it be like this? Arguably, yes. If you don't organize and communicate your efforts well, they "just" save money and help the environment (meaning, all of us). If you do organize and communicate them well, your efforts can grow more powerful over time, as they can influence your own stakeholders and others. The "stakeholders" include customers; so, in addition to saving money, your company has the opportunity to make more money as well.

One of the best things about the Newsweek Green 500 is that you can use it for "greening" your supply chain. (The Greenpeace Guide to Greener Electronics and other listings are useful, too, but the Green 500 is the most comprehensive resource.) Just include Green 500 rankings in your evaluation process; you can give industry group leaders extra points, or even use a cutoff to eliminate companies with poor scores from the comparison. That last approach will get your vendors' attention!

For suppliers whose companies are too small to appear in the Green 500 rankings, you can use the Green 500 framework to contribute to your own ranking approach. And you aren't stuck if you come from a medium-sized or smaller company yourself. Even if your company isn't part of the Fortune 500 or Global 500, you can get your own green ranking, as shown in Figure 11.3.

**Figure 11.3**  You can get a Green 500-type ranking for a medium-sized or smaller company. (*Source*: http://www.thedailybeast.com/newsweek/2012/08/28/newsweek-green-rankings-benchmarking-service.html)

Newsweek and its research partners will assess medium-sized and smaller companies, for a fee, and compare them to other companies in their industry segment(s). This opportunity is publicized on the Newsweek website, referred to as the Daily Beast. (The Daily Beast is a website that Newsweek acquired, and now uses as its web presence.)

Perhaps luckily for you, the results will be delivered confidentially. You can then use them to assess your own efforts, and even publicize them if they're favorable. You can get information by emailing Newsweek at greenrankings@newsweekdailybeast.com.

The Newsweek Green 500 gives you a powerful tool for demonstrating the importance of taking a careful, thoughtful approach, of "bigging up" your green efforts into full-scale projects with their own planning, budgets, and internal and external publicity. "Just Do It" is an appealing slogan for a shoe company, but effective management in a company often requires much more than that.

## 11.2.1 *Why the Newsweek Green 500 Approach Works*

The Newsweek Green 500 works because it ranks companies against each other (http://www.thedailybeast.com/newsweek/2011/10/16/green-rankings-2011.html). By giving the winners bragging rights, it creates a "virtuous spiral." If you want those bragging rights, you have to do better than the other people. They're trying to do better than you, too, so companies are pressed to ever-greater efforts. This is similar to Greenpeace's Guide to Greener Electronics, as mentioned in Chapter 10.

The old story about two hikers and a bear applies here. Two hikers come to a river, set down their backpacks, take off their shoes, and sit with their bare feet (no pun intended) dangling in the river. Suddenly, a bear approaches the river 100 yards downstream. The bear sees the hikers and starts lumbering toward them. One of the hikers calmly reaches in his backpack, fishes out a pair of running shoes, and starts putting them on. The other hiker laughs bitterly and says, "Sorry; even with running shoes on, you're not going to outrun a bear." The first hiker says, "I don't need to outrun a bear; I just need to outrun you."

The Green 500 listing works as free publicity for the top companies. Newsweek publishes the results as a lead story for one issue (amplified by extensive coverage on TV and radio), in the print press and online. In addition, leading companies can repeat the results in their own marketing for the following year, making hay while the sun shines.

In fact, the Green 500 listing is even better than free publicity. Because the listing comes from a reputable, independent source, it's more credible than anything a company might say about its own effort. The leaders in the Green 500 listing can "borrow credibility": By invoking Newsweek's name, they gain the imprimatur of a brand that people worldwide know and respect. So the cost–benefit ratio of green efforts, including green computing efforts, moves sharply upward if they're rewarded by positive results, such as a top Green 500 listing.

There's a stick to go with the carrot. A poor Green 500 listing can be quite damaging to a company's reputation—not only with customers, but with the press, analysts, and activist groups. A poor listing gives external stakeholders something to beat a company up about for a whole year; a series of poor listings can become part of a bad reputation that can be very hard to overcome.

This process isn't all-powerful, of course. There are a huge number of concerns for corporate management to worry about, and green concerns are only part of a complicated whole. Every project in a typical company has to meet stringent cost-justification criteria. The Newsweek Green 500 approach, though, does give more weight to green initiatives than they might otherwise have, and keeps pushing standards upward.

There's also a problem with using a comparative evaluation when a problem is more serious than people realize. For instance, the world is moving far too slowly in addressing greenhouse gas emissions and climate change. If companies use current performance as a baseline, and incremental improvements are rewarded by positive feedback like strong Green 500 listings, companies can believe that they're doing well even as climate change spins out of control.

Climate change, like other environmental challenges, is a bear all of us have to outrun; the "winners" won't feel very good if half of us get caught by the bear.

So clearly, for the most serious problems, more than comparative listings are needed, and soon. However, the companies that do well in today's competitive environment will be much more ready to act—and to continue leading—than companies that are ignoring environmental concerns, or that are ineffective in efforts to meet them.

For your efforts in thinking up green computing projects, "selling" then internally, and assessing the results, however, the Green 500 listings are very powerful indeed. Study them carefully, and use them in your green computing efforts.

## 11.2.2 Looking at Industry Segments

The Green 500 listings divided all companies up into 19 groups (http://www.thedailybeast.com/newsweek/2012/10/22/newsweek-green-rankings-2012-browse-by-industry.html):

1. Capital Goods
2. Consumer Goods
3. Energy
4. Financials
5. Food, Beverage & Tobacco
6. Healthcare
7. Hotels and Restaurants
8. Information Technology & Services
9. Materials
10. Media & Publishing
11. Professional Services
12. Real Estate
13. Retailers
14. Technology Equipment
15. Telecommunications
16. Textiles, Apparel & Luxury Goods

17. Transportation & Logistics
18. Utilities
19. Vehicles & Components

The overall Green 500 list is dominated by a few companies that make a real science of "going green." Notably, the top of the list for 2011 is made up largely of technology companies:

1. IBM - Information Technology & Services
2. Hewlett-Packard - Technology Equipment
3. Sprint Nextel - Telecommunications
4. Baxter - Healthcare
5. Dell - Technology Equipment
6. Johnson & Johnson - Healthcare
7. Accenture - Information Technology & Services
8. Office Depot - Retailers
9. CA Technologies - Information Technology & Services
10. Nvidia - Technology Equipment

Note that seven of the top 10 companies are familiar names in technology—IBM, HP, Sprint Nextel, Dell, Accenture, CA Technologies (Computer Associates), and Nvidia. They come from three related segments: Information Technology & Services, Technology Equipment, and Telecommunications.

In the next few sections, we'll look at the results and some of the highlights for the most technology-related industry groups—Information Technology & Services, Technology Equipment, and Telecommunications. This will give you a feel for how to better evaluate suppliers based on their Green 500 score and show you some takeaways for green computing initiatives.

Although it's very valuable indeed to appear in the top of the overall listings, it's probably more realistic—and more relevant—for most companies to appear in the top of their industry group. If that's not possible, it's important, at least, to not appear in the lowest part of their industry group.

In fact, this last consideration might be particularly relevant for green computing initiatives. If your company is a leader in its industry group—or, even better, a leader in the overall Green 500 list—you probably have a lot of support internally for green computing initiatives, and they're just part of a bigger picture. But if a company is looking to get off the bottom of its industry group rankings in a hurry (and believe me, it happens), a green computing initiative might be a big part of moving up the depth chart. This is equally true whether the company itself is in a technology-focused industry group or not.

## 11.2.2.1 The Green 500: Information Technology & Services (http://www.thedailybeast.com/newsweek/2012/10/22/ newsweek-green-rankings-2012-u-s-500-list.html)

The Information Technology & Services industry group has 28 companies in it, and their average position is 95, whereas the average for the entire Green 500 is, of course, 250. So the whole Information Technology and Services segment ranks very highly indeed on the Green 500.

Names from the top of the list are in the Top 10 shown above. Microsoft, Oracle, and Google are also in the top half. MasterCard, Visa, and Electronic Arts are in the lower part of the list. Companies in this sector have an average Environmental Impact score of 78, Environmental Management score of 55, and Disclosure score of only 22. In fact, many companies ranked lowest in the sector, such as Western Union, VMWare, and the aforementioned Electronic Arts, which have Disclosure scores of 0.

This compares to the overall list, where the average Environmental Impact score is 56, the average Environmental Management score is 52, and the average Disclosure score is 29. The Disclosure score was new in the 2011 rankings, and companies can be expected to do better on it once they see how badly this low ranking hurt most of their standings.

Overall, you can say that companies in Information Technology & Services are better when it comes to being green—at "doing it" (Environmental Impact score of 78, way above the average) rather than "organizing it" (Environmental Management score of 55, a little above the average) or "talking about it" (Disclosure score of 22, well below the average).

You can regard your IT organization as an Information Technology & Services company, and compare yourself directly to such companies on the Green Computing list. You can also use the list to vet suppliers who fall into this category, and as a framework for assessing companies that aren't large enough to qualify for the Green 500.

Compare your efforts to the top companies on this list. How well do you do at reducing your impacts, at managing your efforts, and at being transparent with the public? One advantage of the Green 500 is that these are large companies that tend to make a lot of information publicly available on their websites. With the new Disclosure score taking effect, we can expect to see far more information posted online in the future.

The company with the highest Green score overall—the "winner" of the Green 500 listings—is IBM. They also have an extremely high Disclosure score of 83, which is higher than any other company in the Information Technology & Services segment, and among the very best Disclosure scores in the entire Green 500.

**Figure 11.4** An IBM manager's blog includes a mention of IBM's leadership in green supercomputing. (*Source:* https://www.ibm.com/developerworks/ mydeveloperworks/blogs/benchmarking/entry/ibm_aces_the_green500?lang=en)

Take a careful look at the information that IBM makes available. It ranges from detailed hardware specifications to a mention of IBM's green supercomputers in an IBM technical manager's blog, as shown in Figure 11.4.

### 11.2.2.2 The Green 500: Technology Equipment (http://www. thedailybeast.com/newsweek/2012/10/22/newsweek-green-rankings-2012-u-s-500-list.html)

There are 36 companies in the Technology Equipment industry group, with an average position of 131—much higher than the Green 500 average of 250, but a bit lower than the Information Technology & Services average of 131. Both groups rank way up there on the Green 500.

(If you know a bit about statistics, you'll be just as impressed by the 36 companies achieving an average position of 131 as you are by the 28 companies in

Information Services & Technology achieving an average score of 95. It's just harder for a larger group to achieve a given deviation from the mean.)

As with Information Technology & Services, names from the top of the list for Technology Equipment are in the Top 10 shown above—HP (#2), Dell (#5), and Nvidia (#10). Intel, Motorola, and Cisco are in the top 50. Apple is in the middle of the group, at position 50 exactly, and Qualcomm, NCR, and Broadcom are in the bottom half of the group. Companies in this sector have an average Environmental Impact score of 62 (compared with 78 for Information Technology & Services), an Environmental Management score of 65 (better than the other group's 55), and a Disclosure score of 31 (also better than the score of 22 above). As with Information Technology & Services, several companies ranked lowest in the sector, such as Tech Data, Arrow Electronics, and Amphenol, which have Disclosure scores of 0.

This compares well with the overall list, where the average Environmental Impact score is 56, the average Environmental Management score is 52, and the average Disclosure score is 29. Note that this group is lower in Environmental Impact score, but better for both Environmental Management and Disclosure.

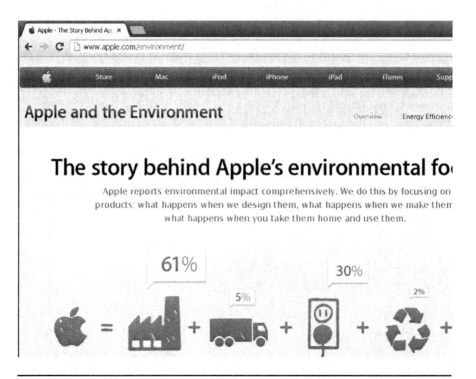

**Figure 11.5**   Apple details its environmental impacts. (*Source:* http://www.apple. com/environment/)

Compared with Information Technology & Services, this group is not as good at doing it but better at organizing it and talking about it. As an infrastructure fan, I'd guess that these supporting factors will lead to stronger performance in "doing it" in the future, whereas the Information Technology & Services group may fade in its environmental impact scores.

For a typical IT organization, companies in the Technology Equipment sector are going to include many top suppliers (and suppliers to suppliers, such as Intel). You can use this list to vet your suppliers and as a framework for assessing companies that aren't large enough to qualify for the Green 500.

You can also use this sector as a comparative framework for your own efforts, but less directly than with Information Technology & Services. (That sector is a pretty direct analog to most IT departments.) These are large companies, with a lot of data on their websites, in financial reports, in the press, and so forth. Use this information to develop comparisons with your own efforts.

Apple is such a star in business and technology that everyone is curious about how they do—well, everything. So take a look at Apple's site for their green disclosures. The best place to start is the Apple and the Environment pages at www.apple.com/environment, shown in Figure 11.5. You can use Apple's approach as a comparative framework for your own efforts.

### 11.2.2.3 The Green 500: Telecommunications (http://www. thedailybeast.com/newsweek/2012/10/22/newsweek-green-rankings-2012-u-s-500-list.html)

There are just nine companies in the Telecommunications industry group, with an average position of 212—a bit higher than the Green 500 average of 250.

Only one company in the Telecommunications group is in the overall Top 10 shown above—Sprint Nextel (#3). AT&T and Verizon rank above 100, and other, less-known companies round out the group. Companies in this sector have an average Environmental Impact score of 72 (relatively high, where the Green 500 average is 56), an Environmental Management score of 45 (a bit below the Green 500 average of 52), and a Disclosure score of 45. As with the previous two groups, several companies ranked lowest in the sector, such as US Cellular, Frontier, and NII Holdings, which have Disclosure scores of 0. So this group is good at "doing it" and "talking about it," but is a bit weak at "organizing it."

As with the Technology Equipment group, you can use this list to vet your suppliers, and as a framework for assessing potential suppliers that aren't large enough to qualify for the Green 500. You can use the websites of these large companies to get information to compare with your own efforts.

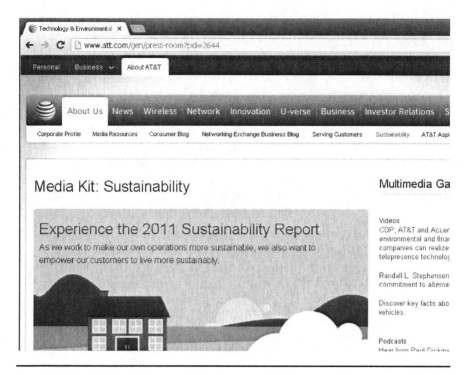

**Figure 11.6**   AT&T puts out an entire Sustainability Report. (*Source*: http://www. att.com/gen/press-room?pid=2644)

AT&T, with its long and varied history, is the "name" company that you can use as a starting point for comparison to your own efforts. AT&T puts out an entire Sustainability Report, as shown in Figure 11.6.

## 11.3  Analyzing Your Own Initiatives, Company, and Sector

Your green computing efforts take place in two contexts. One is your overall company, including the computing effort. Your overall company will fit into one group (or two or more groups) in the Green 500. Your green computing efforts, viewed narrowly, will compare most directly with the Information Technology & Services group. You'll also primarily use companies in that group, the Technology Equipment group, and the Telecommunications group, as suppliers.

Your own company, and specific suppliers, may or may not be large enough to show up in the Green 500 listing. But some of your competitors, companies you benchmark against, your own suppliers, and your suppliers' suppliers definitely will. So use the sections above for direct comparison of your own efforts, and for assessing your suppliers. Then, also, look at your overall company within its industry segment in the Green 500.

I'm going to give a demonstration here of how to assess your own company, using the Media and Publishing group as an example.

If your company is large enough to be in the Green 500 itself, follow this process:

- Use the pull-down menu in the Green 500 listings to pull up a list of the companies in your industry segment.
- View the list that comes up for interesting companies and interesting numbers.
- Copy the entire list into a spreadsheet.
- Calculate the averages for the following: Company position in the list; green score (the overall score); and the Environmental Impact, Environmental Management, and Disclosure scores. (In Microsoft Excel, the formula is =AVERAGE(x:y), where X and Y are the top and bottom cells in the list.)
- Compare your own company's rankings compared to the Green 500 average. Use an index converted to a percentage. For instance, if your sector has an average Green Score of 50, and your company's score is 60, then your index is 1.2. As a percentage, that's 120% of the average. (Say it that way; your bosses will understand.)
- Pick an emblematic company to focus your comparisons on. The emblematic company should be well known (especially within your own company), relatively successful in the Green 500 listings, and have a website with lots of relevant information. (This tends to go with a high Disclosure score.)

You can then follow up by recommending ameliorations (fixes) for areas where you're weak, or weaker than you'd like to be. A green computing effort can improve your results, and set an example, in all three areas that the Green 500 evaluates: Environmental Impact, Environmental Management, and Disclosure.

Here's an example for Media & Publishing (http://www.thedailybeast.com/newsweek/2012/10/22/newsweek-green-rankings-2012-u-s-500-list.html). I used the pull-down menu in the Green 500 list to pull up Media & Publishing companies. I then copied and pasted the list (of X companies) into a spreadsheet. I then copied the listings—18 companies included—into a spreadsheet. I used the Average function to find the following:

- The average list position for media companies is 135, well above the average for all companies of 250.

- The average green score is 58—a bit above the average for all companies of 51.
- The average Environmental Impact score is 73, well above the average for all companies of 56.
- The average Environmental Management score is 52, matching the average of 53.
- The average Disclosure score is 29, well above the average for all companies of 16.

So the summary for green accomplishments is as follows: The Media & Publishing group is good at doing it, average at organizing it, and good (as you might hope) at talking about it.

If I were working for a particular company, I'd then go on to note strengths and weaknesses for my company versus the averages. I'd also pick a company to compare with, on an ongoing basis. Depending on my own company's focus, I might pick the Walt Disney Company (second best in the sector) or Time Warner (fifth best). These are broad, strong, well-known companies without strong political leanings. (News Corp., the owner of Fox News, is an example of a company that does have strong political leanings.) Having picked a comparison company, I'd beat the comparison nearly to death. I'd identify the three strongest strengths, and weakest weaknesses, of my company's green efforts, and compare it with—for example—Walt Disney, for better or worse.

This kind of work brings green efforts to life for your peers and upper management. Consider using the Newsweek Green 500 and other relevant listings as a framework for benchmarking your own green computing efforts, and green efforts at your company as a whole.

## 11.4 Summary

In this chapter we discuss the public face of green computing—what makes companies green, how to use the Newsweek Green 500 to evaluate "greenness," and comparisons of different tech-oriented groups of companies. The next chapter discusses deep green computing by industry segment.

# Chapter 12

## The Future: Deep Green Computing

### Key Concepts

In this chapter we discuss the future of green computing:

- Green computing megatrends
- The need for sustainability
- Decreasing core computing costs
- Telepresence replaces travel
- Toward deep green computing

This chapter summarizes trends discussed throughout the book and points out directions for the future.

## 12.1 Green Computing and the Future

There's an old saying that it's difficult to make predictions, especially about the future. In fact, this saying is so popular that it's been attributed to everyone from former Mets baseball team manager Yogi Berra to quantum physicist Neils Bohr (each of whom had excellent reasons for having said it).

However, people in organizations have to make predictions about the future all the time. There's actually a well-established methodology for doing so. It requires that you look at the drivers of change and at the most desirable possible outcomes. Then you surf the waves of change toward where you want to go.

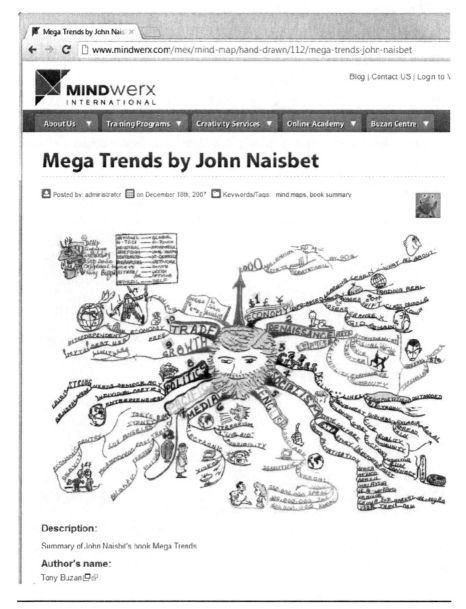

**Figure 12.1**   John Naisbet's *Megatrends* drawn as a mind map. (*Source:* http://www.mindwerx.com/mex/mind-map/hand-drawn/112/mega-trends-john-naisbet)

So let's follow that process to look at the future of green computing. All the material in the previous chapters, plus your own computing and green computing experience, actually give you a lot of information and expertise to draw on in determining your own path within the new computing environments of the future.

## 12.2 Megatrends for Green Computing

The book *Megatrends*, by John Naisbet,[1] was a worldwide hit in the mid-1980s, just as personal computers were really catching on. (A "mind map" of the trends Naisbet identified is shown in Figure 12.1.) Of course, no one's perfect: One of Naisbet's trends was the growth of capitalism in socialist countries, but his book was published just a few years before the fall of the Berlin Wall. And he hardly included the environment at all.

But Naisbet's idea of looking at big trends continues to be useful. It's not critical that you get all the specific, underlying trends right; by setting out what you think they are, you can adjust as new trends fade and emerge.

At present, the really big trends driving green computing are as follows:

- An increasing need for sustainability in everything people do
- The continually decreasing cost of core computing capabilities
- The continually increasing ability of computing to replace other industries and activities

Even three trends is "too many words," compared to a really concise summary: People will do more and more on computers, which cost less and less. The word "cost" is here understood to include the overall environmental impact as well as the overall financial impact, but financial cost is a great way to lead your argument with most audiences.

We'll take a closer look at each of these trends and why each is likely to continue. Then we'll look at what the key costs of computing are and how a new model for future computing can drive them down.

## 12.2.1 An Increasing Need for Sustainability

There's an ever-increasing need for sustainability in everything people do. There are several main drivers for this key need:

- **The world is getting warmer.** The Earth looks certain to warm past the "limit" of 2°C that scientists have called the safe upper bound before unmanageable consequences kick in.

- **The population keeps growing.** The Earth is currently at 7 billion people and adding nearly a billion people per decade. Unless and until disaster strikes, strong population growth looks likely to continue for decades to come.
- **Increasing public concern.** People are concerned about climate change, extreme weather, pollution, toxic materials, and more. This drives companies to try to clean up their acts along many dimensions.

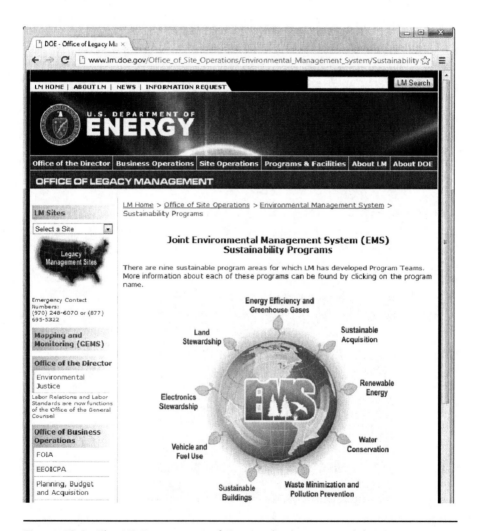

**Figure 12.2**  The US Department of Energy divides sustainability into nine programs. (*Source*: http://www.lm.doe.gov/Office_of_Site_Operations/Environmental_Management_System/Sustainability_Programs.aspx)

The US Department of Energy has sustainability programs grouped into nine areas, as shown in Figure 12.2. Expect to see a lot more like this as sustainability-related trends unfold.

Are these trends likely to continue? It looks like all of them are, for the near term. In the future, though, increasing global temperature, if unchecked, will make it harder and harder to grow food, which means the population can't keep rising. This collision of trends is nearly certain to keep stoking the third trend, which is increasing public concern. Hunger has a way of concentrating the mind, and hunger on a worldwide basis will cause huge concern.

We can briefly summarize the impact of these trends on computing. The key word is greener. I believe that everything organizations do, in and out of IT, will have to justify itself in terms of its sustainability impact. Computing can do more than reduce its footprint in terms of the functions it already handles; computing can also cut activities such as travel, which has a high environmental impact.

Of course, some savvy marketing is required all along the way. For instance, if the computing group keeps taking over more activities, the footprint of the computing group won't decline nearly as fast. Let's see how this works when it comes with reducing travel impacts:

- **Before.** Computing group: Impact 20% (out of a total of 100%). Corporate travel: Impact 30%. Total: 50%.
- **After.** Half of travel is replaced with telepresence, at the cost of a 10% increase in the computing group's impact. Computing group: Impact 22% (a 10% increase). Corporate travel: Impact 15%. Total: 37%.

Note that the total footprint of computing plus travel has declined by about one quarter—but, focusing only on the computing group, its impact rose by 10%.

This is where savvy marketing is required. You need to help stakeholders, inside and outside your company, see the big picture. Otherwise, some of your green computing efforts can look like part of the problem, rather than part of the solution.

## 12.2.2 The Continually Decreasing Cost of Core Computing Capabilities

Moore's law is the most famous law in computing. Gordon Moore, co-founder of microprocessor giant Intel, said that the number of transistors on an integrated circuit doubles roughly once every two years. Because the transistors get faster as they get smaller, this means that chip performance, for a fixed cost, doubles every 18 months.

Another way of saying the same thing is that the cost of computing is cut in half every 18 months. A US Government chart showing this drop over a recent 30-year period is shown in Figure 12.3.

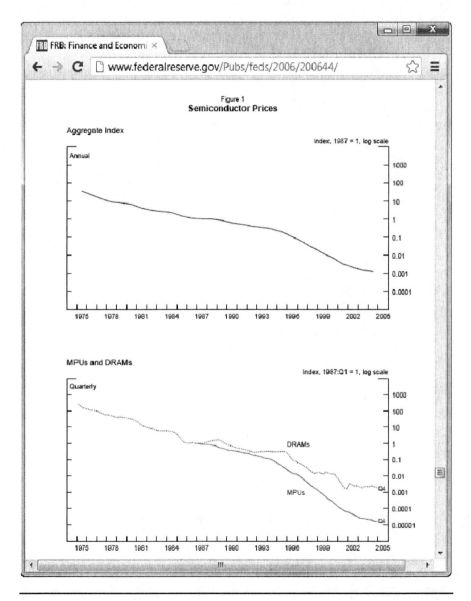

**Figure 12.3**   Processing costs plummet by 50% every 18 months. (*Source*: http://www.federalreserve.gov/Pubs/feds/2006/200644/)

This trend is quite promising for green computing. If costs are plummeting, everything "green" gets easier:

- Energy usage drops by half every 18 months
- Materials requirements drop by half every 18 months
- Costs for these more-efficient devices drop by half every 18 months

Are these trends likely to continue? Very much so. There is some controversy over whether highly complex devices such as microprocessors can keep going at the full Moore's Law pace of improvement. Transistors are becoming so powerful and are positioned so close together that they generate too much heat, slowing the pace of improvement.

But we are now seeing Moore's Law–type improvements in related technical areas, such as hard disk densities and networking speed. Even solar panels are said to be moving toward a Moore's Law–type pace of change. So the improvements that Moore cited look set to largely continue in computing, as a whole, and in green computing, in particular, even if they slow down for a while in transistors themselves. (I say "for a while" because some farther-out advances, such as quantum computing, could make Moore's Law run even faster than it has in the decades since Moore came up with it.)

So why can't the computing group get the same job done for half the money every 18 months? There are a few big reasons:

- Manufacturers pack more into each device so they can slow down the rate of price decreases.
- Software developers pack more into their software so they can sell more features—and raise, not lower, their prices—while running on cheaper underlying hardware.
- The greater complexity of devices and software leads to higher costs for software, in-house software development, support, training, maintenance, and more. People, of course, are far more expensive than processing (and salaries don't drop 50% every six months).

These trends are also set to continue, but they have limits. The price of PCs has steadily dropped, though not as fast as the price of transistors. Software packages reach limits of complexity, so people only use a small fraction of their features. Eventually, for both hardware and software, smaller, "good enough" alternatives can take over—as with people reading and writing emails on their cell phones.

The best way for you to get on top of these countervailing trends—and to get the benefit of increasing hardware efficiency—is to work very hard to take advantage of hardware improvements. Further on in this chapter, I suggest that moving more and more computing activity onto tablets, backed by software running mostly in the cloud, is the way to reap these benefits.

Again, you need to do some marketing. You need to have an answer ready when the Board of Directors asks why computing costs are going up, or are remaining steady, in the company, while the cost of everything that makes up those costs seems to be going down.

You also need to exercise some leadership. Costs won't go down fast—or perhaps not at all—if you just take what the computing mainstream gives you. For instance, Microsoft comes out with a new operating system every few years. Many companies wait years to upgrade—or skip some upgrades entirely. The jury is still out on whether Windows 8 will get very much upgrade attention from large companies (http://www.techrepublic.com/blog/cio-insights/does-windows-8-make-sense-on-business-desktops-tech-chiefs-are-split/39749562). A green computing point of view is that upgrading should be a last resort, rather than the first choice.

## 12.2.3 The Ability of Computing to Do More and More

Computing is increasingly able to take on other kinds of functions. Let's take a look at a few of the devices and activities that computing can partly or largely replace:

- **Snail mail.** People growing up today have no idea of the excitement—and business activity—that used to accompany the daily arrival of the postman. Bad news, good news, even interesting advertising was all committed to paper and sent by air, rail, truck, car, and foot on its way to reach, well, everybody. The quarterly arrival of the Sears department store catalog was a real thrill to many.

   Of course, the postal service still operates today, but at a fraction of its former importance. Mail largely serves to back up electronic delivery—of news, of transactions, of interpersonal communication.

- **Transistor radios, Walkmans, stereos.** People used to listen to music on transistor radios. Now they carry their entire music library on their (mobile) telephones (!) and manage it on their personal computers, tablets, or on the phone itself. Alternatively, people stream music online and don't own it at all.

   And yes, that sounds like a move back to the future of AM radio in the 1950s and 1960s! But now people have more choices than just switching among a few different rock and roll radio stations. (I've noticed, however, at sporting events, that people who used to have transistor radios now just go without the radio coverage they once enjoyed. Not every change is progress.)

- **TVs and movie houses.** More and more entertainment and information that used to reach people on TV, or at the movies, is now delivered through computers. During World War II, the Why We Fight short films helped inspire Americans across the country to support the war effort. Now people watch movies on their telephones and use a personal computer or tablet as an entertainment hub to drive television viewing. Movie ticket sales continue to lag other economic indicators.

Are these trends likely to continue? Certainly. In fact, the new digital approaches are driving some of the old school right out of business. *Newsweek* magazine, a proud print publication for 80 years, has now gone all digital. The US Postal Service continues to close post offices, and it may have to restructure dramatically to survive.

It's important to remember that, even though they took decades to realize, these big, big changes seem commonplace today. That's because remembering the past can actually help us "think big" when we look at the future.

In the following sections, I'll give some examples of activities that can be virtualized—moved onto computers—at great savings in direct costs and environmental impact.

## 12.3 Telepresence Instead of Travel

Flying, or not flying, is the single largest environmental decision that individuals make (or that their organization makes for them). A single round-trip flight of more than a few thousand miles easily generates as much $CO_2$ as everything else you do in a year—buying stuff, driving, leaving the office lights on overnight, all of it. So reducing—even, where possible, eliminating—flying is a huge win for the environment.

Telepresence is an advanced form of videoconferencing. The goal of telepresence is to very closely approach the experience of actually being in the same room with someone, or with a number of people.

Most meetings that occur via the Internet today don't even use videoconferencing. Services such as WebEx and GoToMeeting make it easy to share a PowerPoint presentation or to screen share. Interaction takes place by voice or by typing into a chat window. These services are "palliative"—they fill in the gap from people not being in the same place. They aren't substitutes for actually working in the same office, or meeting in the same conference room.

Telepresence is an effort to make remote meetings as similar to in-person as possible. Cisco is a leader in creating telepresence spaces. The most complete solutions include both physical spaces as well as telecommunications equipment.

One instance of telepresence is a full conference room implementation. Here's how the physical and electronic space works in conference-room telepresence:

- The physical room is, in a sense, cut in half. Half a room goes at one end of the telepresence connection; the other half of the room goes at the other end.
- Cameras and microphones are set up to cover each half-room.
- Each half-room includes a half-moon conference table with chairs on one side.
- The half-moon conference table faces a wall of monitors, which displays the corresponding half-moon conference table on the other side.
- Networking is used to transmit video and audio with as little lag as possible between the two half-rooms.

**Figure 12.4**  Telepresence makes two places feel like one. (*Source:* http://www.cisco.com/en/US/products/ps12453/prod_view_selector.html)

The idea is to create a whole conference room out of two disparate halves. Each organization in telepresence creates one or more half-rooms. The half-rooms are then knitted together electronically during each meeting. Figure 12.4 shows one telepresence setup in operation. It gives some feel for the level of interactivity that's possible with this kind of setup.

The experience of telepresence is amazing. I had the opportunity to use it while working for a major global company on a worldwide video portal, all using Cisco gear. Cisco wanted the company to up its telepresence usage, so they made sure to include telepresence meetings in the project I was working on.

The experience was very much like being in the same room. Because the wall colors, furniture colors, types of chairs and so on all matched, the brain bridged the gap by knitting everything together. The meeting felt a bit eerie at first—but after a little while, the technology faded from my awareness and I clicked into the project we were all "there" to work on.

There were a few oddities. When one party wanted to display something from their computer screen, it showed up at the foot of the table—a good use of space, but lacking verisimilitude. And there was a barely noticeable lag in speech. It was odd to see the other party's lips moving, but not hear the resulting sound until a fraction of a second later.

These oddities were minor, though, as shown by the existence of another big problem around the technology: It's so popular that getting time in the company's telepresence rooms became a major issue, as they were fully scheduled, almost around the clock. The nearby Cisco offices had similar problems, with sales, technical teams, and others competing for precious telepresence time.

Cost is another concern. Setting up the rooms is expensive, and setting up the needed telecommunications connections adds to the cost. Also, Cisco is almost alone in offering the best versions of this technology. All that means a premium to cover Cisco's R&D costs and profits on top of the unavoidable costs of physical and telecommunications setup.

Clearly, though, telepresence points the way to a future in which traveling to meetings can become much less common, replaced by telecommunications. The greener the underlying IT infrastructure, the greater the savings.

## 12.4  Telecommuting Instead of Commuting

What's the difference between telecommuting and telepresence? Telepresence replaces one-off trips for specific meetings—trips that often involve flying. Telecommuting replaces an employee's daily trips into the office. With telecommuting, an employee can work from home—or, less often, from a small satellite facility tied to the office electronically.

Telecommuting is a big potential energy saver, as the gasoline used in the morning commute doesn't need to be burned. When telecommuting becomes a big part of an employee's workweek, it can even support an employee in not owning a car (or for a family to have one car fewer than otherwise).

In one ten-year period (from 1994 to 2004), the US Department of Energy estimates that telecommuting doubled—from fewer than 10% of employees to a figure not far south of 20% (see Figure 12.5). If the same rate of growth has continued, the percentage may be closer to 25% today.

My anecdotal experience, working for a software company in Silicon Valley, is that most of my colleagues work from home, telecommuting, roughly one day a week. Just about all the employees have laptops with webmail, which allows

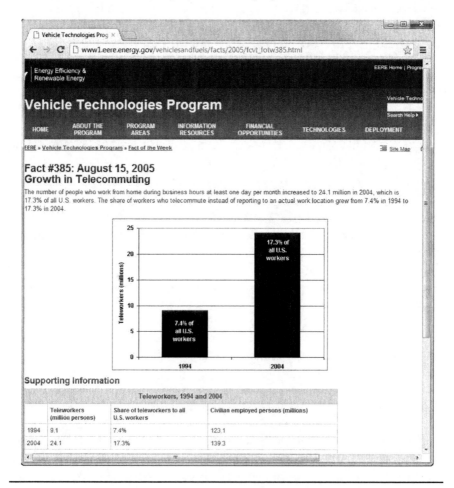

**Figure 12.5** Telecommuting in the United States more than doubled in just ten years. (*Source:* http://www1.eere.energy.gov/vehiclesandfuels/facts/2005/fcvt_fotw385.html)

email access from anywhere, and Virtual Private Network (VPN) capability, which allows access to company resources such as Exchange email servers and shared network resources.

Telecommuting allows people to avoid commuting, which saves time as well as an environmental footprint. It also helps accommodate people who have an appointment near home, who have a need to be at home, or who are feeling a bit poorly—still well enough to work, perhaps, but not wanting to risk spreading some infection to others in the office.

Telecommuting can also support bigger changes in how people work. My current company has field salespeople who only come into the office occasionally. Even one senior executive is based halfway across the country and is only in the company's main office about half the time.

It's important, in these situations, to have safeguards so that productivity isn't impaired by a remote working situation. Regular phone meetings and videoconferences can be a big help. Telepresence, as described in the previous section, can close the gap even further (although telepresence may not work for a remote employee when a full telepresence meeting is held with, say, a big customer). The best telepresence setups only support two sites at once, so the remote employee may have to travel to one or the other of them.

My company is also fairly typical in *allowing* telecommuting. It doesn't really *encourage* telecommuting. The global company that I worked for previously was more on the encouraging side. They made large areas of their offices hot desk friendly. Employees no longer had assigned desks; they used any available desk in a shared space when they were in the office and had to make appointments before coming in to prevent overcrowding.

Some employees, though, are almost demanding extensive telecommuting options. I've had candidates for technical writer positions, for instance, look at me funny when I suggested that my company wanted them to be in the office four or five days a week.

Casual telecommuting is not going to do much for your green credibility these days—it's more an expected option, even though it remains a green option. Instead, telecommuting should be part of a broader approach to reducing the energy footprint from commuting:

- Housing assistance for employees who want to relocate closer to work. (This can mean help finding a place, and maybe a small bonus to cover costs—not necessarily long-term help in paying for rent or a mortgage.)
- Shuttle buses to popular residential destinations. My current employer uses a shuttle service that runs a green fleet of buses and supports Wi-Fi for all trips, allowing employees to work in transit.
- Active encouragement of telecommuting, on top of full technical support and equipment provision for telecommuters. This encouragement can

include establishing "meeting-less Mondays" and similar tactics to reduce the need for employees to be at work every day.

- Active encouragement of remote access options for most or all meetings. This is telecommuter friendly and also helps people who find, shortly before the meeting starts, that they can't get to the meeting.
- Establishing satellite offices to drastically reduce commuting needs, with full networking and even telepresence support.
- Recognition of accomplishment by employees who telecommute, including sharing any barriers or difficulties overcome in getting the work done well.

You can move toward a model in which you reverse traditional assumptions, and coming into the office becomes more of a special event than a daily expectation. With this kind of approach, technology can make a major difference in your environmental footprint.

## 12.5 Toward Deep Green Computing

Replacing more and more of your organization's travel and commuting with digital alternatives is a huge step toward a green future. But you also need to make the underlying digital infrastructure as green as possible.

Going all the way toward a minimal-footprint computing environment is, at this point, something of a thought experiment. No organization that I know of is actually doing this, either in part or in whole. However, there once was a time, more than a century ago, when companies generated their own electricity and heat. (There was no air conditioning at this time.) It took decades for power utilities to evolve, providing power from plugs on the wall and natural gas delivery that customers don't even need to think about. (The very rare instances of natural gas explosions, often fatal, just show how much we take this infrastructure for granted.)

Computing is expected to head in the same direction. So I'm going to set out an idealized model here, extrapolating current offerings and trends to a truly sustainable future.

The key elements in this transformation are as follows:

- **Moving software to the cloud.** This is where Software as a Service (SaaS) follows the path set by electricity production. You move software usage aggressively to Internet delivery, with the browser as a user interface. This steadily reduces your need for expensive, energy-intensive data centers.
- **Moving usage to voice and tablets.** A tablet is a lot less resource intensive than a personal computer, but a phone is a lot less resource-intensive than

even a tablet. Also, both voice and browser interfaces are a big step toward simplicity for the user.

- **Reducing deployments of computers and monitors.** Computers and monitors attached to them become specialty items for people who need particular software that's not able to be converted sensibly to a tablet or voice interface. For instance, graphic designers will probably be using a keyboard and mouse, with big monitors, for a long time to come. But many others can get their work done with occasional or no use of a personal computer and mouse.

Apple's Siri, shown in Figure 12.6, and Android's voice features are examples of voice interfaces. A voice interface is completely cloud dependent; both voice recognition and the functionality offered are supported by deep computing resources. In fact, voice recognition is a perfect example of the value of green computing. It can use several CPUs at once for fractions of a second—for instance, to decipher a particularly complicated bit of speech—while using much less computing power most of the time.

The same operation can be drawing on many gigabytes of stored speech data for comparison, when needed. Providing the power needed for this kind of flexibility simply isn't possible for voice recognition running on a personal computer.

The graphic designer and voice recognition examples show the real key to moving to deep green computing: Software availability. Software delivers computing functionality, and moving software functionality to the cloud is key to delivering it across any device needed. For word processing today, it's fairly easy to use a notepad-type app to enter text on a tablet. For formatting and editing, however, a personal computer is much easier. Simple graphics creation and photo editing can be handled on the tablet; more complex work requires a personal computer.

Video creation presents an interesting edge case. It would seem that video creation would require a big, powerful desktop computer and several monitors—and, for most professionals, it does. However, video editing apps are available on newer, more powerful iPads, for instance. And the work that gets done on the iPad isn't necessarily "less than" what many users do on a personal computer; it's just different. The tablet-plus-app version makes different functionality available, which influences the kind of work that gets done.

## 12.6 Platforms for Deep Green Computing

To move to deep green computing, you need to carefully consider the software functionality that's available on each platform—voice, phone, tablet, laptop, and personal computer (laptop or desktop) with extra monitors.

**Figure 12.6**   Apple's Siri is helping to make voice a new platform. (*Source*: http://www.apple.com/ipad/features/)

Here's a list of some capabilities available at each level of functionality:

- **Voice.** Have text messages, voice messages, email read aloud; create brief replies via voice or text. Answer simple queries—for example, "Where's the nearest gas station?"
- **Phone.** Check email and make brief replies. Simplified Web access. Making and sharing photos. Location-based functionality.
- **Tablet.** Check email and make longer replies. Good Web access. Taking and sharing photos. Location-based functionality. Simplified versions of most computer functions.

- **Laptop.** Most computer work, limited sometimes by lack of screen space.
- **Personal computer plus multiple monitors.** Intensive computer work, including computer programming; graphics creation; movie editing; and complex tasks, such as writing a book, or researching and writing a report.

You can analyze everything your organization does on various computing platforms against this "pyramid" of functionality. You can find instances in which a single application or task keeps people from moving to a different platform.

For instance, many salespeople use Salesforce.com for contact and task management, Excel for filing expense reports, and Word for writing sales letters. Salesforce has recently announced a tablet version of their app. Excel and Word are available on some tablets but are hard to use. To move salespeople to the iPad, for instance, you might have to simplify the expense-reporting and letter-writing tasks so they can be handled by iPad apps or completed by workers back in the office.

This is how you identify employees—individuals or groups—who can get all, or almost all, of their work done at a given level of the pyramid.

Another big issue, from a deep green computing point of view, is the increasing use by office workers of one or two very large monitors attached to a desktop or laptop computer. Computer programmers, graphic artists, and others pioneered the use of this kind of computer setup. Now, with hardware having become less expensive, it's becoming common for many other users, as well. Unfortunately, it's fairly resource intensive.

There are two difficulties here:

- **High resource usage for basic tasks.** The same user who cheerfully checks and replies to email in a laptop or tablet can, an hour later, be doing the exact same thing on a powerful laptop or desktop computer with multiple attached monitors. The environmental footprint in the second scenario is far higher.
- **Distraction of workers from key tasks.** The reason given for running multiple monitors is to keep email, chat programs such as Yahoo! Chat or Salesforce Chatter, and social networking tools available and in sight. However, a worker deep in thought, focused on a task such as writing a report, can be very much distracted by all that extra functionality. Being able to check a quick fact in a Web browser can speed the work up; responding to emails and chat alerts can greatly slow it down.

So there's a lot to think about in moving to a deep green computing approach. More hardware is not necessarily better, and a lower-footprint approach can be liberating for productivity, as well as beneficial to the planet.

## 12.7 Selling Deep Green Computing

Deep green computing can be implemented in phases:

- **Individual employees.** Specific employees can be offered the opportunity to only use a tablet, or can be moved to a tablet-only approach by management.
- **Specific job functions.** As we keep mentioning, because it's such a good example, salespeople can usefully be moved to tablets. Some executives might follow. Then, for instance, the Human Resources (HR) staff, which might require moving to cloud-based HR software. And so on, throughout your company.
- **Departments.** You can make tablet use the norm across a department, with exceptions approved by senior management.
- **Companies.** You can then make tablet use the norm across a company—with exceptions, of course.

The benefits of such a move are not only toward becoming more and more green. You're greatly simplifying the work lives of your employees and nearly removing entire functions from your company. Employees will spend more time interacting with each other, with partners, and with customers. The need for internal help desk staff, for instance, will greatly diminish.

In order to make this happen, software companies will need to move most capabilities into the cloud, at least as an option. (Microsoft, for instance, is making cloud versions of software from Word to its Microsoft Dynamics Customer Relationship Manager, but has not yet made its software easily usable on tablets.) You will have to pressure your suppliers on this issue, and also make tablet versions of specialty or in-house software. This isn't just a technical task; you need to "refactor" your software to only ask users to do things that they absolutely need to do. Complex options and settings need to be eliminated.

I once had the privilege of working with a software developer who had developed satellite navigation systems—called "sat nav" devices, or GPS systems—which were delivered as built-in systems in cars. My company was making standalone GPS devices. We offered customers many configuration options and set-up choices. Our friend from the built-in world reacted heatedly to this tendency. "If you're too stupid to figure out the right answer," he huffed, "what makes you think the user is going to want to bother to do it for you?" This was a live, in-person version of the radical approach to simplicity that the late Steve Jobs brought to products like the iPhone and iPad.

As you proceed, you'll need to sell the benefits of what you're doing. Unfortunately, people tend to focus only on feature lists, such as the speed of a microprocessor or the multilingual capabilities of a word processing program, and ignore more subtle qualities like the speed of completing a task or ease of use. You can help educate them. You can also "big up" the savings you're achieving and the positive environmental impact of your work.

Let's highlight some of the benefits of different types of deep green computing:

- **Voice access.** You probably can't move many employees entirely to voice-supported, Apple Siri-type services. But, if you can move even a few, all these employees need is a smartphone. Other employees who use voice access for some of their tasks are likely to experience great speed, ease of use, and flexibility in getting crucial tasks done.
- **Phone access.** You may be able to move some employees to a combination of voice-access services and cell phone apps. This hugely reduces the environmental footprint, since employees are going to have smartphones and have them turned on nearly all the time, anyway. It might be asking a lot, though, to present employees with tasks such as accessing websites designed for big screens on the much smaller screen of a phone.
- **Tablet access.** Moving more than a few employees to all-tablet computing (including voice tasks) is tough today. You need to start working and planning now to open the door for this kind of movement in the future. Employees who can use an all-tablet approach should benefit from the simplicity of tablet interfaces and the ease and flexibility of carrying and using a tablet. Tablets are also great for casual videoconferencing. Done right, moving employees to tablets can greatly liberate them, making their lives—and the organization's life—much easier.
- **Laptops (no extra monitors).** The benefits of extra monitors are sometimes offset by the interruptions and distractions available on a larger screen. (Putting the Gangnam Style video on infinite replay on a big screen is fun, but distracting.) For many users, the consistency of the laptop-only interface may be a benefit rather than a loss.

These changes have a deep and far-reaching effect on the environmental footprint of your computing operation:

- **Cloud computing.** Cloud computing moves environmental impact from relatively inefficient data centers that are on your books to highly efficient data centers that are on someone else's. You can then help pressure your providers to become even more efficient.
- **Lower electricity usage.** Using a smaller device uses far less electricity than a larger one. You get this benefit even when users have access to larger devices, as long as they spend more of their time using the smaller ones.

- **Lower embodied energy.** The smaller the device, the less embodied energy, the fewer hazardous chemicals, the easier waste disposal at end of life. However, to get this benefit, you have to cut some users off—if you give a user a big-screen monitor, for instance, it still has a life cycle, even if it's not used all that much.
- **Cost savings.** All of these advantages translate, of course, to cost savings. Getting rid of data centers—or not building them at all; using smaller and smaller devices; helping employees work faster; and reducing the internal IT infrastructure of help desk people, data center staff, and so on, all save money. You can spend much more of your money on developing and delivering products and services, and on sales—the money-making parts of the company.

## 12.8 Summary

In this chapter we discussed the future of green computing, including green computing megatrends, the need for sustainability, the decrease in core computing costs, and the increase in telepresence as a replacement for travel. We also described deep green computing as a new trend. This chapter summarized trends discussed throughout the book and pointed out directions for the future.

# References

## Preface

1. Carson, R., *Silent Spring*, Houghton Mifflin Co., New York (NY), 1962.
2. Geyer, R. A., *A Global Warming Forum: Scientific, Economic, and Legal Overview*, CRC Press, 1992.

## Chapter 3

1. Carson, R., *Silent Spring*, Houghton Mifflin Co., New York (NY), 1962.
2. Gore, A., *An Inconvenient Truth: The Planetary Emergency of Global Warming and What We Can Do About It*, Rodale Books, 1st ed., 2006.

## Chapter 4

1. McBay, A., Keith, L., and Jensen, D., *Deep Green Resistance: Strategy to Save the Planet*, Seven Stories Press, New York, 2011

## Chapter 5

1. Nader, R., *Unsafe at Any Speed*, Grossman Publishers, New York, 1965.
2. Greenpeace, Greenpeace Guide to Greener Electronics; http://www.greenpeace.org/international/en/campaigns/toxics/electronics/Guide-to-Greener-Electronics/Previous-editions/how-the-companies-line-up-17/.

## Chapter 7

1. Murugesan, S., Harnessing Green IT: Principles and Practices, *IT Professional*, January–February 2008, pp. 24–33.
2. *Best Practices Guide for Energy-Efficient Data Center Design*, prepared by the National Renewable Energy Laboratory for the U.S. Department of Energy, Federal Energy Management Program, March 2011.)
3. Schulz, G., *The Green and Virtual Data Center*, CRC Press, Boca Raton (FL), 2009.

## Chapter 8

1. Schulz, G., *The Green and Virtual Data Center*, CRC Press, Boca Raton (FL), 2009.

## Chapter 9

1. Gore, A., *An Inconvenient Truth: The Planetary Emergency of Global Warming and What We Can Do About It*, 1st ed., Rodale Books, 2006.
2. *An Inconvenient Truth*, a documentary film, released 2006.

## Chapter 12

1. Naisbet, J, *Megatrends: Ten New Directions Transforming Our Lives,* Warner Books, 1982.

# Index